Christian Faith and the Theological Life

℘ *Romanus Cessario, O.P.*

Christian Faith and the Theological Life

The Catholic University of America Press
Washington, D.C.

Copyright © 1996
The Catholic University of America Press
All rights reserved
Printed in the United States of America

The paper used in this publication meets the minimum requirements
of American National Standards for Information Science—Permanence of Paper for Printed Library materials, ANSI Z39.48-1984.
∞

Library of Congress Cataloging-in-Publication Data

Cessario, Romanus
   Christian faith and the theological life / Romanus Cessario.
   p. cm.
   Includes bibliographical references and index.
   1. Faith. 2. Christian life—Catholic authors. I. Title.
BV4637.C38 1996
234'.2—dc20
   ISBN 0-8132-0868-8 (cloth : alk. paper).
   ISBN 0-8132-0869-6 (pbk. : alk. paper)

For the McPhersons and Honey White
with grateful appreciation

Contents

Acknowledgments

In his "Dry Salvages," T. S. Eliot notes, "It seems, as one becomes older, / That the past has another pattern, and ceases to be a mere sequence—." This book on the life of faith points to the accuracy of Eliot's observation. So I am very grateful to my colleagues and friends for helping me to realize this transition. First of all, I am pleased to acknowledge the invaluable assistance of Father J. A. DiNoia, O.P., who carefully read the manuscript and suggested many improvements. Recognition is also due to Mrs. Lisa Lickona and Mr. John Janaro, who commented on the style of the volume, both theological and literary, to Dr. Gary Culpepper, who read a penultimate draft, and to the Dominican nuns at North Guilford, Connecticut, who encouraged me by listening to these chapters in the form of conferences on the life of faith, which Eliot calls "the ground of our beseeching." Sister Susan Heinemann, O.P., of the same monastery, devoted significant energies both to reading the text, which is much improved as a result of her insightful remarks, and to preparing the index. Once again, I owe my good friend Father John P. McIntyre, S.J., an expression of gratitude for his close reading of the manuscript and for improving it with the best of Jesuit pedagogy. The present book embodies my reflection on the virtue of faith, which took place for the most part at the Dominican House of Studies (Washington, D.C.), where many Dominican and other students helped me to recognize that proper instruction in the theological virtues lies at the heart of pursuing the theologal life. I am grateful to

His Eminence, Bernard Cardinal Law, and to the rector of St. John's Seminary (Brighton, Mass.), Monsignor Timothy Moran, for providing me the opportunity to continue this instruction in the theological schools of Boston. I dedicate this volume to my maternal aunt and uncles, Mrs. Helen White, Mr. Daniel A. McPherson, and Mr. Thomas R. McPherson, as a sign of familial affection and sincere gratitude for their consistent support. They too have nourished me on the "life of significant soil."

Brighton, Massachusetts
28 January 1996
Feast of St. Thomas Aquinas

ℬ Introduction

Faith and the Theological Life

To acquire knowledge about God is one thing; to commit oneself to him is another. Though these actions are obviously related, they constitute discrete moments in the development of the Christian life. In order to maintain this distinction, spiritual authors of the classical French tradition distinguish between the terms "théologique" and "théologal." The former term describes what pertains to theological study and learning, whereas the latter denotes what pertains to the divinized life and practice of the Christian believer. Thus in French, *la vie théologale* directly signifies a life transformed by grace and animated by the virtues of faith, hope, and charity—in short, the godly life. In the seventeenth century, the English poet John Donne wrote that the "Theologall vertues, Faith, Hope, and Charity, are infus'd from God," but today the English term "theologal" is not widely employed.[1] Still, the nuance that the term connotes is important for speaking correctly about the Christian life. So in order to emphasize the utter uniqueness of a human life that is infused with divine grace and shaped by the theological virtues, we have adopted in English the phrase "the theological life."

When St. Paul describes the immediate and affective union with the

---

1. See John Donne, *Pseudo-martyr*, 190 and 210: "This is not meant onely of Charitie, as it is a Theologall vertue." The 1994 English version of the *Catechism of the Catholic Church* speaks about the "theologal path of our prayer" (2607) and describes the first three petitions of the Our Father as "more theologal" (2803).

divine Persons that God offers to all persons, the Apostle speaks about the state of being justified through conformity to Christ (Rom. 8:29–30). In simpler terms, then, the phrase "theological life" means the Christian life, but with the important precision that a life is Christian to the extent that it is both elevated by divine grace and actualized by infused virtues. The infused virtues include the theological virtues, namely, faith, hope, and charity, as well as the moral virtues that fall under one of four cardinal virtues of prudence, justice, fortitude, and temperance. Together, the infused virtues enable the Christian to answer the call to holiness that Christ extends to all peoples. The Second Vatican Council affirms the permanent validity of the vocation to lead a theological life. For "the Lord Jesus, the divine master and model of all perfection, preached holiness of life, which he himself both initiates and perfects, to each and every one of his disciples no matter what their condition of life: 'You, therefore, must be perfect, as your heavenly father is perfect' (Matt. 5:4–8)."[2] By living the theological life, we advance in holiness of life. The universal call to holiness is fulfilled in those who, according to the divine purpose and design, complete the pattern that God has established for the theological life.

The Infused Virtues

Because living the theological life supposes the justification of the whole person, each human capacity must undergo the transformation of grace. Therefore, an analysis of Christian life and practice requires attention to a wide range of virtues. "Virtue" signifies a class of qualities that are stable or "habitual" features of the personality. Virtues display firmly rooted dispositions for specifically good human activity that both constitute and describe the moral character of the human person. A full and adequate account of theological ethics requires attention to both the acquired and the infused moral virtues. Acquired virtues we develop over a period of time and by means of repeated instances, or patterns,

---

2. The Second Vatican Council's Dogmatic Constitution on the Church, *Lumen gentium*, chap. 5, no. 40. Translations of conciliar texts are from *Decrees of the Ecumenical Councils*, ed. Norman P. Tanner, S.J. (Washington, D.C.: Georgetown University Press, 1990), though in some cases with minor modifications.

of good human activity, and so, since the transforming power of the Holy Spirit is not at work in them, acquired virtues influence exclusively the sphere of human decision making and action. These are the virtues about which moral philosophers write and, sometimes, dispute.[3] As the acquired virtues belong to the inherent capacities of human nature, their development in an individual by definition presupposes neither the energy of divine grace nor the assent of Christian belief. To borrow the image of St. Augustine, these are the virtues whose exercise develops the human city, for they shape the moral character of the good citizen within the social and political community. Infused virtues, on the other hand, are spiritual endowments that originate entirely in the sanctification that Christian theology attributes to the work of the Holy Spirit. They do not depend originally for their existence on the free exercise of human energy and capacities. Rather they are freely bestowed graces that enable the believer, who nonetheless continues to act freely under their impulse, to undertake and to persevere in a complete and perfect Christian life. These are the virtues that build up the City of God, that mark the lives of those who "are citizens with the saints and also members of the household of God, built upon the foundation of the apostles and the prophets, with Christ Jesus himself as the cornerstone" (Eph. 2:19, 20).[4]

In his systematic exposition of Christian theology, the *Summa theologiae*, Saint Thomas Aquinas explains that the acquired moral and intellectual virtues perfect the natural seeds of virtue that lie within human nature as created by God and that remain even after original sin. The infused moral virtues, however, develop only within the theological life of the believer, that is, a life suffused with faith, hope, and charity.[5] Since

3. For a recent survey of the multiplicity of issues that virtue and character raise for moral and political philosophers, see Martha Nussbaum, "Times Literary Supplement," July 5, 1992.

4. Biblical citations are from the 1989 New Revised Standard Version Bible.

5. Aquinas raises this issue in a general way in *Summa theologiae* Ia-IIae q. 63, a. 3, when he inquires whether any moral virtues are infused in us by God, but he provides a fuller discussion in Ia-IIae q. 62, aa. 1–4. (References to the *Summa theologiae* follow the accepted practice, namely, the part of the work, e.g., Ia-IIae for the *prima secundae*; the question, e.g., q. 62; the article, e.g., a. 4; the specific part of an article where required, e.g., ad 3, for the reply to the third objection. References to the other works of Aquinas

each infused virtue constitutes a uniquely supernatural, grace-given attribute, God, "who is rich in mercy, out of the great love with which he loved us even when we were dead through our trespasses" (Eph. 1:4, 5), bestows them without consideration for a person's natural talents or actual state of moral character. God loves us because he is good, not because we are; and because God loves us, we can acquire "the riches of his glorious inheritance among the saints" (Eph. 1:18). Indeed, St. Paul claims that this exercise of loving condescension not only exemplifies the divine generosity but also reveals God's purposes and strategy for our salvation: for "God chose what is foolish in the world to shame the wise, God chose what is weak in the world to shame the strong, God chose what is low and despised in the world, even things that are not, to bring to nothing things that are, so that no human being might boast in the presence of God" (1 Cor. 1:27–29). As the work of God's love within us, the infused moral virtues of prudence, justice, fortitude, and temperance along with their allied virtues enable the believer to live that complete transformation of human life into which the Christian mysteries, especially baptism, inaugurate us.

There are theologians who prefer to explain the dynamics of the theological life without any appeal to the infused virtues. The Franciscan doctor John Duns Scotus (c. 1265–1308), for example, held that a person who possesses theological faith and divine charity already enjoys sufficient divine aid to direct his or her human life toward heavenly pursuits.[6] And still today, some theological traditions view infused moral

---

specify the title of the work along with the usual way of citing it.) Most quotations from the *Summa theologiae* come from the sixty-one-volume Blackfriars edition published in London by Eyre & Spottiswoode between 1964 and 1980. Other texts of Aquinas come from available English translations, though sometimes with modifications.

6. See his *Quaestiones in librum III Sententiarum*, dist. 36, no. 28 (Vivès edition, vol. 15, p. 701). What Scotus is discussing, in part, at this text is the problem of children who die prior to the age of reason and what kind of supernatural graces and gifts belong to them as a result of their baptism. Scotus argues that there is no need to postulate that the theological virtues are infused within such children to account for their preparedness for the heavenly communion; nor, in general, is there a *need* to postulate the infused virtues in addition to the acquired virtues. Of course, Scotus in no way eliminates the need for the acquired virtues in the wayfaring state; the thrust of his remarks is rather to give the greatest scope possible to the acquired virtues. Furthermore, as a purely historical matter, the position that Scotus adopts is a variant of the position already taken by Henry of Ghent in his *Quodlibeta* VI, q. 12 (ed. G. Wilson, pp. 140–42). I am indebted to Dr. Timothy Noone

virtue as a superfluous category of moral qualities. But in reply to this line of argumentation, those who develop the position of Aquinas accept his bold claim that though the "theological virtues [faith, hope, and charity] are enough to shape us initially to our supernatural end, that is, to God himself immediately and to none other, still the soul also needs to be perfected by the infused moral virtues in regard to other things, though as subordinated to God."[7] To put it differently, in order to render a complete account of the theological life, the theologian must explain how God's holiness suffuses the whole person. The grace of the infused moral virtues shapes and energizes our human operative capacities, intellect, will, and sense appetites, so that a human person can act promptly, joyfully, and easily in those areas of human conduct that are governed by the Gospel precepts.

The Theological Virtues

Theological warrant for speaking about infused virtue lies principally in the New Testament's insistence on the radical change that the grace of Christ accomplishes in the person incorporated into his Body. When Aquinas uses the phrase "infused moral virtues," he wants to make it abundantly clear that every dimension of human behavior lies open to being transformed by God's grace. At the same time, Aquinas recognizes that the foundations—the first principles—of authentic Christian behavior remain the "theological virtues": faith, hope, and charity. For the human person, the foundational basis for Christian living is explained in terms of habitual grace, which establishes a personal and permanent relationship between God and the justified believer. Within this unique embrace that God extends only to intellectual creatures, the theological virtues of faith, hope, and charity first of all specify the acts that distinguish the justified man or woman from those who are not living the Christian vocation to beatitude. For these virtues constitute the supernatural capacities given to the Christian that enable him or her to adhere personally to the triune God. As such, they

---

of the School of Philosophy at The Catholic University of America for this expert commentary on the text of Scotus.

7. *Summa theologiae* Ia-IIae q. 63, a. 3, ad 2.

remain the foundation of God's generous work within the Christian believer. For only the Persons of the blessed Trinity acting together can establish the personal and proper relationships of a creature with Father, Son, and Holy Spirit—commonly referred to as the "divine indwelling"—that believing in God, hoping in God, and above all, loving God accomplishes in "everyone whom the Lord our God calls to him" (Acts 2:39).[8]

In his treatise on the new law of grace, Aquinas makes clear that the bestowal of the grace of the Holy Spirit properly pertains to the Christian dispensation.[9] In other words, the grace of the Spirit is at work in the world only because Christ has accomplished the mission given to him by the Father. As the principal instrument of God's work in the world, Jesus inaugurates the theological life through his preaching but especially by his salvific death. For this reason, Aquinas steadfastly maintains that the efficacy of the Church's sacraments derives uniquely from Christ's Passion.[10] The theological life, then, is nothing other than the gift of redemption, "the righteousness of God through faith in Jesus Christ for all who believe" (Rom. 3:21). Accordingly, the theological virtues remain inseparably united with the work of sacramental reconciliation that the New Testament situates within the context of preaching the name of Jesus: "Repent, and be baptized every one of you in the name of Jesus Christ so that your sins may be forgiven; and you will receive the gift of the Holy Spirit" (Acts 2:38). Similarly, in his *Commentary on the Gospel of John*, St. Cyril of Alexandria (d. 444) draws together some of the themes that characterize the theological life as it is lived in the Church. He writes:

8. Since Aquinas defines the theological virtues as the several ways in which the human person reaches "a happiness surpassing man's nature" (Ia-IIae q. 62, a. 1), the theologian must clearly distinguish between the natural capacity of the human person to reach the God of this happiness and what the human person remains constitutionally unable to accomplish without a special divine aid: "Reason and will are naturally ordered to God inasmuch as he is the principle and end of nature, though in proportion to nature. But reason and will by their nature are not sufficiently ordered to God as he is the object of supernatural happiness" (ad 3).

9. *Summa theologiae* Ia-IIae qq. 106–14.

10. For example, in *Summa theologiae* IIIa q. 68, a. 1, Aquinas holds the view that whereas baptism, the "door" to the sacraments, was instituted at the moment of Christ's own baptism in the Jordan, the obligation to seek baptism became incumbent on all peoples only after Christ's death, since only then did the sacraments possess their efficacy.

Let the wisdom of John teach us how we live in Christ and Christ lives in us: "The proof that we are living in him and he is living in us is that he has given us a share in his Spirit." Just as the trunk of the vine gives its own natural properties to each of its branches, so, by bestowing on them the Holy Spirit, the Word of God, the only-begotten Son of the Father, gives Christians a certain kinship with himself and with God the Father because they have been united to him by faith and holy resolve to do his will in all things. He helps them to grow in love and reverence for God, and teaches them to discern right from wrong and to act with integrity.[11]

The theological life forms the heart of Christian discipleship and of that imitation of Christ which discloses the Church as a universal cause of salvation. Needless to say, this is precisely what must be preached today. The new evangelization aims to proclaim once again that the theological life is indispensable for every human creature, even though it is true that "God, through ways known to himself, can lead those who through no fault of their own are ignorant of the Gospel to that faith without which it is impossible to please him (see Heb. 11:6)."[12]

Because of its proven worth and fruitfulness, the authoritative treatment of the theological virtues that Aquinas provides in his *Summa theologiae* guides the present effort to reclaim the classical teaching on theological faith.[13] Aquinas principally argues for the existence of the theological virtues on the basis of the twofold end of human life, the natural and the graced: "One [the natural end] is proportionate to human nature . . . the other, a happiness surpassing that nature."[14] But

11. St. Cyril of Alexandria, *Commentary on the Gospel of John* Bk. 10, chap. 2 (PG 74: 331–34), trans. International Committee on English in the Liturgy in *The Liturgy of the Hours*, vol. 2 (New York: Catholic Book Publishing Company, 1976), p. 834. Cyril's works (Migne PG 68–77) were translated into English during the Oxford Movement. See Library of the Fathers of the Holy Catholic Church, volumes 43 (1832) and 48 (1885).

12. The Second Vatican Council's Decree on the Missionary Activity of the Church, *Ad gentes*, no. 7. It is this truth that grounds the Church's missionary efforts, as the same document makes clear: "Sent by God to the nations to be 'the universal sacrament of salvation,' the Church by the innermost requirements of its own catholicity and in obedience to the command of its founder, strives to proclaim the gospel to all humankind. The apostles themselves, on whom the church is founded, following in the footsteps of Christ, 'preached the word of truth and brought churches to birth' (St. Augustine, *Expositions on the Psalms* 44, 23 [PL 36: 508]). It is the duty of their successors to carry on this work unremittingly, so that 'the word of God may speed on and triumph' (2 Thess. 3:1) and the kingdom of God be proclaimed and established all over the world" (no. 1).

13. In *Summa theologiae* Ia-IIae q. 62, Aquinas devotes a single question to the three theological virtues as part of his general introduction to morals.

14. See *Summa theologiae* Ia-IIae q. 5, a. 5. For a discussion of how the twofold end

because the realization of beatitude—the theological name for the perfect happiness that comes from being united with God—surpasses the abilities of human nature, human knowing and loving must be readied to achieve this immediate union of knowledge and love with God. The theological virtues establish such a proportion in each of the dynamic capacities—the operative potencies—of the human soul. And again, since human nature possesses no inherent operative capacities capable of theological loving, hoping, and believing, these virtues must be received as God's special gifts to his creatures. Thus, the theological virtues remain entirely distinct from the intellectual and moral virtues, even when the latter exist as infused virtues. Why? Only the theological virtues have "God himself" as their proper objective. St. Paul in 1 Corinthians 13:13 points to this truth when he explains the ways, of both intellect and will, in which the human person reaches out for union with God. Furthermore, the theological virtues stand in a particular relation to one another, as determined both by their objective value and according to the sequence of their developing in the human person. As mother of the virtues, charity ranks hierarchically first among them. But because, as Aquinas puts it, "no human appetite moves toward anything, either by hoping or loving, unless it be apprehended by sense or mind," faith precedes the other two virtues in the order of their coming to exist in a person.[15]

The theological virtues form an indispensable element of the Church's instruction about Christian living. During the Council of Trent (1545–63), the Fathers included a reference to the theological virtues in chapter 7 of the Council's Decree on Justification:

Consequently, in the process of justification, together with the forgiveness of sins a person receives, through Jesus Christ into whom he is grafted, all these infused at the same time: faith, hope, and charity. For faith, unless hope is added to it and charity too, neither unites him perfectly with Christ nor makes him a living member of his body. Hence it is truly said that faith without

---

of human existence affects the moral life of the Christian believer, see Benedict M. Ashley, O.P., "What is the End of the Human Person? The Vision of God and Integral Human Fulfilment," in *Moral Truth and Moral Tradition. Essays in Honour of Peter Geach and Elizabeth Anscombe*, ed. Luke Gormally (Dublin: Four Courts Press, 1995): 68–96.

15. See *Summa theologiae* Ia-IIae q. 62, a. 4.

works is dead and barren (see James 2:17, 20), and in Christ Jesus neither circumcision is of any value nor uncircumcision, but faith "working through love"
(Gal. 5:6).

Christian salvation embodies God's own personal initiative to enter into
loving communion with the entire human family; no one, therefore, is
excluded from the call to share in the divine glory. This call is spoken
by Jesus Christ, whose Gospel of grace is preserved only in the Church.
Christ is the incarnate Son of the Father; his words and deeds efficaciously communicate divine power to those who receive them. While
the capacity for the new life of divine grace is found in every person
born into the world, it belongs to God alone to quicken the aptitudinal
image of God in the creature, so that the human person can enjoy a
loving conformity with each of the divine Persons. This act of justification begins with hearing the Truth of God's proclamation and receiving it in faith. "For I am not ashamed of the gospel; it is the power
of God for salvation to everyone who has faith, to the Jew first and also
to the Greek. For in it the righteousness of God is revealed through
faith for faith; as it is written, 'The one who is righteous will live by
faith'" (Rom. 1:16, 17). Through her formal teaching, the Church affirms that the righteousness to which Paul refers is manifest in the
Christian who puts the theological virtues into practice.

Theological Faith

A study of the theological virtues, one can argue, ought to begin with
a treatment of the virtue of faith. The Letter to the Romans clearly
indicates that the preaching of the Gospel inaugurates the Christian life.
In fact, St. Paul raises a basic question for Christian evangelization:
"And how are they to believe in one of whom they have never heard?"
In his reply to this rhetorical question, the Apostle supplies this important commentary: "So faith comes from what is heard, and what is
heard comes through the word of Christ" (Rom. 10:14b, 17). Some
schools are reluctant to distinguish sharply among the three theological
virtues, but the example of Aquinas and other theologians provides ample warrant for stressing the distinctive characteristics of theological
knowledge—the virtue of faith—and theological love—the virtues of

hope and charity. Aquinas insists that in order to comprehend the Christian life the theologian must clearly establish the radical, reciprocal interdependence that exists between a complete knowledge of divine truth and a specifically Christian love of God, self, and neighbor. Commenting on the unity of the Christian life as contained in the truth of all sacred Scripture, the Franciscan theologian and doctor St. Bonaventure (c. 1217–74) explains that no one can achieve the understanding of this truth unless he or she first receives the gift of faith in Christ: "As long as our earthly state keeps us from seeing the Lord, this same faith is the firm basis of all supernatural illumination, the light guiding us to it, and the doorway through which we enter upon it."[16]

The spiritual formation of those who receive the gift of faith in Christ takes place within the Christian Church. The Second Vatican Council points out that the communication of divine truth is ordained for our happiness: "By divine revelation God has chosen to manifest and communicate both himself and the eternal decrees of his will for the salvation of humankind, 'so as to share those divine treasures that totally surpass human understanding.' "[17] In light of this teaching, the *Catechism of the Catholic Church* first sets forth the "divine treasures" contained in the articles of the Apostles' Creed and then explicates in what the practice of this faith consists: the sacraments, the moral life of the virtues and commandments, and Christian prayer and meditation. In the Christian life, divine truth necessarily informs the practice of truth, and so we can speak of living by faith.

In order to instruct the faithful in these important matters, the Church draws on the richness of the complete Christian tradition. Everyone must possess a true knowledge about the Persons of the blessed Trinity and about the mysteries associated with the life of Christ. Incorporated into Christ through baptism, all the baptized, as St. Bonaventure reminds us, are said to enjoy a special illumination that opens up their minds to know the mysteries about the inner life of God

16. St. Bonaventure, *Prologus* in *Opera omnia* 5, 201–2, trans. International Committee on English in the Liturgy in *The Liturgy of the Hours*, vol. 3 (New York: Catholic Book Publishing Company, 1975), p. 834.

17. The Dogmatic Constitution on Divine Revelation, *Dei verbum*, chap. 1, no. 6, which includes a citation from the Dogmatic Constitution on the Catholic Faith, *Dei Filius*, chap. 2 [*DS* 3005] of the First Vatican Council.

and the economy of salvation. So far from being an endowment reserved for only a few, the illumination that accompanies the theological virtue of faith plays a central role in the life of every believer. There can be no true practice of the faith without a proper instruction in the faith. This book seeks, then, to explain in what instruction about the truth of faith consists and, furthermore, how this truth shapes and influences the lives of those who accept the preaching of the Gospel.

The following chapters each treat a different aspect of theological faith. To situate the theological virtues within the larger picture of Christian revelation, chapter 1 discusses the humanity of Christ, the gift of grace, and the creation of human beings in the image of God as prerequisite elements in any effort to understand the life of faith. The design of the three middle chapters of the book is derived from the Aristotelian notion that objects specify actions and actions reveal the specific kind of capacity required for their production.[18] In accord with this principle, chapter 2 identifies the object of faith as God, the First Truth, who is known in a truly human mode (propositional statements) by means of a light that exceeds mere human powers (the *lumen fidei*). Chapter 3 investigates the act of faith from the perspective of the believing subject, beginning with the interior act of belief that comes to fulfillment in the outward profession or confession of belief's content in public witness. As chapter 4 demonstrates, Christian faith is to be understood not as an isolated intellectual act but as a virtuous form of life, or *habitus*, that affectively transforms the mind of the believer unto a share in the eternal life of the divine Persons of the Trinity. The final chapter examines those gifts of the Holy Spirit that the theological tradition beginning with St. Augustine associates with the fruition of the virtue of faith. The gifts of understanding and knowledge provide, as Aquinas realized, special endowments of grace for the righteous one who lives by faith.

Because revealed truth lies at the heart of the Christian life, it is appropriate to remember that both the concrete witnesses of the saints and the conceptual elucidations of theology can serve as sources for our

---

18. In *Summa theologiae* IIa-IIae qq. 1–4, Aquinas reverses the order of inquiry: first, the object of faith, secondly, the act of belief, and then the human capacity or potency, the intellect that receives the infused *habitus* of faith.

instruction about the dynamics of Christian faith. The present study uses a full range of sources in order to illumine the virtue of faith. Although the theological synthesis achieved by Thomas Aquinas serves as the principal guide for organizing such a large amount of material, other witnesses to the importance of faith and its place within the theological life are cited frequently throughout the chapters of this book. These sources of ecclesial experience and pedagogy include the sacred Scriptures, the magisterial tradition, especially as presented in the texts of the Second Vatican Council, the authoritative writings of the early Christian period, and the testimony of saints and of classic spiritual authors.

Chapter 1

A Perfect Praise of Glory

In her short spiritual treatise "Heaven in Faith," Blessed Elizabeth of the Trinity wrote: "A praise of glory is a soul that gazes on God in faith and simplicity; it is a reflector of all that he is; it is like a bottomless abyss into which he can flow and expand."[1] The opening verses of the Letter to the Ephesians that describe the heavenly Father's design for all the members of the human race prompted Elizabeth to reflect on the meaning of the Pauline phrase "a praise of glory:"

In Christ we have also obtained an inheritance, having been destined according to the purpose of him who accomplishes all things according to his counsel and will, so that we, who were the first to set our hope on Christ, might live for the praise of his glory. In him you also, when you had heard the word of truth, the gospel of your salvation, and had believed in him, were marked with the seal of the promised Holy Spirit; this is the pledge of our inheritance toward redemption as God's own people, to the praise of his glory [Eph. 1:11–13].

By likening the person whom God loves to the adopted child in a household, the New Testament—we see this especially in the letters of St. Paul—appeals to human experience as a way to describe the growth of

---

1. "Heaven in Faith," no. 43, p. 112. The text of "Heaven in Faith," which the young Carmelite nun wrote some three months before her death on November 9, 1906, is contained in volume 1 of the complete works, *I Have Found God,* ed. Conrad De Meester, trans. Aletheia Kane (Washington, D.C.: ICS Publications, 1984). This edition also contains a complete "General Introduction" to the life and works of Elizabeth of the Trinity, pp. 7–82.

the Christian life. Just as a natural son or daughter is taught within a family structure how to live a good and happy life, those whom God "destined for adoption as his children through Jesus Christ" (Eph. 1:5) require a new instruction about the things of God. And although they receive this instruction within the community of the Church, all true wisdom has its origin in God, who both instructs the mind and transforms the heart. It is principally, then, the grace of the Holy Spirit that makes of the Christian person a living "praise of glory," an ever more spacious vessel of the divine wisdom and love. For Blessed Elizabeth of the Trinity, the practice of theological faith fulfills the divine promise of salvation, ensuring that those whom the Holy Spirit is making into a perfect sacrifice of praise are entirely transformed by his love.

In order to attain a more profound understanding of the virtue of faith, we need to consider the coordinates that connect the theological virtues to the Christian life. Three affirmations concerning the theological virtues are particularly significant. First, the theological virtues belong exclusively to the Christian dispensation; second, they express concretely the supernatural gift of habitual grace; third, they represent authentic perfections in the human person. In this chapter, we will consider in turn each of these three topics that serve as the coordinates for a study of the theological life.

The first topic concerns Christology. Jesus Christ, the one Mediator between God and humankind, communicates the theological life to those who hear and accept the preaching of the gospel. Cyril of Alexandria explains the significance of the fact that Christ as man mediates the divine life to us: "From Christ and in Christ, we have been reborn through the Spirit in order to bear the fruit of life; not the fruit of our old, sinful life but the fruit of a new life founded upon our faith in him and our love for him."[2] The theological virtues are the principles of a "new life" for those who share the same common nature with the Incarnate Son of God. By living this new life, we realize the inheritance that Christ's saving work makes possible for every human being. Aqui-

---

2. St. Cyril of Alexandria, *Commentary on the Gospel of John*, Bk. 10, chap. 2 (PG 74: 331–34), trans. International Committee on English in the Liturgy in *The Liturgy of the Hours*, vol. 2 (New York: Catholic Book Publishing Company, 1976), p 833.

nas describes Christ's mediation of this divine treasure as the grace of his headship over the Church.

The second topic explores the gift of grace as it exists in the human person. Because Christ bestows a new life on those who already live a natural life, theologians speak about the configuration and dynamism of the theological life as rooted in habitual or sanctifying grace. Furthermore, they speak about this habitual grace as a "created form." Why a form? Grace produces a qualitative change that radically affects the believer's human life, a change that renders the human person "fit" for a supernatural union with God. But why link the theological life with a distinctive created form, one over and above what God provides in human nature? Is it not sufficient that men and women are created in the image of God, in order for them to be fully apt to follow the Christian way and attain union with God their Creator? St. Augustine and with him the Christian tradition unanimously reply in the negative. The inherent power of human nature, writes St. Augustine, "is not the grace that the Apostle commends to us through the faith of Jesus Christ. For it is certain that we possess this nature in common with ungodly men and unbelievers; whereas the grace that comes through the faith of Jesus Christ belongs only to them to whom the faith itself appertains."[3] Habitual grace effects the divinization of the person; as such it can come about only from a special working of God. No created nature—not even a created nature "in the image of God"—can claim a participation in the divine life by its own power.[4]

This leads to the third topic, an account of the relation between creation and redemption. Christian anthropology recognizes different senses in which the phrase "in the image of God" can describe the

---

3. St. Augustine, *On Grace and Free Will*, chap. 13, 25 (PL 44, 896; NPNF 5, 454).

4. Still, creation in the image of God means something for the Christian life; for there does exist a real continuity between belonging to the human family and becoming children of God and sharers in God's life. For God has willed to give himself to his human creatures. So some authors speak of human nature's "obediential potency" for beatific union with God. In any event, such a capacity in the intellectual creature remains passive; it does not signify a proleptic protrusion of human nature into the active world of Christian meanings and values. Servais Pinckaers prefers the expression "capacité passive" instead of obediential potency to explain what exists in spiritual creatures as a disposition for beatific union with the blessed Trinity. For his argument, see "Le désir naturel de voir Dieu," *Nova et Vetera* 51 (1976): 255–73.

religious condition of human beings. One should distinguish in particular between created human nature (which by intelligence and freedom
images God within the physical universe) and human nature elevated
by grace to supernatural life—an image of God in a more radical sense.
Only the latter incarnates in the human person a grace-given perfection
that is in conformity with the fullness of the divine plan. As we shall
see, we can also identify other meanings of the term "the image of
God." It expresses a dynamic reality in the human creature who, by the
power of God's gratuitous love, undergoes transformation from being
one *capable of* knowing and loving God to one who actually *is* knowing
and loving God. To conceive of the image of God and human perfection
in this way does not introduce an unwarranted and needless fissure into
the Christian cosmos; it does not mischievously create what some have
labeled a two-layered universe. Rather, in the words of St. Leo the
Great, "If we comprehend faithfully and wisely the beginning of our
creation, we shall find that the human creature was made in God's image, to the end . . . that our race attains its highest natural dignity, by
the form of the divine goodness being reflected in us, as in a mirror."[5]
The Fathers were fond of making the point that whereas the human
being was created in God's image, the achievement of a "likeness" *(similitudo)* to God required the perfection of sanctifying grace, which embodies the form of the divine goodness reflected in us. In the Platonic
idiom of the early Fathers, we pass from shadow to reality.

To sum up, three topics—the mediation of Jesus Christ, the gift of
habitual grace, and the anthropology of the image of God—form the
coordinates in which the theological life of faith, of hope, and of love
finds its appropriate setting within the larger context of revealed truth.
No one who enters into faith's relationship with God does so in any way
other than or apart from the one who is the only Way. So to introduce
our study of the theological life, let us consider these three issues, man,
grace, and Christ, in greater detail. Each discussion aims to illumine
different aspects of God's transformation of our lives into a perfect
praise of glory to his name.

---

5. *Sermons*, no. 12, 1 (PL 54, 168; NPNF 12, 121).

Christ: Source of the Theological Life

The Humanity of Christ

The New Testament announces the central and unsurpassable place of Christ in the communication of divine life to humankind. Through the Incarnate Son we receive the grace of adoption and are drawn into the Trinitarian life. With Blessed Elizabeth of the Trinity, therefore, we read in the Letter to the Ephesians that "[God] destined us for adoption as his children through Jesus Christ, according to the good pleasure of his will, to the praise of his glorious grace that he freely bestowed on us in the Beloved" (Eph. 1:5–6). Because the Incarnate Son is God's very own Beloved, the Church holds that Jesus Christ illustrates and illuminates to the highest possible degree the ultimate measure and concrete essence of the human person.[6]

As a way of explicating the New Testament teaching on adoptive sonship (see Rom. 8:14–17), classical Christology developed the thesis that the humanity of Christ serves as a unique "instrument" for communicating God's life to the Church. The suggestion that Christ's human nature serves as an instrument of his divinity originates with the early Greek Fathers, who adapted the Neoplatonic notion of instrument—*organon*—precisely in order to explain how the complete human nature assumed by the Second Person of the blessed Trinity plays a real and authentic role in our salvation.

The theological use of the notion of instrument is not an entanglement of gospel truth with alien philosophical systems. As we shall see, "instrument" in this usage pertains to the notion of *cause*, a basic philosophical principle—rooted in common experience—that identifies the sources of *change* in created beings. The distinction between principal and instrumental causality illuminates the variety of *ways* that change comes about in any creature. In particular, the distinction between principal and instrumental *efficient* causes helps us to see how, as an instrumental cause, Christ's complete and entire human nature stands in an

---

6. See Pope John Paul II, *Redemptor hominis*, 8–10. In this context, "human person" refers to the ultimate perfection of a human nature, whose laws and values, as *Veritatis splendor*, no. 38, affirms, are open to human investigation.

active relationship to his divinity. The Persons of the blessed Trinity acting together remain the principal efficient cause (the ontologically adequate source) of every good thing that happens in the world, of every movement that benefits the human person. We say therefore that the Trinity is the principal efficient cause of grace and of our salvation. Christ's humanity, however, is the instrument through which this causal work of the Trinity is accomplished, through which a saving "change" in the human being is effected.

Philosophers explain that when any entity possesses the capacity to be moved, this potential implies a certain kind of imperfection. The possibility for change indicates that the being has not yet achieved the full and perfect realization of its potential. Change itself, then, involves a state of becoming in a given reality; it signifies motion *toward* a term or "end," toward a fuller achievement of the being's specific nature. When considered as a true becoming, as an increase in the being of a thing, motion indicates the existence of a cause greater than that which is moved. It is well known that Roman Catholic theology traditionally considers the brute fact that things move in the world among the more manifest persuasions for the existence of a God who can account for such movement. As T. S. Eliot says, "At the still point of the turning world" ("Burnt Norton"). Moreover, when the Book of Wisdom records that divine wisdom is more active than all active things (Wis. 7:24), the Old Testament itself applies the philosophical notion of the "unmoved mover" to the God who "created the heavens and the earth" (Gen. 1:1).

The claim is made in philosophy that there exists a relationship of dependence between what is moved and whatever causes the thing to move. When a cause produces an effect, one usually can distinguish further between a principal cause and an instrumental cause. "A principal cause," Aquinas explains, "acts from itself by its own inherent quality . . . thus sun lights the air, and fire heats water, whereas an instrumental cause acts not precisely by its own quality, but in virtue of the influence of the principal cause."[7] As a source of heat, the sun can act directly on something cold and wet, such as a Monday morning wash.

7. *Quaestiones disputatae de veritate,* q. 27, a. 4.

In this example, the principal cause (the sun) accounts for the total cause of a total effect (the heating and drying of the clothes). But another causal influence can exercise a distinct, though subordinate, effect upon the thing that is moved (in this example, the freshly laundered clothes). When this happens, the instrumental cause allows for a new deployment of the principal cause: for example, when clothes are dried in a machine, whose source of energy is ultimately solar. The heat of the sun (principal cause) still dries the clothes, but the specific structure of the automatic dryer—its instrumentality—causes them, as any launderer will testify, to come out differently than if they were to hang out in the parched, hot climate of a Mediterranean afternoon. So there are two operations in play, one from the instrument, and the other from the principal cause, which surpasses the native capacity of the instrument.

Most instruments remain separate from the principal agents who employ them. To return to the example above, the solar-powered clothes dryer is not a physical extension of the sun. Some other instruments, however, are joined to and do make a single piece with the principal agent cause. Christ's humanity is one of these. The fifth-century Council of Chalcedon determined that a single person or, to use the technical term, *hypostasis*, unites the two natures, human and divine, of Christ. A later ecumenical council, Second Constantinople, gave further precision to this dogma: "There is but one *hypostasis* [person], which is our Lord Jesus Christ, one of the Trinity."[8] Christian doctrine on the Incarnation confesses that in the God-man there exists but one personal reality—one personhood—to which everything in Christ's human nature is to be attributed as its proper subject.

In order to take full account of the dogma of faith that Christ's human nature is united to his divine Person, Aquinas affirms that the humanity of Christ is a "conjoined" instrument of his divinity. Christian theology develops this usage when it inquires how the humanity of Christ discharges a real, though instrumental, role in God's activities. In one place, Aquinas argues in this fashion: "To give grace or the Holy Spirit belongs to Christ inasmuch as he is God, authoritatively; but

8. See Council of Constantinople II, anathemas against the "Three Chapters," no. 4 (*DS* 424).

instrumentally it belongs to him as man, inasmuch as his humanity is the instrument of his Godhead."[9] By affirming the instrumentality of Christ's full human nature, Aquinas passes on the rich teaching of St. John Damascene (675–749) who, in his *De fide orthodoxa*, argues that there must be a direct or physical (not merely moral or juridical) influx of Christ's meritorious actions on his members.[10] This explanation reflects a typically Greek emphasis in talking about the mysteries of the Christian faith, for, as is generally agreed, Eastern theology especially focuses on the actual, ongoing reality of the divine presence that the Incarnation achieves in the world. On the other hand, looser accounts of the relationship between God and the creature (for instance, the notion of "moral union") seem to recur more frequently in the history of Western theology, especially after the Reformation.

Let us consider some philosophical principles that guide the operation of instrumental causes. First, there is the general principle that every cause in acting produces a thing somewhat like itself.[11] Thus, any efficient cause, whether principal or instrumental, must be proportionate to the activity that it exercises on another being. This proportion or order that exists between both instrumental and principal causes and what is caused implies first of all a certain "fit" or consonance between mover and moved. Next, whenever a certain activity is communicated through an instrument, the activity requires a commensurate match between the instrument and the principal agent. And finally, there must also be a suitable union between the instrument and the beneficiary of the activity.

Were it not for the unsurpassable Christian message that God, for

9. *Summa theologiae* IIIa q. 8, a. 1, ad 1. See also Ia-IIae q. 112, a. 1, ad 1: "Christ's humanity is 'a kind of instrument of his divinity,' according to Damascene. Now an instrument performs the action of the principal agent not by its own power but by the power of the principal agent. And so Christ's humanity does not cause grace by its own power but by the power of the conjoined divinity, in virtue of which the actions of Christ's humanity have saving efficacy."

10. This work is a Latin translation of Book Three of the saint's *Pêgê Gnôseôs*, or *Fount of Wisdom*. For further information on the merit of Christ and his efficient causality, see Colman E. O'Neill, O.P., *The One Mediator*, vol. 50 of *Summa Theologiae* (New York: McGraw-Hill, 1965), pp. 238–44.

11. See *Summa theologiae* Ia q. 4, a. 3: "Omne agens agit sibi simile inquantum est agens, agit autem unumquodque secundum suam formam, necesse est quod in effectu sit similtudine formae agentis."

whom "all things are possible" (Matt. 19:26), actually establishes a proportion between himself and creatures, so that the spiritual creature can be drawn into a communion of holiness and beatific fellowship, there would of course be no grounds for imagining that God causally engages humankind in so fully personal a way, that is, by making human creatures real lovers of the divine Persons. In the *Summa theologiae*, Aquinas uses the example of merit to illustrate the order that exists between Christ and his members, for whom he acts as an instrument of sanctification. "Grace was bestowed upon Christ," he writes, "not only as an individual but inasmuch as he is Head of the Church, so that it might overflow into his members; and therefore Christ's works are referred to himself and to his members in the same way as the works of any other man in a state of grace are referred to himself."[12] In this text, Aquinas evokes the Pauline teaching on the Body of Christ: "For just as the body is one and has many members, and all the members of the body, though many, are one body, so it is with Christ" (1 Cor. 12:12). In sum, because Christ's humanity remains personally united with the divine Word, one of the Trinity, and as much as we (along with the angels) are joined to Christ as members of one Body, our share in the divine life flows from God through Christ and from Christ to us. The humanity of Christ— conjoined to the divine Person of the Word and united with other human beings in virtue of a shared human nature—remains the instrumental cause of God's saving work: Christ's humanity is the instrument through which and by means of which God "moves" human beings toward their destiny of union with him.

Our Involvement in the Life and Destiny of Christ

Membership in the Church of Christ is one of the questions that we study today in the branch of theology known as ecclesiology, the study of the Church. But until the early nineteenth century, reflection on the Church did not divide off a special discipline or branch of theology, with its own methods and set of questions. Rather, theological reflection on the Church developed out of specific questions in Christology, even though, by the early medieval period, canon law and Church polity in general had developed into their own disciplines and generated their

---

12. *Summa theologiae* IIIa q. 48, a. 1.

own treatises.[13] For example, Aquinas discusses the fundamental constitution of the Church as part of his treatment of Christ's special prerogatives, in particular, his threefold grace. More specifically, Aquinas identified Christ's capital grace or his grace of headship as the constitutive element of the Church.[14] There is reason to believe that this approach to the Church is more faithful to the biblical revelation than some later ecclesiological views developed with too much dependence on the methods and the conclusions of the social sciences. The theologian needs to say more about the Church of Christ than scientific theories about individuals and their relationship to groups can supply, even when the social theorists are sympathetic to Christian belief.

A properly Christian view of the Church must be rooted in the Pauline teaching on Christ as Head of the body: "He is the head of the body, the Church; he is the beginning, the first-born of the dead, so that he might come to have first place in everything" (Col. 1:18). Three points about Christ's capital grace deserve particular emphasis: First, as Head, Christ himself remains preeminent among the members; second, Christ's ability to impart grace to the other members ultimately derives from his divinity; finally, the specific identity of human natures in the Incarnate Word and in each member of the human race provides a ground to explain the joining of member to Head.[15] We now turn to the implications of the grace of headship for the theological life of those who are members of Christ's body.

Because Christ shares in a common nature with all the members of the human race—that is, he possesses the same kind of human nature that we possess—he is able to communicate to us his divine benefits.

---

13. It is interesting to observe that the canonists of the pre-Gratian period were accustomed to placing doctrinal canons side by side with ecclesiastical law; John P. McIntyre describes this practice as the "ecclesiology of the *unum* . . . : the unity of the Godhead: the unity of Christ: the unity of the Church: rendered visible in the one see of Rome." See his review of *Liber canonum diuersorum sanctorum patrum siue Collectio in CLXXXIII titulos digesta*, ed. Joseph Motta in *Monumenta Iuris Canonici*; Series B: *Corpus Collectionum* 7 (Vatican City: Biblioteca Apostolica Vaticana, 1988) in *Christianesimo nella Storia* 12 (1991): 420–22. The Jesuit theologians of the sixteenth-century Catholic Reform developed certain implications of the ecclesiology of the *unum*.

14. Aquinas develops this theme in *Summa theologiae* IIIa q. 8: "The Grace of Christ as Head of the Church."

15. Aquinas further elaborates on these three points in his *Commentary on the Letter to the Ephesians*. For further information, see his *In Ephesios* I, 8.

The Letter to the Hebrews suggests one practical advantage of this arrangement: "Therefore he had to become like his brethren in every respect, so that he might be a merciful and faithful high priest in the service of God, to make a sacrifice of atonement for the sins of the people" (Heb. 2:17). Following the framework provided especially by St. Paul, Aquinas develops a persuasive theology of the "mystical body." In order to emphasize the analogical character of his comparison, however, Aquinas consciously inserts in his Latin text the phrase "*quasi una persona*": Christ and his members remain united *as if* they formed one person. We should remark, nonetheless, on the philosophically strong language that is used to affirm the kind of bond that unites Christ "mystically" with other human persons: "Just as the natural body remains a 'one something,' although made up of a diversity of members, so we reckon the whole Church, which is the mystical body of Christ, as one person, together with its head who is Christ."[16] The force of the comparison derives from the ontological unity of the human person: body and soul together form the undivided unity of the person. Aquinas wants us to think likewise about the unity of believer and Christ within the Church.

As a result of the strong unity between Christ and the members of the Church, each believer derives spiritual benefits from Christ the Head and enjoys a distinctive kind of communion in Christ. The Christian society *(societas christiana)*, which for the present time only Christian utopian literature can depict in any complete way, promises to give concrete expression to Jesus' final witness: "The glory that you have given me I have given to them, so that they may be one, as we are one" (John 17:22). But the work has begun. In this text, Jesus is referring to his disciples, whose lives ought to become a praise of God's glory. In his *Commentary on Ephesians*, Aquinas sketches something of what this glory means for those who live the theological life:

Every spiritual sensibility, every gift, everything which can exist in the Church—all of which are in Christ superabundantly—derive from Christ and develop in the members of the Church. . . . Whoever is a member of the Church, Christ makes wise according to that perfect wisdom which is in him; whoever is just, Christ makes to be so according to his perfect justice.[17]

16. *Summa theologiae* IIIa q. 49, a. 1, *corpus.*
17. *In Ephesios* I, 8.

This teaching reflects a long-held view among the Church's pastors concerning the practical effects of sacramental incorporation into Christ. For example, we find it clearly expressed in the catechetical instructions of the fourth-century Greek Father Cyril of Jerusalem. His contemporary Gregory of Nyssa makes the same point in his *Treatise on Christian Perfection* when he uses the image of the sun and its rays to explain how Christ influences the moral lives of his followers:

> When we consider that Christ is the true light, having nothing in common with deceit, we learn that our own life also must shine with the rays of that true light. Now these rays of the Sun of Justice are the virtues which pour out to enlighten us so that "we may put away the works of darkness and walk honorably as in broad daylight."[18]

A classical thesis in Christology, as noted above, speaks about the *triplex gratia Christi*, the threefold grace of Christ. Christ as man possesses, first, the grace of union, that grace belonging exclusively to the uncreated Person of the Incarnate Logos; next, Christ's own habitual or sanctifying grace, which accounts for the substantial holiness of his human character; third, the grace of headship or leadership, which establishes Christ as the life of the Church. As the saints of every generation remind us, the believer's participation in Christ's spiritual benefits flows from his pierced side, the source of sacramental life in the Church. Catholic teaching always keeps the theological life and the sacramental life together.

Christ's capital grace includes his capital virtue. Aquinas explicitly inquires whether Christ possesses the moral and theological virtues.[19] According to the principle that motion belongs more perfectly to the mover than to the moved, the Christian tradition clearly affirms that Christ possesses each one of the moral virtues in its perfect state. As the Sun of Justice, Christ becomes the source of all moral goodness in the Church. Of the three theological virtues, however, Christ possesses only charity. The One who reveals the heavenly Father lived not in the darkness of faith but by a light that derives from the beatific vision.[20] In

---

18. *On Christian Perfection* (PG 46: 259–62), trans. International Committee on English in the Liturgy in *The Liturgy of the Hours*, vol. 4 (New York: Catholic Book Publishing Company, 1975), p. 107.

19. See *Summa theologiae* IIIa q. 7, aa. 2–4.

20. For further information see my article, "Incarnate Wisdom and the Immediacy of

like manner, the certainty deriving from that vision removed for Christ the expectancy inherent in theological hope. Christ remains, however, preeminent in redeeming love—his created charity; and "from his fullness we have all received, grace upon grace" (John 1:16).

Grace: Form and Dynamism of the Theological Life

The Notion of Created Grace

According to the promise of Jesus himself, whoever confesses Father, Son, and Holy Spirit within the Church of faith and sacraments enjoys a personal union with the blessed Trinity. The Dominican theologian William Hill calls this union "the New Being by grace [that] means entry into God's being *as it is proper to him,* i.e., entrance into the uncreated divine life of Father, Son, and Spirit—possible to the creature only as the term of its intentionality of knowledge and love."[21] As real *habitus* that transform and perfect human knowledge and love, the theological virtues of faith, hope, and charity belong to the order of the New Being.[22] Although debates concerning the proper way to express the relationship between grace and nature recommence with each new round of theological discussions, the scriptural witnesses and the tra-

---

Christ's Salvific Knowledge," in *Problemi teologici alla luce dell'Aquinate (Atti del IX Congresso Tomistico Internazionale). Studi Tomistici* 44 (Vatican City: Libreria Editrice Vaticana, 1991): 334–40.

21. William J. Hill, *The Three-Personed God: The Trinity as a Mystery of Salvation* (Washington, D.C.: The Catholic University of America Press, 1982), p. 276. For a fuller explanation of the Thomistic use of intentionality to explain the Trinitarian indwelling, see Fr. Hill's *Proper Relations to the Indwelling Divine Persons* (Washington, D.C.: The Thomist Press, n.d.). There has been a development of the term *intentionality* since the time of Aquinas. St. Thomas and his contemporaries used the term to designate a mental sphere of logical relations as well as initial primary intelligible species. The Renaissance Thomists, such as John of St. Thomas, spoke about *media quo* in describing first-order concepts. Finally, by way of Brentano (for whom intentionality meant the mind's relation to its psychic contents), Husserl understood intentionality as the relational act whereby the subject pointed its relation to a more or less determinate content. Some philosophers are rightly wary of the notion insofar as it seems to suggest a strategy for getting the knower out of the hole dug by Descartes and subsequent idealists. The theologian, however, uses the term in treating of the virtue of faith only in order to show the full implications of St. Thomas's axiom that theological faith terminates in the *res*.

22. The Latin term *habitus* belongs to the fourth conjugation of nouns, and so it looks the same in both the nominative singular and plural.

dition of the Fathers so explicitly affirm the gratuity, profusion, and utter distinctiveness of divine grace that to conceive of this spiritual enrichment in men and women as other than real and ontological can result only from a selective reading of the sources. Furthermore, because this New Being is new for the human creature, but not for God, theologians designate the New Being as possessed by us a "created" grace. Aquinas equates habitual grace with that "special love, whereby God draws the rational creature above the conditions of its nature to a participation in the divine Good."[23] The theological virtues are concrete expressions of the believer's participation in the divine Good. They enable the human person to move beyond the limits of creatureliness by assenting to divine Truth and by loving the divine Goodness. For intelligent creatures, no greater good can be conceived.

The steadiness and stability in pursuing divine Goodness that belong to the theological life urge the theologian to compare grace with the quality of *habitus*. This is an example of analogical thinking. *Habitus,* one of the qualities of being, refers to the way in which a particular being possesses the features or traits that characterize its specific nature. Grace is called habitual because this divine gift creates the proximate principle or foundation for the theological life, resulting in a real modification of the human person. In other words, because divine grace not only produces good actions but also radically modifies the person who acts, the theologian needs to account for the soul-penetrating transformation of the justified person that enables him or her to perform deeds worthy of eternal life. Insofar as it seeks to account for this mystery, the view that sanctifying or habitual grace is a created gift of God remains an indispensable concept for the theology of grace.[24] For this philosophical intuition about how the New Being permeates our created beings establishes the grounds for an ontological precision that succeeds

23. *Summa theologiae* Ia-IIae q. 110, a. 1, *corpus.*

24. In the middle decades of the twentieth century, the *ressourcement* theologians called the attention of the Catholic world to the need for a realignment of theological categories. The neo-scholastic theologians, they remarked, had developed ways of speaking about habitual grace that seemed strangely foreign to the biblical and patristic teaching about the personal relationship into which God invites intelligent creatures. At the end of the twentieth century, there exists a general agreement that the texts of the Second Vatican Council, especially the celebrated *Gaudium et spes*, no. 22, have contributed much toward re-tooling theological categories.

in communicating the depths of how grace works both on human nature and in human freedom. At the same time, as Thomists in particular like to observe, the view that God's complete self-giving to intelligent creatures remains a *created* perfection of the person enables the theologian to address fully other important theological truths, such as the total dependence of the creature on God, the certitude of divine providence, and the sovereign independence of the divine will in the governance of the world.[25]

Theologians working out of the Thomist commentatorial tradition describe habitual grace as a formal physical (although analogical) participation of the divine nature as such. Each element of the definition requires explanation. First, the term "formal." This adjective derives from the Latin word *forma,* and it designates the form or structure that a given reality takes on in the world. In the context of a definition of divine grace, form refers to the condition that grace establishes in the justified soul. The scholastic theologians distinguished between substantial forms, which establish the basic kind or quiddity of a being, and accidental forms, which modify the substance in some significant way. Now grace radically changes us, but it does not accomplish this at the price of changing the kind of beings that we are, namely, human beings. In other words, although habitual grace represents a real, ontological endowment in the spiritual order, it does not turn human beings into pineapples, canaries, or angels. Thus, preferred Thomistic parlance speaks about divine grace perfecting human nature, and about habitual grace as an accidental modification of the human person.

Because many students of theology understand accidental in the sense of superfluous or expendable, this theological usage has given rise to much misunderstanding in the area of Christian anthropology. Aquinas, who read carefully St. Augustine's manifold instruction on grace, was clear about the utter necessity of divine grace for living the theological life. In fact, in order to emphasize that accidental does not mean incidental, Aquinas consciously chose to explain the "accidental" presence of grace in the human soul by comparing the divine life in us to the way in which something known comes to exist, such as an intelligible

---

25. For further development of this claim and one of the best presentations of the Thomist position, see J.-H. Nicolas, *Les profondeurs de la grâce* (Paris: Beauchesne, 1969).

species or form, in a knowing subject. Knowledge affects the human person in a most fundamental way, and yet what is known remains distinct from the one who knows. In a concise phrase, Aquinas summarizes this comparison as follows: "For what in God is a substantial mode comes to be in the soul that participates in the divine goodness in an accidental mode, as is clear in the case of knowledge."[26] His recourse to the intentionality of human knowledge illuminates the abiding presence of the divine life in those who are justified by faith and continues to provide the best model for speaking theologically about the proper relations of the indwelling Trinity to each member of Christ's body. As I have said, to speak about the accidental character of grace does not mean that Christian theology considers grace of secondary importance or something extrinsic to or merely cosmetic for human nature. The accidental character of the form simply implies that divine grace shapes the human person in the way that a known object affects the person who knows; in short, divine grace, like the knowable object, is foreordained to being-in a subject.

The above explanation of how grace affects the personal lives of believers avoids suggesting a conflation of human nature and divine grace. Before the Second Vatican Council, ecclesiastical authority cautioned against certain theological positions that threatened to confuse God's creative presence to the human creature with the realization of the same person's call to beatitude.[27] The danger here is the risk of emphasizing the pervasive and inclusive character of divine grace in a way that practically eliminates the need for a real grace of justification— one that effectively transforms an impious person into a holy one. But the New Testament makes it exceedingly difficult to glide over the fact that the justification won by the blood of Christ really involves a movement from our being "by nature children of wrath, like everyone else"

---

26. *Summa theologiae* Ia-IIae q. 110, a. 2, ad 2.

27. For example, Pius XII's *Humani generis* (1950): "Alii veram 'gratuitatem' ordinis supernaturalis corrumpunt, cum autument Deum entia intellectu praedita condere non posse, quin eadem ad beatificam visionem ordinet et vocet" (*DS* 3890). For a contemporary discussion of this issue, see my "Is Aquinas's *Summa* only about Grace?" in *Ordo Sapientiae et Amoris. Image et Message de Saint Thomas d'Aquin à travers les récentes études historiques, herméneutiques et doctrinales,* ed. Carlos-Josaphat Pinto de Oliveira, O.P. (Fribourg: Editions Universitaires, 1993): 197–209.

to our being "alive together with Christ—by grace you have been saved" (Eph. 2:3, 5).

Since the Church's theological tradition recognizes the intrinsic relationship between form and activity, the scholastics were accustomed to speak about grace as both an entitative *habitus* (that is, an accidental form) and a kind of motion. The distinction still serves theological discussion well. Philosophers tell us that any created nature is a principle of motion and rest that specifies and regulates the movement of the entity to which it belongs. Since, as we have seen, grace is a kind of form, this spiritual endowment must account for uplifted human activity. Moreover, such a special principle is necessary to explain the supernatural life in us, for no human person properly speaking can perform a supernatural action. The sixteenth-century Italian theologian Cardinal Cajetan, in his commentary on the *Summa theologiae*, summarizes this teaching on grace conceived after the fashion of a form or nature: "Grace first perfects being *[esse]* and not operation *[operari]*; and therefore grace does not, in a primary way, perfect an object or act, but secondarily; for first it makes one a son [or daughter] of God and then makes one capable of meriting eternal life."[28] While it is true that both the infused and the theological virtues describe how a graced person conducts his or her daily life, Cajetan further explains that divine "grace is not primarily concerned with works, for its principal concern is divine fellowship, which remains prior to all virtue or virtuous activity."[29] Cajetan here interprets Aquinas's teaching on the relationship of divine grace, which transforms the human person, to the moral life, which is the expression of the New Being. This teaching reflects Aquinas's own study of the Church's controversies with the Pelagians, who mistakenly taught that salutary acts were possible apart from the transforming power of divine grace. When we speak about the theological life, then, we are not giving one more example of how world religions develop ethical schemes. The theological life is first of all a transformed life.

When by appeal to analogy theologians consider divine grace as a

---

28. *In Iam-IIae* q. 110, a. 4, no. vii. See Hebrews 9:15: "For this reason he is the mediator of a new covenant, so that those who are called may receive the promised eternal inheritance, because a death has occurred which redeems them from the transgressions under the first covenant."

29. Ibid., no. viii.

type of motion, they speak about "actual grace." Actual grace supplies the immediate principle for Christian activity, when, as Aquinas says, "the human soul is moved by God to know or will or do something."[30] By developing this analogy, the tradition further distinguishes two kinds of actual grace, identified by the terms operative or cooperative. God intervenes with operative grace in the life of a person who, because no soul can adequately prepare itself for the divine initiative, remains purely passive in the face of the divine movement. The scholastics called such a soul moved rather than moving—*mens mota et non movens*. As the Church learned during the course of the long controversies with the Pelagians, the grace of initial justification, which accounts for the first moment of conversion, falls within this category. On the other hand, the one who benefits from cooperative grace participates personally in the graced activity in such a way that, while the gift remains the fruit of divine initiative, the graced action has roots in human freedom and in the human person. Unresolved quarrels about the manner in which human freedom operates under the impulse of divine grace make it difficult to find an easy and uniformly agreed upon way to explain, or even speak about, this cooperation.[31] Since most of what Christians do in the theological life falls within the category of cooperative grace, current theology is struggling to find an appropriate way to express the relationship between the divine *motio* and personal resolve. In fact, the activities of Christian life that figure most in a person's eternal salvation, our works of merit and satisfaction, concretely express movements of cooperative grace (when the Christian soul both is moved and moves— *mens mota et movens*).

In the celebrated seventeenth-century disputes with the Molinists, representatives of Baroque Thomism stoutly defended the view that

30. *Summa theologiae* Ia-IIae q. 110, art. 2. In this text, Aquinas distinguishes between grace as a movement *(motus)* and grace as a *habitus* or quality; he describes "actual grace" as "a certain movement of the soul."

31. These controversies developed in their classical forms at the end of the sixteenth century. The principal positions were developed by Thomists, such as Domingo Bañez (1528–1624), Augustinians, such as Henri Noris (1631–1704), Molinists, such as the Spanish Jesuit Luis de Molina (1535–1600), who gave his name to the school, Congruists, such as the Jesuits Francisco de Suarez (1548–1617) and St. Robert Bellarmine (1542–1621), who modified the more enthusiastic claims of Molina, and Syncretists, including, later, St. Alphonus Liguori (1696–1787). Nicolas, *Les profondeurs*, pp. 189–97, gives a brief but compelling account of the Thomist doctrine on physical premotion.

every human action occurred as a result of a divine "physical pre-motion" that causes the human will itself to cause: in causing the creature to act, God operates fully, and not partially in the way that some who defended versions of the divine concurrence theory seemed to imply.[32] The Thomists involved in the *Congregatio de Auxiliis* (1598–1607) correctly reckoned that a number of important theological issues were at stake in the discussion. Christian life conceived as a partnership with God borrows almost exclusively from the model of human solidarity, and so results in a highly anthropomorphized vision of God's love. The concordist view, so called because of the *Concordia* by the sixteenth-century Jesuit Luis de Molina, holds that the divine omnipotence is constrained by its cooperation or simultaneous concursus with created agents; God's influence is thus partial, even half-hearted. On the other hand, the view that God exercises a full, causal influence on human freedom emphasizes the permanence and efficacy of the divine action as it enfolds the unsteady and frail created self, a self that always enjoys, according to the Thomist account, a complete though admittedly subordinate exercise of freedom.

When theologians say that grace is something "physical," they obviously are using the term "physical" in a technical sense. Both the metaphoric imagery and the straightforward teaching of the New Testament make it plain that God's action in the world results in real changes and produces real effects in people. St. Paul expresses this realism when he compares the effects of Christian baptism to Christ's own death and resurrection: "We have been buried with him by baptism into death, so that, just as Christ was raised from the dead by the glory of the Father, so we too might walk in newness of life" (Rom. 6:4). The scholastics chose to describe this real action as "physical" in order to distinguish it from causes of a lesser efficacy, such as "moral" causes. Roman Catholic theology refuses to consider divine grace as something extrinsic that simply inspires or motivates the life of the believer; no

---

32. Theories of divine concurrence include classical Molinism and its later refinement in Congruism. For a fuller explanation of these two views about how God interacts with human freedom, see T.C. O'Brien, "Premotion, Physical," in *The New Catholic Encyclopedia*, vol. 7:740a–742b. Also, Bernard Lonergan, S.J., discusses this point in his *Grace and Freedom. Operative Grace in the Thought of St. Thomas Aquinas* (New York: Herder and Herder, 1971).

explanatory account that reduces grace to a special influence, an inspiration, a call, or any sheerly moral reality suffices for an orthodox account of the theology of grace. Thus, to call grace "physical" does not imply that it is something material, as when we speak about physics or a physical plant. Rather, such language affirms, as St. Jerome explained to some newly baptized Christians, that for those who have been raised up by the Word of God from the mire of this world, "the very nature of things has been changed."[33] "Physical" also distinguishes habitual grace linguistically from other kinds of authentic divine activity—such as mystical graces, mystical phenomena—that represent transitory gifts of the Holy Spirit, which, because they are transitory, do not necessarily shape the character of the one who receives them.

In the scholastic definition of grace, the terms "formal" and "physical" both modify the substantive "participation." Grace principally signifies a participation in God's own life. From the perspective of participation, divine grace belongs to the inner reality of the soul. In other words, grace does not stop at the margins of the human person. Aquinas makes this point clearly: "One must say that grace is in the essence of the soul, perfecting it, insofar as it gives to the soul a spiritual being, and makes it through some kind of similarity a participator of the divine nature [precisely as such]."[34] In the definition of grace, the phrase "of the divine nature precisely as such" indicates that grace finds its origin in the very reality that makes God to be God: the three Persons of the blessed Trinity.

The notion of participation enjoys a long history in both theology and philosophy. Today, scholars generally agree that Aquinas's doctrine on participation reflects as much certain Platonic influences on his thought as it does straightforward Aristotelian elements.[35] In his *Commentary on Boethius's De hebdomadibus*, Aquinas explains: "To participate is, as it were, to take a part; and therefore, when anything receives in a

---

33. St. Jerome, *In Psalmos XXXXI, Ad Neophytos* in *S. Hieronymi Presbyteri Opera* Pars II, Opera Homiletica (Turnhout: Brepols, 1958), 64–66: "Dicite ergo, qui Xpistum nunc induistis, et ductum nostrum sequentes, quasi pisciculi hamo, ita sermones Dei de gurgite saeculi istius subleuamini: In nobis rerum natura mutata est."

34. *De veritate* q. 27, a. 6.

35. See for example, L.-B. Geiger, O.P., *La participation dans la philosophie de S. Thomas d'Aquin*, Bibl. thomiste 23 (Paris: 2d edition, 1953) and Cornelio Fabro, *La nozione metafisica di partecipazione secondo S. Tommaso d'Aquino* (Turin: 3d edition, 1963).

particular manner that which belongs to another in a universal [total and absolute] manner, it is said to participate it."[36] Since to participate (from the Latin *partem capere*) means to possess in a partial manner something that subsists in total perfection as a pure, unlimited source, this definition of participation requires a certain modification in order to clarify the limits of a creature's capacity to participate in the divine nature. For this reason, our proposed definition of grace further modifies the term "participation" by the qualifier "analogical." Analogy means that the same name is applied to a number of different things in virtue of all of them being related, though in different ways, to a single primary thing. Because the authentic Christian tradition outrightly rejects all intimations of pantheism, the theologian is obliged to qualify as analogical the participation in the divine nature that grace realizes in the human person. By this appeal to analogy, the tradition simply signals that our participation in the divine nature does not entail our complete absorption into the divine being. Given the nature of the divine being, any unqualified union of God and the creature would result in the effective annihilation of created personhood; therefore, correct theological practice refers to an analogical participation of the creature in the divine life.[37] This qualification allows us to affirm a real communion of the Christian with the blessed Trinity but at the same time to safeguard the human creature with his or her personal distinctness and freedom.

The relationship that grace enables the human person to enjoy with the persons of the blessed Trinity forms the essence of the Christian life. Aquinas summarizes his understanding of habitual grace in the following way:

For just as by its intellectual power the human person participates in the divine knowledge through the virtue of faith, and in the divine love through the virtue of charity in its power of will, so too through the nature of the soul do we participate, by way of a kind of likeness in the divine nature, in consequence of a certain rebirth or recreation.[38]

36. *In Boethii de hebdomadibus,* lect. 2. For further information, see Gerard Casey, "An Explication of the *De Hebdomadibus* of Boethius in the Light of St. Thomas's Commentary," *The Thomist* 51 (1987): 419–34.
37. For a detailed discussion of this question, see William J. Hill, *Knowing the Unknown God* (New York: Philosophical Library, 1971), especially pp. 131–44.
38. *Summa theologiae* Ia-IIae q. 110, a. 4. The English theologian Cornelius Ernst, O.P., explains that "in God alone are being and doing one and the same; in all creatures

The spiritual authors translate this important feature of Christian theology into a language that conveys the seriousness of the matter. In his long poem, the *Living Flame of Love*, St. John of the Cross speaks about God as the center of the soul. His spiritual heir in the tradition of Carmel, Elizabeth of the Trinity, summarizes his teaching in a way that illumines "the kind of likeness" that grace effects in the Christian saint.

"God is the center of the soul. So when the soul with all" its "strength will know God perfectly, love and enjoy him fully, then it will have reached the deepest center that can be attained in him." Before attaining this, the soul is already "in God who is its center," "but it is not yet in its *deepest* center, for it can still go further. Since love is what unites us to God, the more intense this love is, the more deeply the soul enters into God and the more it is centered in him." When it "possesses even one degree of love it is already in its center"; but when this love has attained its perfection, the soul will have penetrated into its *deepest* center. There it will be transformed to the point of becoming very like God.[39]

While the expressions of the saints vary, their teachings always disclose the coherence of divine truth, offering a unified instruction about the theological life. In this case, we see that grace establishes the Christian believer "at the still point of the turning world."

The Humanization of Grace

Divine grace discloses God's work in our present lives according to two types of causality, classically termed formal and efficient. A cause is a principle on which something else depends in some way for its existence. A formal cause constitutes the structure or quiddative element, which is the foundation of a thing's definition; an efficient or agent cause brings about the perfection of a thing. God alone gives grace, for he alone makes the creature share in his divine life. But how does divine grace shape our human nature? In the order of logical priority, the hu-

---

there is a real distinction between essence and powers. The theological interest of [Aquinas's] use of the distinction here is that it establishes an 'ontological' rather than a 'personalist' perspective for grace. Grace is prior to its 'personal' expression in man." See his *The Gospel of Grace*, vol. 30 of *Summa Theologiae* (New York: McGraw-Hill, 1972), pp. 122–23.

39. Elizabeth of the Trinity, *Heaven in Faith*, pp. 96–97; for the original text of St. John of the Cross, see *The Living Flame of Love*, Stanza 1:13, in *The Collected Works of St. John of the Cross*, trans. Kieran Kavanaugh, O.C.D., and Otilio Rodriguez, O.C.D. (London: Nelson, 1966), p. 583.

man person first receives the status or form of a participant in the divine nature. Following a long tradition of patristic exegesis, Aquinas considers one New Testament text central to the discussion.

His divine power has given us everything needed for life and godliness, through the knowledge of him who called us to his own glory and goodness. Thus he has given us, through these things, his precious and very great promises, so that through them you may escape from the corruption that is in the world because of lust, and become participants of the divine nature. (2 Pet. 1:3–4).

Pastors and theologians since the patristic period have appealed to this New Testament text in the course of preaching about or explaining the mystery of transformation in Christ. Thus, in his *Book on the Holy Spirit*, St. Ambrose—associating the transforming work of grace with the action of the Holy Spirit—asks, "Who, then, can dare to say that the Holy Spirit is separated from the Father and the Son, since through him we attain to the image and likeness of God, and through him, as the Apostle Peter says, are participants of the divine nature?" (2 Pet. 1:4).[40]

In developing his teaching on the structure of created grace, Aquinas takes the human person's participation in the divine life as a *point de départ*. Contemporary biblical theologians evoke the same lines of argument when they draw our attention to the figure of the *Deus praesens* or the motif of realized eschatology, particularly associated with the Johannine writings. The category of formal causality seems especially congenial to this scriptural pattern. Moreover, certain texts of Aquinas compare grace to a formal cause: "Grace in the sense of a quality is said to act on the soul not in the manner of an efficient cause but in the manner of a formal cause; so whiteness makes something white and justice makes something just."[41] But we need to make another distinction here. The formal cause under consideration is a special kind of formal cause, namely, formal *exemplary* causality. An exemplary cause accounts for a thing's being of a certain kind, but it does not determine the thing's formal constitution or quiddity.

Although he hesitates to capitalize on the category of formal causality to account for the humanization of grace, Aquinas does not settle for

---

40. St. Ambrose, *On the Holy Spirit*, Bk. 1, chap. 6 (PL 16, 723; Fathers of the Church 44, 80; hereafter FOTC).

41. *Summa theologiae* Ia-IIae q. 110, a. 2, ad 1.

an extrinsicist account of sanctifying grace. In fact, a true reading of Aquinas considerably distances him from a substantialist view of divine grace, according to which the accidental character of grace is formally connected only tenuously with human nature—as if human nature were nothing more than a kind of receptacle for divine grace. The substantialist view is extrinsicist in a negative sense. At the same time, the Thomist commentatorial tradition does not square easily with an overly formalist account, according to which the congruities between human nature and divine grace are explained in such a way that it is difficult to discern where nature ends and where grace begins. The classical Thomist commentatorial tradition—authors such as Cajetan and John of St. Thomas—were always alert to the risk of conflating grace and nature. But they also refused to reify divine grace, as if human nature served as a container for it. Rather they stressed the gratuitous and relational character of this gift in ways that strike a discordant note with many later views on Aquinas's meaning.[42]

We have seen that grace accounts for change in the human person. Just as in the natural order form begets movement, so also does the transformation that grace effects in the believer. The new life or New Being that God's goodness and glory generate in the believer inaugurates an authentically personal movement whose goal is the permanent possession of divine life: "Beloved, we are God's children now; what we will be has not yet been revealed. What we do know is this: when he is revealed, we will be like him, for we will see him as he is" (1 John 3:2). In other words, there remains an eschatological dimension to the Christian life, one that introduces another line of causal analysis, namely, final causality. In order to achieve a balanced theology of grace, the Catholic tradition emphasizes both our realized ("already") participation in the divine life here and now and the final ("not yet") vision of God's glory. Grace and glory differ not in kind but only in degree,

---

42. Thus, Cardinal Cajetan qualifies his reading of Aquinas in a way that sounds strikingly contemporary: "Grace is not properly said to be created; but it can be so termed inasmuch as it is not educed from the power of the subject nor given on the basis of merits." And nearly a century later, John of St. Thomas makes a similar point: "Grace is not created, since it is produced as an accident inhering; thus, it is produced in and from its subject and not from nothing. . . . With respect to its reality, it is nothing other than the very nature of the soul; relationally it has that reality inasmuch as it is subordinated to an agency exceeding its nature."

and in the mode whereby we are united with God. The wayfarer lives by faith, whereas the saints, in vision, behold face to face. Christian life, then, proposes a sacramentalized journey in faith that leads to beatific fellowship with the saints in vision. An excessively eschatological approach to God, in which the believer can only expect some future encounter with him, eclipses the reality of grace as a true, though analogical, participation in the divine nature. Too much emphasis on an absent God obscures the Catholic truth that God here and now is working at the still center of our still-moving world.

The Catholic stress on the reality of divine grace in our present lives leads to two further considerations regarding the virtues of the Christian life. First, habitual grace is the root and font of the theological and infused moral virtues. Thus, Aquinas affirms that grace "is not simply a virtue; rather it is a kind of habitual state which is presupposed by the infused virtues, as their origin and root."[43] Recall that virtue also falls under the category of a *habitus*, a permanent characteristic that is difficult to modify and that disposes a person to act either well or ill. With an eye for greater precision, theologians traditionally distinguish between two types of *habitus*. One type—called entitative *habitus*—affects the subject in its very being. As we have seen, the New Being of sanctifying or habitual grace belongs to this type. The virtues, on the other hand, are operative *habitus*: they modify the way a subject performs or acts. The theological life commits us to both being and doing, to both life and living a life. St. Augustine compares our sanctification to a new birth: "From this begetting by grace," he writes, "we distinguish that son who, although he was the Son of God, came that he might become the son of man, and might give us, who were children of the human family, the power to become the children of God."[44]

There is a second consideration. Because the graced person participates in the divine nature, we can also consider the theological virtues from the viewpoint of the triune God. According to Aquinas's explanation, created grace is related to the divine nature as participating to what is participated in—or as T. S. Eliot puts it, "say that the end precedes the beginning." In the blessed Trinity, the divine Being remains

---

43. See *Summa theologiae* Ia-IIae q. 110, a. 3, ad 3.
44. *Letters*, No. 140: 3,9. (PL 33, 541; FOTC 20, 64).

identical with God's knowing and loving, but in the intelligent creature, created existence is not identical with acts of knowing and loving. Still, divine grace ennobles these human acts. For just as the Christian soul participates through habitual grace in the deepest center of God, so through the theological virtues of faith, hope, and charity the believer participates in God's own knowing and loving. In this way, the life of grace replicates in the human person the image of the inner life of the blessed Trinity. Quoting the fourteenth-century Flemish mystic Jan van Ruysbroeck on graced souls, Elizabeth of the Trinity explains: "They live, in St. John's expression, in 'communion' with the three adorable Persons, 'sharing' their life, and this is 'the contemplative life'; this contemplation 'leads to possession.'"[45] We could add that this experience, which the saints recognize with special clarity, also describes the theological life that the virtue of faith initiates.

In the Image of God: The Anthropology of the Theological Life

The Notion of an Image

Basing themselves on the inspired biblical witness (for example, in Genesis 1:26 and Wisdom 2:23), Christian writers have developed the theme that each instance of human nature is made after and abides as the image of God, the *imago Dei*.[46] St. Leo the Great encouraged his congregation with these words: "Dearly beloved, if we comprehend faithfully and wisely the beginning of our creation, we shall find that man was made in God's image, to the end that he might imitate the Creator."[47] The doctrine of the *imago Dei* continues to influence strongly the Church's teaching on the dignity of the human person. The documents of the Second Vatican Council explicitly employ the motif at least six times, in a variety of appropriate contexts. The substance of

---

45. Elizabeth of the Trinity, *Heaven in Faith*, p. 98.

46. For a basic study on the history and origins of this doctrine in Western theology, see John Edward Sullivan, O.P., *The Image of God. The Doctrine of St. Augustine and Its Influence* (Dubuque, Iowa: The Priory Press, 1963). *Man in God's Design* (Newcastle-upon-Tyne: Studiorum Novi Testamenti Societas, 1953) contains a collection of essays by non-Catholic biblical scholars, such as C. H. Dodd, P. I. Bratsiotis, R. Bultmann, H. Clavier.

47. St. Leo the Great, *Sermons*, no. 12: 1 (PL 54, 168; NPNF 12, 121).

the theological teaching holds that "man was created 'in the image of God,' with the capacity to know and love his creator, and was divinely appointed with authority over all earthly creatures, to rule and use them and glorify God."[48] In order to grasp the full significance of this central concept for the theological life and virtues, we must further investigate the theoretical notion of an image.

Using distinctions developed in philosophy, the theological tradition treats the generic notion of an image in two ways. An image belongs either to the genus of similitude (likeness) or to the genus of signs. As a sign, an image makes something manifest to those capable of grasping its significance.[49] As a likeness (similitudo), an image resembles something other than itself. But not every likeness qualifies as an image. In order to be an image, the likeness must resemble the thing imaged either in species or in some mark of a species.[50] Three qualifications must be met in order to realize the genuine meaning of an image.

First, for a likeness to qualify as a true image, the likeness must resemble the thing imaged with respect to its highest perfection. Thus, the human creature is not said to be an image of God under the more common aspects of possessing being or having life, but only on account of its highest perfection, namely, that the human creature possesses and acts in accord with an intellectual nature. St. Augustine offers an authoritative witness to this feature of an image: "Herein lies man's eminence, that God made man after his own image in so far as he gave him an intelligent mind, which is where he surpasses the animals."[51] Second, the image must resemble that of which it is an image according to the latter's proper species. Since this condition means that an image must participate in the imaged thing's species or form, it could prove restrictive for talking about a human being as a true image of God. For nothing participates specifically in divinity except the Persons of the blessed Trinity. Aquinas therefore recognizes the need to introduce an important distinction here: participation in the same species can happen

48. Pastoral Constitution on the Church in the Modern World, *Gaudium et spes*, chap. 1, no. 12.

49. St. Augustine popularized this notion for the West; see for example *De doctrina christiana*, Bk. 2, chap. 1, 1–2 (PL 34, 35–36).

50. See *Summa theologiae* Ia q. 35, a. 1, and also q. 93, a. 1.

51. See *Summa theologiae* Ia q. 93, a. 2, s.c. where Aquinas quotes Augustine's *In Genesim ad litteram*, Bk. 6, chap. 12 (PL 34, 348).

either by actually being in the same species, or by proportionally or analogically sharing in its characteristics.[52] To apply this distinction, an image can exist as perfect and equal to what is imaged, as the eternal Son personifies the image of the Father, or an image can remain imperfect and unequal to the archetype. This is the case of our human nature, which, since it neither equals nor naturally possesses the perfectness of God, enjoys only an analogical community with the specific nature of what is imaged. Third, an image must derive or proceed from that of which it is an image—as a child is the image of its parents. Two individuals who look alike yet are unrelated may possess a strong physical resemblance to one another, but, strictly speaking, one is not the image of the other. Since every creature comes forth from God, each human person fulfills this requirement for being a true image of the Creator.[53]

Post-conciliar theology stresses the close affinities of theological anthropology and Christology, so today theological discussion about the *imago Dei* is inseparably bound up with reflection on the one who preeminently embodies "the image of the invisible God, the firstborn of all creation" (Col. 1:15). The Genesis text that records that humankind was made "ad imaginem Dei" (after the image of God) gave patristic theology and exegesis a way to distinguish the diverse ways that Christ and humankind are said to be images of God. Aquinas summarizes their efforts thusly:

The firstborn of all creation is the perfect image of God, perfectly realizing that of which he is the image, and so he is said to be "the image" quite simply, and never to be "after the image." But man is both said to be "the image," because of its likeness to the original, and "after the image," because the likeness is imperfect.[54]

A central text of the Second Vatican Council expands on this distinction by clearly pointing out the salvific import of the doctrine of the *imago*:

52. By this distinction, Aquinas anticipates a difficulty that later theology, especially within the Reformed tradition, will raise, namely, that no created being can enjoy any sort of real community with God: "Since one means being undivided, a *species* [image] is called similar in the same way as it is called one. Now something can be called one not only numerically or in kind or class, but also by a certain analogy or proportion; and in this way a creature can be one with God, or consort with him" (*Summa theologiae* Ia q. 93, a. 1, ad 3).

53. See *Summa theologiae* Ia q. 93, a. 1.

54. *Summa theologiae* Ia q. 93, a. 1, ad 2.

"He who is 'the image of the invisible God', is the perfect human being who has restored to the offspring of Adam the divine likeness which had been deformed since the first sin."[55] In a fallen world, to be "after the image" of God means that, in Christ, we need to pursue the work of image-restoration and image-perfection.

What Is Imaged in Us: The Divine Nature in Three Persons

The Christian faith confesses that Father, Son, and Holy Spirit together imprint their image on human nature. All divine action in the world originates in the communion of Persons in the blessed Trinity. St. Basil the Great can thus write: "The Father, the Son and the Holy Spirit alike hallow, quicken, enlighten, and comfort."[56] Theologians cite the creating and hallowing of humankind as an example of God's work *ad extra*, and they distinguish this from the immanent movements of divine knowledge and love that constitute the very Persons of the Trinity.

Each of the divine Persons is equally God. "For," says Gregory Nazianzen, "one is not more and another less God; nor is One before and another after; nor are they divided in will or parted in power; nor can you find here any of the qualities of divisible things; but the Godhead is, to speak concisely, undivided in separate Persons."[57] The divine nature remains identically that in and of the three divine Persons, except the mutual and subsistent relations by which it is the nature of each Person. These, moreover, are distinguished from each other only relationally, and not as possessing distinct or separate shares in the divine nature.

The divine image that belongs to the human person is an image both of the divine nature and of the divine Persons. After all, Aquinas explains simply, "That is what God actually is, one nature in three Persons."[58] In his *De Trinitate*, St. Augustine used the human soul and its powers to explain the Trinitarian image in the human person.[59] The

---

55. Pastoral Constitution on the Church in the Modern World, *Gaudium et spes*, chap. 1, no. 22.
56. St. Basil the Great, *Letters*, no. 189: 7 (PG 32, 693; NPNF 8, 231).
57. St. Gregory of Nazianzus, *Orations*, no. 31 (PL 36, 148; NPNF 7, 322).
58. See *Summa theologiae* Ia q. 93, a. 5.
59. For further information, see the seminal article by Charles Boyer, "L'Image de

operative concepts were mind *(mens)*, self-knowledge *(notitia sui)*, and self-love *(amor sui)*. And so from the beginning of the fifth century, Western theology began to develop the view that the specific representation of the blessed Trinity in the human creature consists in like processions of a mental word and love from a principle within.[60] Perhaps the best fruit of this protracted theological reflection appears in the mystical tradition that identifies the Trinitarian image as the archetype for the relational character of human loving as well as the ultimate principle for the proper ordering of right reason and human appetite in human conduct. Since this is true, we can make such affirmations as "divine truth measures human freedom" or "Christian virtue puts the mark of the Trinity on our human actions," although conclusions such as these belong to a more developed phase of the image doctrine.

What does it mean to say that the human creature images the divine nature? Facilitated by both the Aristotelian conception of potency and act and the account in Exodus of God's revelation to Moses, Aquinas speaks about God as sheer subsistent act, that is, as unreceived and unlimited by any essence other than itself. Only God is free simply to

---

Trinité. Synthèse de la Pensée Augustinienne," *Gregorianum* 5 (1946): 173–99; 333–52, and Sullivan, *The Image of God*, p. 106, n. 1.

60. On Aquinas's account, the personal names of the divine Persons as found in the canonical Scriptures ground the Trinitarian theology that distinguishes one divine Person from the other. First, for the Word/Son: because in God "to be" *(esse)* denotes simply "to know" and "to speak" *(intelligere/dicere)*, there is an intelligible emanation or intellectual procession in God's self-knowledge. Formally taken, knowing entails the speaking of what is known. This procession terminates in the Word Spoken, which is not simply the Knower (although it is the actuality of the knower precisely as such and consubstantial with him), nor the knowing-act itself (which, in this instance, is simply the divine nature itself), nor the content of the knowing (the Father's knowledge of the divine nature as Principle), but merely the formal concept or inner word whereby the knower knows. Since what the Father knows is the divine nature (in its simplicity as unreceived act of being), this knowing-act is also simple. That is, the knowing act is also the speaking-act of the being of what is known. Further, because knowing is a generation of a terminal likeness of what is known and because likeness is the ground of love, there is a further procession in God, i.e., of love. This term of immanent operation is neither the lover himself nor the love-act nor the object loved (all of which are identically the divine nature, saving only the relations of mutual opposition whereby the Father is the Unprincipled Principle and the Son the Principled Principle). Rather, the term of this procession is the very reality of love itself whereby the beloved is in the lover. It is the *impulsus* or *pondus amoris*—the being-in-love itself, the expansion of the intellectual nature abidingly in the direction of and after the shape of the beloved, the inner dynamic orientation the lover bears toward the beloved. Thus, the one whom we call the Holy Spirit.

be, as the text,"I am who I am" (Exod. 3:14), suggests. The identity of essence and existence in God means that God's being is identically both his truth (the substantive true and the act of knowing and speaking the truth) and his goodness (the substantive good and the act of loving). When the human person participates in the divine being and in these entitative and operative perfections, he or she shares those perfections in a differentiated and complex mode, even though the perfections remain essentially identical and simple in God.[61] Philosophically, this is the case because it does not belong essentially to the human person to exist—a distinction that helps the theologian clarify the Christian doctrine on the radical distinction between the Creator and everything that is created. Our imaging of the divine nature establishes the foundation for Christian anthropology.

To render a complete account, however, of the human person created in the image of God, we need to consider the mark of the Trinity that is impressed on every human being.

The Structure of the Trinity in Us

The natural image of the Trinity resides in the whole intellective part of the human soul—that is, not only in the intellect itself, but also in the will in its coordination with the intellect. Soul signifies the spiritual principle in man. Furthermore, as much as the divine nature remains sheer subsistent act and the procession of the Persons occurs by way of immanent operations, the image provides a source of dynamic movement in the human being. In fact, Aquinas contends that we should look for the image of God, not primarily in the intellectual capacities of the soul, but in the very acts of those operative capacities or powers.[62] Be-

61. Aquinas makes this point in the course of explaining why divine Logos, the Second Person in God, remains consubstantial with the Father: "For us to be and to know are not the same thing; this is why something having existence in our thought does not form part of our nature. But God's *esse* and his knowing are the same; this is why the Word of God is not either an accident in God or an effect, but is the divine nature" (*Summa theologiae* Ia q. 34, a. 2, ad 1).

62. See *Summa theologiae* Ia q. 93, a. 7. Through his teaching on the nuptial meaning of the body, Pope John Paul II has emphasized that "the human body shares in the dignity of 'the image of God': it is a human body precisely because it is animated by a spiritual soul, and it is the whole human person that is intended to become, in the body of Christ, a temple of the Spirit." For further references, see *The Catechism of the Catholic Church*, nos. 362–68.

cause the processions of the Word and of the personal Love of God
are by way of God's self-knowing and self-loving, the image of God
consists not in knowing or loving acts of whatever kind, such as those
specified by created objects in the world. Rather, the Trinitarian image
can be realized only in acts of self-knowledge and self-love or in acts
of knowing and loving God. Aquinas, then, accepted St. Augustine's
view that self-knowledge and self-love provide grounds for an authentic
representation of the Trinity. But with St. Augustine, Aquinas also realized that inquiry about the native structures of human knowledge and
love can advance Christian anthropology only to a certain point.

Before we examine the difference between the image of representation and the image of conformity, we should first mention the pro-
gressive stages in the call to holiness in which the image exists. By
referring to a standard medieval commentary on the Bible, the *Glossa
ordinaria*, Aquinas identifies three theological moments in which the
image of God exists. He recounts that "on the text of Psalm 4:7, 'The
light of thy countenance O Lord is sealed upon us,' the *Gloss* distinguishes a threefold image, namely the image of 'creation, of re-creation,
and of likeness.' The first stage of image then is common to all humankind, the second belongs only in the justified person, and the third
comes only to the blessed ones in heaven."[63] In this text, Aquinas points
out the various states or conditions of human nature with respect to
beatific communion. He provides us, then, with a theological view of
history that accepts divine providence as the ultimate explanatory feature for the sequence of human events—what St. Augustine calls the
"temporal dispensation of divine providence."[64]

---

63. See *Summa theologiae* Ia q. 93, a. 4. The image of God exists in man in three
distinct ways: First, by nature, as the connatural human dynamism toward our ultimate
end. As part of the created order, however, human nature remains aptitudinal for ultimate
communion. So the natural image of God can not know and love God in his very own
divinity, but only commonly under the generic aspects of Principle of being and ultimate
End. Second, the image can exist actually and habitually, though only imperfectly, in those,
who by reason of their conformity to the divine nature by grace and to the divine knowing
and loving by the theological virtues, actually know and love God as a Trinity of Persons.
Finally, there remains the perfect imaging of God that belongs to the creature only in the
state of glory, in which the divine Essence itself mediates the knowing act that unites each
of the blessed to God.

64. See his *De vera religione* 7 (PL 34, 128).

The Image of Representation

One way that every human being bears the image of God is called the image of representation. This natural image of the Trinity emerges out of the working of the human soul, which through knowing and loving itself dynamically images the divine self-knowledge and love constitutive of the Trinity of Persons. St. Augustine held the view that "the mind remembers, understands, loves itself."[65] Recall that in the Augustinian conception of the mind, memory ranks among the rational powers of the human soul. Therefore, St. Augustine was able to discover the image of representation in the trinity of powers that comprise the rational soul. Aquinas demonstrates, however, that even when the memory is described, and correctly so, as a sense power, the two remaining powers of the rational soul, the capacity to know and the capacity to love, are sufficient to account for the Trinitarian image as it exists in every human person.[66]

The image of representation shows how the structure of the human psyche reflects—or *represents*—the pattern of knowledge and love in the Trinity. It does not imply, however, that the human person is actually engaged in the saving actions of knowing and loving the Persons of the Trinity, or in any conformity with God as an object of knowledge. So the image of representation can be compared with a photographic image that is being stored on film; it is like a diaphanous negative of an image that still needs to be developed. By possessing the image of representation, man is not said to realize the image of God in the most perfect sense, though every human person is called to such perfection through

65. *De Trinitate*, Bk. XIV, 8 as quoted in *Summa theologiae* Ia q. 93, a. 8.

66. The standard account runs as follows: We come to know the nature of our soul's intellectual powers, not through an immanent act, but only after we know external things and experience what our knowing something involves. Realist epistemology postulates a medium or "intelligible species" for every act of knowing something outside of the self, but the soul's self-knowing is achieved without such an impressed species. Still, Aquinas argues, the grounds for discerning a Trinitarian image are found even within the immanent structure of self-knowing. This happens in the interplay of the mind with its own similitude, which in turn generates an impulse toward self-loving. The operative analogy can be expressed thus: Human knowing and loving is to the essence of the soul as divine knowing and loving is to the divine essence. For further treatment of this important element of Trinitarian theology, see Aquinas's *Quaestiones disputatæ de veritate* q. 10, aa. 7, 8.

the theological life. For whereas self-knowledge and self-love can represent the Trinity, these immanent actions leave the human creature, who is made for the ecstatic embrace of love, incomplete and unfulfilled. Because only God satisfies, the theological tradition also speaks about a more perfect form of the Trinitarian image—the image of conformity.

The Image of Conformity

The natural image of conformity exists in the human person, for whom God is in some way an object of contemplation and love. The soul most perfectly and dynamically images the divine Trinity in knowing and loving God himself.[67] In this actualization of the image, what is imaged is not merely the structure of immanent operations whose object is the self, but the divine knowledge and love whose object constitutes the Trinity of Persons. The image of conformity can be compared, then, to an electronic image on a television screen that communicates the full vitality and quality of whatever is televised. For through it, the powers of the human soul not only represent the Trinity of Persons but they display their real capacity to conform to them in knowledge and love.

Because punishment for original sin entails the loss of fellowship with God, the image of conformity is realized differently during the periods of salvation history, namely, after sin but before the time of Christ's coming and after the fullness of grace is revealed. Consider two points: First, we can speak about an image of God, wherein God is attained not as he is in himself but rather according to the soul's own proper mode of being and as the cause of that being. While still more intimate to us than we are to ourselves, God is not loved as he is in himself, as a Trinity of Persons, but only under the common aspect of the good, and as its principle. This imaging is the lot of man without Christ. Even the revelation made to Israel does not radically relieve its frustation, which arises from man's being made for an ultimate communion that only Christ makes possible. Second, we know that Christ, through his Paschal mystery, makes it possible for every member of the race to image God precisely as a Trinity of Persons. That which is only potentially and aptitudinally an image of the divine Persons by nature, and is this defectively because of human sinfulness, becomes actually

67. For a fuller treatment, see *Summa theologiae* Ia q. 93, a. 8.

an image of God only by the conformity that grace bestows. In an especially important text about human love, Aquinas spells out this distinction:

Charity loves God above all things in a higher way than nature does. For nature loves God above all things insofar as he is the source and end of natural good; but charity loves him above all things inasmuch as he is the object and source of blessedness and inasmuch as humankind has a certain kind of spiritual communion with God. Charity also gives the natural love of God a certain extra quick responsiveness and delight; just as any virtuous *habitus* gives something extra to a good act as performed through natural reason alone by one who lacks the virtuous *habitus*.[68]

By establishing the person within a communion of friendship with God, divine grace personally and ontologically shapes human nature, so that those who enjoy the *koinonia* of divine friendship begin to act in a distinctive fashion. For Aquinas, Christ reveals the difference that grace makes for human life. Participation through grace in the inner-Trinitarian life of God completes the image of conformity.

In the graced image of conformity, the Christian believer enjoys the full measure of God's favor. Commenting on a verse of the psalms, St. Augustine remarked: "If we have been made children of God, we have also been made gods, but this is the effect of grace adopting, not of nature generating."[69] The image of conformity theologically interprets what St. Paul refers to as the "spirit of adoption" (Rom. 8:15) and what St. Augustine here calls the grace of adoption.

We can discern three levels of realization in the one image of conformity: First, as much as the adopted children of God formally participate in the divine nature, the remote principles of our knowing and loving are analogically the same as the divine processions themselves. Next, since by faith the human person shares in the divine knowing-act, and, by hope and most especially by charity, in the divine loving-

---

68. *Summa theologiae* Ia-IIae q. 109, a. 3, ad 1. In my judgment, this text clarifies Aquinas's understanding of the specificity of Christian ethics, for while on the one hand he affirms that the "new law did not have to prescribe any external works by way of precept or prohibition," on the other it is clear that the infused virtues, especially prudence, function in a way that reflects the status of the Christian believer as an adopted child (see the discussion in *Summa theologiae* Ia-IIae q. 108, a. 2). One must, however, take account of Aquinas's complete discussion of the moral life and not compare isolated texts.

69. St. Augustine, *Expositions on the Psalms*, Ps. 49:2 (PL 36, 565; NPNF 8, 178).

act, the proximate principles of our knowing and loving are analogically the same as the knowing and loving within the Trinity. Finally, the objects attained in these knowing-acts are analogically the same as within the blessed Trinity, for those who enjoy the image of conformity know God as he is in himself, namely, as First Truth-Speaking by faith, and love him in the same way by hope and charity as the supreme Friend.

We gain a full appreciation of the theological virtues, and of the virtue of faith in particular, only within the context of the whole of divine revelation. This follows from the patent fact that only the believer who remains personally united with God enjoys the activity of faith, hope, and charity. In this chapter, we have identified three important elements of Christian doctrine that provide the proximate coordinates for understanding the virtues of faith, hope, and charity: (1) Christ, the one who communicates divine grace; (2) sanctifying or habitual grace itself, and this as a proper endowment of a human nature created in the image of God; and (3) the image of God, which reveals the harmonies between creation and redemption. Only by grace can the human creature become what God is; this transformation of human nature occurs originally and preeminently in the Incarnation of the divine Word. As the opening chapters of Ephesians insist: "But each of us was given grace according to the measure of Christ's gift" (Eph. 4:7). Those who are members of Christ's Body enjoy a relationship with the three divine Persons that the virtues of faith, hope, and charity render specifically unique and entirely unlike any natural form of kinship between God and humankind. We call this relationship the theological life. Elizabeth of the Trinity summarizes the Christological teaching about both the transformation and the life of grace as follows: "A soul that permits the divine Being to satisfy in itself his need to communicate 'all that he is and all that he has,' is in reality the praise of glory of all his gifts."[70]

70. Elizabeth of the Trinity, *Heaven in Faith*, no. 43, p. 112.

Chapter 2

The Riches of His Glorious Inheritance

The sixteenth-century Carmelite mystic St. John of the Cross writes: "As our faith grows more intense, so does our union with God."[1] In this short phrase, the Doctor of Carmel captures the Church's common teaching that theological faith introduces the human creature into a personal relationship with God. Indeed, as long as the Christian abides in this world, he or she can enjoy an authentically personal encounter with the Trinitarian God only through the exercise of theological faith.[2] Hence, theologians distinguish this union, which depends on theological faith, from other instances of human encounter with the living God that do not entail friendship and ensure ultimate communion. In order to enjoy a truly personal union with God, such as only the theological life affords, a person requires instruction in the Church's authoritative teaching on faith and morals.[3]

Because Christian faith requires a knowledge of God's truth, theo-

---

1. In the same text he further elaborates: "For the likeness between faith and God is so close that no other difference exists than that between believing in God and seeing him. . . . Only by means of faith, in divine light exceeding all understanding, does God manifest himself to the soul" (*The Ascent of Mount Carmel*, Bk. II, chap. 9, no. 1).

2. In his Apostolic Constitution *Benedictus Deus* (29 January 1336), Pope Benedict XII specified the roles of faith and hope as virtues of the wayfarer in a negative way by defining "ex cathedra" that the beatific vision brings these two theological virtues to an end (*DS* 1001).

3. Pope John Paul II has made Creed and Catholic identity a constant theme of his Magisterium; see for instance, his discourse to the bishops of the United States in *Origins* 22:42 (1 April 1993): 717–21.

logians customarily explain the dynamics of faith by appeal to the ordinary processes of knowing and understanding. Faith constitutes a kind of knowing: that "you may know what is the hope to which he has called you, what are the riches of his glorious inheritance among the saints" (Eph. 1:18). However, John of the Cross signals an important difference between knowledge in faith and ordinary human cognition. Faith, he says, "causes darkness and a void in the intellect."[4] Indeed since the earliest Christian centuries, spiritual authors have appropriately underscored that knowledge in faith in some ways does leave the mind unsatisfied. Gregory of Nyssa even compares this knowledge to the leaden darkness that surrounded Moses as he advanced to encounter God on Mount Sinai.[5] To sum up: knowledge in faith unites us to "God, the Father of Our Lord Jesus Christ" (Col. 1:3), for through faith we come to see the Truth, though for now we see it, as St. Paul says, "in a mirror, dimly" (1 Cor. 13:12).

From its earliest moments, the Christian tradition taught that theological faith embodies a specific form of intellectual activity, that it involves a search for truth.[6] Tertullian, to cite one example, often speaks about faith in connection with the "rule of truth," and Hilary of Poitiers uses a verb of the head when he says that faith "perceives the mysteries of the Kingdom."[7] The conviction that belief involves the attainment of knowledge explains some central practices of the Christian religion: a catechumen learns about the faith; pastors and laity teach the faith; the bishop of Rome bears a particular responsibility to safeguard the content of faith; Christians should be able to explain what they profess in faith; finally, every member of the Church is under obligation to defend faith's truths, at times even with their lives. In short, although what is believed surpasses the abilities of unaided human intelligence, the one who believes acquires a true knowledge of divine truth, and this illumination changes the whole conduct of a believer's life.

4. *The Ascent of Mount Carmel* Bk. II, chap. 6, no. 2.

5. In technical languages, this feature of knowledge in faith is called its apophatic quality. See Gregory of Nyssa, *Vie de Moise*, ed. Jean Daniélou, S.J. (Paris: Sources chrétienne, 1942–43).

6. For an overview of the terms employed in the canonical Scriptures for theological faith, see Juan Alfaro, "Fides in terminologia biblica," *Gregorianum* 42 (1961): 463–505.

7. St. Hilary of Poitiers (c. 315–67): "Regni mysteria fides percipit" (*De Trinitate*, chap. 2).

Faith is a kind of knowing. But what does a person learn through the exercise of the virtue of faith? In this chapter we shall inquire about the object of knowledge in faith. We have seen that faith introduces the believer into the riches of God's glorious inheritance, which is the Trinitarian life. Knowledge in faith is ordered toward acquiring the truth about God and his richness, so as to draw the believer into the communion of Trinitarian love. Faith introduces believers into the mysteries of the Kingdom, so that they "may have power to comprehend with all the saints what is the breadth and length and height and depth, and to know the love of Christ which surpasses knowledge" (Eph. 3:18, 19). Because knowledge in faith initiates a relationship between the one who believes and the very Persons of the blessed Trinity, the virtue of faith is properly referred to as a "supernatural virtue."[8] Affirming clearly the supernatural character of faith, theologians maintain that the proper object of knowledge in faith is nothing short of God who is the First Truth.

Faith's Object: First Truth

Theologians employ the notion of an "object" in order to explain the specifics of Christian life. The *Catechism of the Catholic Church* defines object as "a good toward which the will deliberately directs itself." The object chosen is one of the constitutive elements or "sources" that determine the morality of a human action.[9] "Object" stands for any reality that is capable of perfecting a person through an engagement with itself. Now only God is entirely self-sufficient; God does not need any object to perfect him. Human persons, however, must achieve perfection by engagement or interaction with other creatures. The proper achievement of this interaction constitutes the virtuous life. Because we need to discover what are the good ways to interact with the world, inquiry into the nature of any virtue begins with establishing its proper object. We read in the encyclical *Veritatis splendor* that "the morality of the human act depends primarily and fundamentally on the 'object' ra-

---

8. The First Vatican Council's Dogmatic Constitution on the Catholic faith, *Dei Filius*, explicitly refers to faith as a supernatural virtue: "Hanc vero fidem, quae 'humanitatis salutis initium est,' Ecclesia catholica profitetur, virtutem esse supernaturalem . . ." (*DS* 3008).

9. *Catechism of the Catholic Church*, nos. 1750, 1751ff.

tionally chosen by the deliberate will."[10] The term "object" here stands for the reality, whether a thing or a person, that both engages and draws forth a particular action, thereby making the action to be of a certain kind.[11] In its moral teaching, the Church uses "objects" to distinguish, for the benefit of the moral agent, good moral choices from bad ones, as well as to differentiate the virtues. We need to consider further the use that the tradition makes of this important notion.

Aquinas wrote: "As a physical thing has its species from its form, so an action has its species from its object."[12] This affirmation grounds the standard thesis that an action is a particular type of action through specification by object. A particular action in turn specifies the capacity and *habitus* from which the action proceeds. This specification provides the foundation for the terminology we use to distinguish both specific kinds of human acts, such as, almsgiving, worship, or adultery, and specific *habitus*, such as, charity, religion, or chastity. The logical classification of acts and *habitus* is rooted in the ability of an object to exercise a real causal influence on human behavior. In other words, the specification of a *habitus* signifies that a virtue (or vice) exists as a specific kind of good (or bad) feature of the human person because of the object that makes it good or bad. Christian morality is always about the real; it is never only a morality of the head. In order to identify accurately what someone is doing in a concrete situation, it is necessary to identify the human action in terms of its relationship to specific realities or objects. Not only must the real object fit the human capacity that engages it; in order to be virtuous, the fit must also be a proper one, that is, according to reason. Virtuous activity means engaging the objects that perfect human nature according to the measure that right reason sets down. Try to put food in your ear, and you will discover how inappropriate for a

10. John Paul II, encyclical letter *Veritatis splendor* (1993), no. 78. For further discussion of this cardinal point in the encyclical, see Martin Rhonheimer, "'Intrinsically Evil Acts' and the Moral Viewpoint: Clarifying a Central Teaching of *Veritatis Splendor*," *The Thomist* 58 (1994): 1–39, and "Intentional Actions and the Meaning of Object: A Reply to Richard McCormick," *The Thomist* 59 (1995): 279–311.

11. For some of the important texts where Aquinas explains objects and capacities or *habitus*, see *In III Sent.* d. 33, q. 1, a. 1, sol. 1; *De veritate* q. 15, a. 2; *In de anima* Bk. 2, lect. 6; *Summa theologiae* Ia q. 77, a. 3; Ia-IIae q. 18, a. 2 & q. 54, a. 1 & ad 1; q. 72, a. 1. And for some examples of how the neo-scholastics used this distinction, see George Klubertanz, S.J., *Habits and Virtues* (New York: Appleton-Century-Croft, 1965).

12. *Summa theologiae* Ia-IIae q. 18, a. 2.

human capacity an object can be; appropriately ingest an excessive amount of proper foodstuffs, and you will experience in your digestive system the results of exceeding the measure set down by right reason. In order to see how specification by object works, consider the experience of seeing a red apple. After some reflection, one can distinguish the formal interest of the object from the material aspect of the object. Some commentators identify this distinction between a material and a formal object with the distinction that philosophers make between thing and object.[13] A material object designates the term of an action; it signifies the specifying reality, the thing, from the point of view of its givenness or facticity. In our example, the apple itself. Formal objects, on the other hand, denote the psychological and formal interest that engages the action with the material object. In the example of sense perception, we identify some aspect or aspects of a thing as a formal object when it specifies the formal characteristic (such as color) that allows the thing to be known (in this example, as visible). In our example, the apple precisely as red. By identifying the formal interest of an object, we can differentiate one kind of human action from another and identify the operative capacity that serves as the principle of a specific kind of action.[14] Because the apple is a red-colored object, we can see it with the capacity for vision.

An apple as a simple material object can possess diverse formal notes or objects. As red or colored, the apple constitutes an object for the capacity of sight and its act of seeing.[15] But the same colored apple also possesses other characteristics or attributes that do not relate to seeing

13. For instance, see Yves Simon's editorial comment in *The Material Logic of John of St. Thomas*, trans. Yves R. Simon, John J. Granville, and G. Donald Hollenhorst (Chicago: University of Chicago Press, 1955), p. 623, no. 44.

14. In one text, Aquinas puts it this way: "Because everything acts to the degree that it is actual and so through its form, and because for the passive capacities the object is the actuating element, therefore that aspect of the object to which a passive capacity is proportioned is that which is formal in the object. And because they derive their species from this formal aspect of the object, capacities and *habitus* are differentiated in reference to it" (*In III Sent.* d. 24, q. 1, sol. 1). The translation, slightly modified, comes from T. C. O'Brien, *Faith*, vol. 31 (New York: McGraw-Hill, 1974), Appendix 1, "Objects and Virtues," pp. 181–82.

15. *Habitus* shape an operative capacity to deal, whether for good or ill, with various objects. The brave person must be ready to confront dangerous circumstances of all kinds. Because the power of vision deals only with objects that possess color, no *habitus* exists for seeing.

and do not engage the human capacity of vision. A sweet or sour apple becomes an object for the capacity of taste, while a hard or soft apple engages the capacity of touch. Seeing, tasting, and feeling represent three different activities that engage a person with the same red, juicy, and ripe apple. Thus, we can distinguish one form of engagement from another precisely because of the different formal aspects that exist in the fruit.

Since Christian revelation proposes no complete perfection for humankind other than knowing and loving the three-personed God, the Persons of the blessed Trinity in the unity of the divine nature constitute the unique Object of the theological virtues. St. Augustine describes the end of the theological life as a life centered wholly on God: "He shall be the end of our desires, who shall be seen without end, loved without cloy, praised without weariness. . . . There we shall rest and see, see and love, love and praise. This is what shall be in the end without end."[16] The virtue of faith initiates in the Christian believer the movement toward this fulfillment.

In order to grasp why the deployment of "object" serves any useful purpose in the discussion of the theological virtues, it is important to have a proper understanding of intentionality.[17] As Aquinas makes clear, the analysis of the theological virtues borrows extensively from a philosophical analysis of human knowing: "Every *habitus* of apprehending possesses two aspects: namely, what is apprehended materially, which is like the material object; and that by which it is apprehended, which is the formal account of the object."[18] Because faith constitutes a *habitus* of supernatural knowing, we examine the nature of faith and distinguish it from the other virtues by giving an account of its formal and material objects. The same method holds true for the other theological virtues, which are *habitus* of supernatural loving.

But there exists a deeper significance in the technical use of the intentional model to illustrate God's presence in grace, one that points

16. St. Augustine, *De civitate Dei*, Bk. 22, chap. 30 (PL 41, 801; NPNF 2, 509).

17. For what follows, I am heavily indebted to the magisterial treatment by O'Brien in *art. cit.*, pp. 178–85.

18. *Summa theologiae* IIa-IIae q. 1, a. 1. Translations of Aquinas's treatise on faith, *Summa theologiae* IIa-IIae qq. 1–16 are from *Readings in the Summa theologiae*, vol. 1, *On Faith*, trans. Mark D. Jordan (Notre Dame, Ind.: University of Notre Dame Press, 1990).

up the surpassing excellence of knowledge in faith. The use of "intentional" can also affirm that the act of faith "tends toward" and finds its term in the divine Being itself. By directing the subject toward another being, believing resembles other intentional acts—acts of knowing and loving—that come to completion by resting in their appropriate objects. While the inborn structure of the human capacities can support our knowing and loving of created things, clearly something more is required when the object attained is one of the divine Persons. Even though we study these gifts of the blessed Trinity in terms of the human mode of knowing and loving, faith, hope, and love remain the sources of distinctively supernatural intentional acts.

Since the Christian tradition steadfastly rejects all claims of composition-in-being of the divine with the created, the union between God and intelligent creatures in grace cannot be described in terms of an entitative union. Intentionality entails a distinction between the subject and object, though not the unbridgeable split between the two that has bedeviled so much of modern philosophy since Descartes. This account of the theological life appeals to the most universal and concrete of human experiences, knowledge and love. As a genuine "object" of the human being's knowledge and love, God can be said to be the "friend" of the human being. Only because of the Incarnation, of course, does the Christian believer dare to conceive analogically his or her relationship with God in the terms of human friendship. The blessed Trinity revealed by Christ draws forth the intentionality of the knowledge of faith and the loving adherence of hope and charity. Thus, the Christian believer experiences union with God "in the same way that the knower rests in the known and the lover in the beloved."[19] This intentional union forms the wellspring of the theological life.

Now we are ready to examine in greater detail the specific character of Christian faith. Within the personal relationship that grace establishes, the Christian is able to reach out toward the divine truthfulness: God as First Truth constitutes the formal object of theological faith. In order to understand the precise sense in which God as First Truth can

19. *Summa theologiae* Ia q. 43, a. 3: ". . . there is a special presence consonant with the nature of an intelligent being, in whom God is said be to be present as the known in the knower and the loved in the lover." Intentional acts are a way of conceiving the supernatural relationship between God and his intelligent creatures.

be the formal object of faith, we need to invoke an additional refinement of the nature of the formal object. Since the fifteenth century, theological writers have found it helpful to distinguish between the terminative formal object and the mediating formal object.[20] The terminative formal object refers specifically to the distinctive feature of an object that seizes the attention of an operative capacity and terminates its act, for example, the color of the apple. The mediating formal object signifies a medium or trans-subjective "bridge" thrown across from the side of the object permitting the capacity or *habitus* to make contact with the terminative formal object. Thus in the example of seeing a red apple, the light required for seeing any colored thing illustrates the mediating formal object. In other terms, we can consider the formal object either precisely in itself, namely, terminative, or as it connotes a certain condition for its operation, namely, mediating. Admittedly, introducing a further distinction into the already somewhat foreign notions of formal and material objects risks alienating those skeptical about maintaining the theological categories of earlier periods. On the other hand, making the distinction between the mediating formal object and the terminative formal object provides, as the present discussion demonstrates, the necessary conceptual framework for introducing some important distinctions about the working of theological faith.

We can usefully apply the distinction between the terminative formal object and the mediating formal object to God as First Truth. Recall that the terminating formal object describes the precise feature of the divine nature that interests a particular theological virtue; God as being the very First Truth is the formal object of theological faith.[21] Like every divine attribute, this Truth of course exists identically with the divine Being itself. On the other hand, the mediating formal object represents the light or medium that enables the subject to reach the formal object, as physical light is required in order for the human eye to attain a colored thing, its formal object. Since only the divine nature itself can serve as an adequate medium for the communication of divine Truth, God him-

20. In the Latin of the commentatorial tradition, we find the distinction between the formal object *quod* and the formal object *quo*. However, this development derives from a suggestion that Aquinas himself makes in *Summa theologiae* IIa-IIae q. 1, a. 6, ad 2.

21. In the Renaissance Latin of the Thomist commentator Cardinal Cajetan, *Prima Veritas in essendo.*

self serves as the medium in which theological faith attains to the First Truth. We can imaginatively think of this medium as a "bridge" between the one who possesses theological faith and First Truth. In order to distinguish the medium from the term, the scholastic theologians referred to the mediating formal object of theological faith as the Truth-Speaking of God.[22]

Within the distinction of formal and material objects, God also functions as the material object of theological faith: God himself is the *de facto* "thing" reached by the act of faith. To be sure, God himself cannot be known by the human intellect unless he adapts the revelation of himself to the human mode of knowing. Human knowing entails making judgments about reality, and these judgments are expressed in truth-bearing statements or propositions. Theological faith therefore embraces particular propositions about God and about his saving action in the world. As bona fide objects of faith, these propositional truths are by no means incidental to the life of Christian belief.[23] On the contrary, they give concrete expression to the invisible realities of the Christian religion. Since God's own witness calls forth our assent to these truths, and because the assent of faith comes to term in them as instruments of God as First Truth-Speaking, these secondary material objects, as the propositions of faith are called, share in the single formal definition or meaning that constitutes theological faith, namely, God as First Truth in Being. The reason for designating the articles of the various ecclesial creeds and, by extension, other truths proposed for our belief by the Church as genuine, though secondary, material objects of faith lies in the need to associate explicitly whatever belongs to theological faith with the Truth-Speaking of God himself. Indeed, nothing short of this participation in divine Truth can justify the indispensable role that these propositions play in the believer's relationship with God and the importance they hold in defining the Christian religion.

Given these preliminary distinctions, we can now provide a working definition of theological faith. The virtue of faith is an infused *habitus* that enables the human person to attain the transcendent God who is

---

22. In Latin, *Prima Veritas in dicendo.*

23. Concerning the relationship of the objects of theological faith to revelation, the noted Dominican Reginald Garrigou-Lagrange held that faith's material object includes everything that God reveals *(omne revelatum a Deo).*

the First Truth. Theologians employ the adjective "infused" in order to indicate that God alone can cause the virtue of faith to exist in a person. St. Paul teaches this important feature of Christian life when he reminds the Corinthians that, although there may be many preachers of faith, "neither the one who plants nor the one who waters is anything, but only God who gives the growth" (1 Cor. 3:7). Even the preeminent achievements of unaided human intelligence fall dramatically short of what God, who "dwells in unapproachable light" (1 Tim. 6:16), communicates to us in faith.

Controversies concerning the nature and the gratuity of the supernatural order recurrently mark the history of theology, and especially so since the Modernist crisis in the early twentieth century. All responsible parties to the discussion, however, agree that nothing within the structure of a created human nature enables the human person to know God precisely as a Trinity of Persons, with all of the divine favor and intimacy that such interpersonal communion represents in a person's life.[24] Well does St. Thérèse of Lisieux remind us that everything is grace—"Tout est grâce!" Knowledge of the truths of faith necessarily depends upon God's free initiative and desire to communicate personally his divine truth to men and women. The existence of a graced communion with the blessed Trinity does not of course exclude other divine initiatives in the world, such as are required in the first call to conversion and justification. But these neither transform nature nor elevate nature's capacities such that the human mind can achieve a full knowledge of the highest Truth. Only grace and the faith it generates make possible our supernatural knowledge of God. The First Vatican Council condemned the view that all the dogmas of the faith can be understood and demonstrated from natural principles by reason properly trained.[25] Ear-

24. The *Catechism of the Catholic Church* makes this affirmation a part of the Church's faith and of Catholic doctrine: "Man's faculties make him capable of coming to a knowledge of the existence of a personal God. But for man to be able to enter into real intimacy with him, God willed both to reveal himself to man and to give him the grace of being able to welcome this revelation in faith. The proofs of God's existence, however, can predispose one to faith and help one to see that faith is not opposed to reason" (no. 35).

25. See *DS* 3041. Also, see the interesting witness of George Tyrrell as related in his *Religious Immanence* and the anonymously published *Letters from a Modernist: The Letters of George Tyrrell to Wilfrid Ward, 1893–1908*, ed. Mary Jo Weaver (London: Sheed and Ward, 1981).

lier, Aquinas had recognized the limits that unaided human nature and reason impose on knowing God: "When discussing the capacities of the soul," he affirmed, "philosophers have never even imagined anything like grace."[26]

Because the formal motive for Christian belief—its mediating formal object—remains God himself as First Truth-Speaking, no individual person or community of persons can establish adequate grounds that would oblige an individual to make an act of theological faith. In any person, the virtue of faith, which "is the first stage of human salvation, the foundation and root of all justification," results only from God's free initiative to draw him or her into the divine life.[27] Once this thesis is accepted, the Christian Church is then free to develop apologetical arguments appropriate to the conditions of a given culture.

An influential alternative position on the genesis of theological faith originated in the work of the Franciscan theologian John Duns Scotus (c. 1256–1308), who argued that *fides acquisita* ("naturally acquired faith") remains a prerequisite for *fides infusa* ("supernaturally infused faith"). A particular view about how man can naturally know God led him to advance this thesis. Scotus knew that philosophical learning can develop a reasonably true account of the divine nature, and so he argued that since truthfulness constitutes a divine attribute, unaided human reason should eventually reach the conclusion that God cannot err or deceive.[28] From this premise, one could argue that the motive for belief does center exclusively on First Truth-Speaking. Though criticized by commentators such as the Spanish Jesuit Juan de Lugo (1583–1660) in the seventeenth century, the Scotist position still influenced the treatises on faith well into the modern period, thanks mainly to the persuasive exposition of another Jesuit, Luis de Molina (1535–1600). The Molinist line of interpretation confuses the judgment that the doctrine

26. *De veritate* q. 28, a. 2, ad 7.

27. See the Council of Trent's "Decree on Justification," chap. 8: "How justification of the sinner freely granted through faith is to be understood." To insist on the creature's absolute dependence on God's gracious initiative in receiving theological faith shapes the development of apologetics. For further treatment, see Avery Dulles, *A History of Apologetics* (Washington, DC: Corpus Instrumentorum, 1971).

28. Aquinas also appreciated human reason's quest for the highest truths; see Georges Cottier, O.P., "Les motifs de crédibilité de la Révélation selon saint Thomas," *Nova et Vetera* 1990/2: 161–79.

of the Church has been revealed by God (the judgment of credibility) with the judgment that the articles of faith are true precisely because they participate in divine Truth (the judgment of faith). Although Molina's approach highlights the ecclesial nature of faith, his position in effect suggests that serious reflection on the objective evidence of the Christian religion can itself constitute a *motive* sufficient for an act of faith.

Since it does not explicitly affirm that the unaided human mind can acquire divine truth, the Scotus-Molina perspective on theological faith does not amount to outright naturalism. But this approach does seem to elide the difference between seeing that something is credible and seeing that it is true. To recognize a witness to some truth as compelling is not the same action as to grasp the truth itself.[29] Moreover, this conception of the genesis of theological faith entails an odd conception of the interaction between divine agency and human agency. For Molina affirms that faith becomes a properly supernatural activity only because God transforms what remains a basically natural activity, i.e., belief, into a supernatural reality. On this account, God intervenes in human life as required for those activities that a person is unable to realize entirely through his or her own efforts, such as instructing us in truth (faith) or rewarding our good efforts (merit).[30]

The Catholic Reform of the sixteenth century developed a line of argumentation aimed at establishing a motive for faith on the basis of what human reason can discover with its own resources. Operating on what today in some quarters might be called the precritical assumption that when the New Testament sets forth Christ's salvific words and deeds, it records events as they actually transpired, Renaissance apologists turned to the New Testament itself, especially to the canonical

29. In his commentary on *Summa theologiae* IIa-IIae q. 1, a. 4, no. II, Cajetan aptly observes that if someone accepts something as credible, he does not on that account accept it to be true, but that the testimony is of such a quality that it is worthy of credence. ["Si constat aliquid esse credibile, non constat propterea esse verum, sed testimonia esse talia ut illud sit credibile."]

30. Frequently this apologetic view of theological faith shaped the nineteenth-century scholastic treatises on faith. As early as 1850, the Jesuits, through their newly founded journal *Civiltà Cattolica*, urged the adoption of the scholastic model as a way to refute the Modernist "rampant errors" of the day. For further information on the American experience, see Philip Gleason, *Keeping the Faith: American Catholicism Past and Present* (Notre Dame, IN: University of Notre Dame Press, 1987), pp. 166–72.

Gospels that present Christ as the one who fulfills the Old Testament expectations for a Messiah. From this vantage point, the post-Tridentine apologists argued first that Christ's miracles and especially his resurrection constituted historical proof of his divine and therefore believable message; second that, following Christ's explicit instructions, the Church continues to transmit trustworthily what Christ himself taught. From these premises, Catholic authors, until the eve of the Second Vatican Council, continued to maintain that human reason can discover in the pages of the New Testament a form of empirical verification for the Church's credibility and can therefore supply a rational motive for assenting to the particular truths that the Church proposes for belief. After the 1943 encyclical *Divino afflante Spiritu* gave a new impulse to Catholic biblical scholarship, this approach to apologetics began to decline in Catholic theological circles.

Apologetic interests invariably affect the theology of faith. In the course of determining what forms of human experience dispose a person for receiving the free gift of theological faith, the theologian must carefully preserve the properly divine character of the theological virtues, or risk compromising the gratuity of the divine self-giving and obscuring the character of the Christian life.[31] As a theological virtue, the virtue of faith unites the believer—through the mediation of Christ's human nature and historical ministry—to the persons of the blessed Trinity. Accordingly, in a strict sense, nothing created pertains to the formal object of theological faith.[32] "My teaching is not from myself," Christ affirms, "it comes from the one who sent me; and if anyone is prepared to do his will, he will know whether the teaching is from God or whether my doctrine is my own" (John 7:16, 17). To be sure, the secondary material objects of faith involve created realities such as truth-bearing statements or propositions. But these acquire their dignity and importance within the Christian religion precisely be-

---

31. In her paper on "Faith," in The Collected Philosophical Papers of G. E. M. Anscombe, vol. 3, *Ethics, Religion and Politics* (Minneapolis: University of Minnesota Press, 1981), pp. 113–20, Elizabeth Anscombe develops this point along lines different from, though not incompatible with, what is said here.

32. Strictly speaking, both the material object and the formal object [mediating *(quo)* and terminative *(quod)*] remain properly theological, that is, they are identified with the divine nature.

cause of theological faith's formal object, that is, because they express God's Truth within the context of the Church's life and mission.

Since divine truth is never a portion of the divine reality, First Truth-in-Being and First Truth-Speaking are identical in God. To hold otherwise would amount to cleaving God's truthfulness from the substance of the divine nature. But because the divine nature subsists in three distinct Persons, Father, Son, and Holy Spirit, we can consider the Trinitarian communion in terms of First Truth. It belongs to the incarnate Son to reveal the Trinitarian message of salvation. Those who receive this message in faith become believers who even here and now possess "the riches of his glorious inheritance in the saints" (Eph. 1:19). The theological life is marked with the living sign of the blessed Trinity.

Faith's Object: Truth-Bearing Statements (Propositions)

In the grace and favor of the Incarnation, God allows his truth to be measured out in human words. Moreover, within the logic of the Incarnation, the meaning of these human words adequately represents the divine Truth they signify. Catholic theology gives to the incarnational hermeneutic a privileged place in its understanding of faith. The fact that the truth about God is really communicated in human words forms the basis for the Church's concern to safeguard the deposit of faith. At the opening of the Second Vatican Council in 1962, Pope John XXIII explained that the principal objective of the Council would encompass the task of better guarding and explaining the precious deposit of Christian doctrine.[33] Theologians pursue this same goal by providing an account of what might be called subsidiary material objects of theological faith, and by explaining how they together form an organic unity in the deposit of faith.[34]

As a result of various developments within classical Protestantism, the view that faith provides a guarantee for salvation that can be expe-

---

33. See *Acta apostolicae sedis* 54 (1962), p. 788; cited in the Apostolic Constitution *Fidei depositum* of Pope John Paul II, which presents the *Catechism of the Catholic Faith*.

34. While the medieval theologians did not employ the term "dogma" in the same sense that we find in later ecclesiastical usage (e.g., in the documents of the Vatican councils), they were able to explain the significance that the articles of authoritative creeds held for Christian faith.

rienced in some way by the individual influences experiential-expressive views of religious doctrines.[35] According to such views, doctrines serve as noninformative and nondiscursive symbols of inner feelings, attitudes, or existential orientations. Theologians, both Catholic and Protestant, have drawn attention to important issues in the theology of faith as a result of their research in this area, but it can happen that too much focus on the personal state of the believer can lead to a relativization of faith's content. The main problem, however, is not so much the failure to recognize the full complement of faith's subsidiary material objects, as the preference to view these as nonpropositional, and not truth-bearing.[36] In any event, appeal to personal experience has gained a wide influence in contemporary religious studies—so much so that, even among Roman Catholic authors, one finds approaches to faith that make subjective experience the preponderant criterion for both the authenticity of scriptural revelation and the validity of theological argument. In my view, this circumstance increases the urgency for a new deployment of the medieval notion of an article of faith. Communion in faith requires a common language of faith, and the burden of achieving this unity starts with the articles of faith.

The Articles of Faith and Other Things Believed

A fresh perspective on the content of Christian belief is afforded by retrieving the notion of an article of faith. The evolution of the notion of an article as the basic unit of Christian belief began in the twelfth century. The medieval theologians, it should be noted, had no intention of confining God to the limits of created words. Rather, their concern in associating divine truth with truth-bearing statements was to show that human language can serve as an instrument for raising the creature

35. For one account of this development, see George A. Lindbeck's *The Nature of Doctrine: Religion and Theology in a Postliberal Age* (Philadelphia: Westminster Press, 1984), pp. 16ff. Professor Lindbeck, however, proposes a cultural-linguistic understanding of religion and, consequently, of doctrine; though it can complement the Thomist view, is not entirely congenial to propositions. For a critical review of Lindbeck's proposal from a Thomist perspective, see Colman E. O'Neill, "The Rule Theory of Doctrine and Propositional Truth," *The Thomist* 49 (1985): 417–42.

36. However, Pope John Paul II, addressing American bishops, has argued that certain catechetical approaches are not sufficiently attentive to the full truth of Catholic doctrine: "Certain methods have been adopted in which the *fides quae creditur* is too much neglected" (*Origins* 22: 47 (6 May 1993) 717–21).

to God. Such statements do justice to both the historical and the universal character of Christian revelation. Under the guidance of the Holy Spirit, the Church uses the articles of faith to conceptualize the biblical revelation, so that divine truth remains centered in the historical reality that marks its appearance on earth and at the same time is liberated from the confines that any particular culture or time would otherwise impose on it.[37] The development of a theory to explain the profession of the Christian faith constitutes a singular achievement of scholastic theology.

Early thirteenth-century theologians first gave clear expression to the account of the articles of faith as truth-bearing. In an attempt to explain the content of the articles of faith, their immediate predecessors had tentatively put forward the dialectical juxtaposition of two key notions: the proposition *(enuntiabile)* and the reality *(res)*. As an *enuntiabile*—something that can be enunciated in propositional form—the object of faith embodies a statement or proposition, as for example in the assertion, "I believe that God made heaven and earth." As a *res,* or reality, the object of faith transcends the inherent limitations of language and points to the very being of what is believed. In the example cited, faith would unite the believer to the God who is maker of heaven and earth, with all that such a graced union implies for our attitude toward the physical universe. But the development of a satisfactory account of the article as truth-bearing required the transition from an elementary logic of terms, based upon the Aristotelian *Categories,* to a logic of propositions, based upon Aristotle's *De interpretatione.* The former approach, with its anticipatory nominalistic overtones, risked the suggestion that divine faith is articulated through the arbitrary assignation of symbols or words, while the latter, with its psychological sophistication, opened up a way to explain faith's unitive function in the life of the Christian believer.

The single formal object of theological faith—God as First Truth—

---

37. For further discussion of this point, see Kenneth L. Schmitz, "St Thomas and the Appeal to Experience," *Catholic Theological Society of America Proceedings* 47 (1992): 1–20: "Conceptualization invested with the energy of the human spirit offers us the possibility of an approach to particular situations and to our own particular era from a point of reference that is at once both larger than the particular situation and era, and yet resident at its very center" (15).

provides a unifying principle for what the Christian religion holds as true. At the same time, the Church proposes many things for belief. Theologians agree that the diversity in the number of the articles results from human reason's attempt to seize the objective transcendent intelligibilities of the truths proposed for belief. Faith then appropriates these truths according to the limitations of human cognitional structure, and so the human mind must "articulate" divine truth into different elements or articles.[38]

According to the testimony of St. Ambrose, the practice of the early Church was to identify twelve articles in the Creed, thereby symbolizing through the full number of the apostolic college the entirety of the apostolic faith.[39] The medieval theologians frequently enumerate fourteen articles—twice the perfect number of seven—and thereby symbolically display the same fullness of apostolic faith. In *Summa theologiae* IIa-IIae q. 1, a. 8, Aquinas outlines the articles under two headings: Seven of the articles concern the mystery of the Godhead in itself and seven the humanity of Christ and the mysteries of his life (see Chart 1).[40]

His organic account of the articles of faith raises three related issues: first, a definition of the article as a unit; second, a coordination of the articles with the broader range of everything that is set forth for belief; and third, an elaboration of this coordination by a comparison with science, that is, conceived as an ordered body of knowledge. If we assume that Aquinas offers a representative account of the way that the Catholic tradition understands these issues, examining his explanations will illumine the deeper senses involved in the notion of an article.

First, Aquinas's definition of an article materially depends on its Greek etymology, namely, a joint or juncture.[41] He proceeds to deepen

38. Aquinas first develops this argument in the *Scriptum super libros Sententiarum* III, d. 25, q. 1, a. 1, sol. 1, and later gives it a more sophisticated statement both in the *Summa theologiae* IIa-IIae q. 1, a. 6: ". . . ubi occurrit aliquid speciali ratione non visum, ibi est specialis articulus: ubi autem multa secundum eandem rationem sunt incognita, ibi non sunt articuli distinguendi," and in the *Compendium theologiae* Bk. 1, chap. 246.

39. See St. Ambrose, *Explanatio symboli*, chap. 8 (PL 17, 1158). In the first part of its comprehensive statement of Christian faith and practice, *The Catechism of the Catholic Church* (no. 191) follows the patristic usage.

40. See *In III Sent.* dist. 25, q. 1, a. 2; *Summa theologiae* IIa-IIae q. 1, a. 8; *Compendium theologiae* Bk. 1, chap. 246.

41. In the work of his youth, his *Sentences* commentary (e.g., *In III Sent* d. 25, q. 1, a. 1, sol. 1), Aquinas carefully places his interpretation of the *articulus* in this fashion under

Chart 1

Those things whose vision is eternal life, or the mystery of the Godhead	Those things that lead to eternal life, or the mystery of the Incarnation
1. unity of the Godhead	1. Incarnation
2. Trinity of the Godhead	2. virginal birth
3. works of the Godhead	3. passion, death, burial
-creation	4. descent into hell
-sanctification	5. resurrection
-last things	6. ascension
-eternal glory	7. coming in judgment

this lexical suggestion with a more formal account when he speaks about the article as dispositions of the parts *(coaptatio distinctorum)*. By this phrase, Aquinas intends to describe an organic relationality that, so to speak, is written into the heart of the article. In other words, the articles fit with one another according to a determined order, just as the bones of the human skeleton do. This means that each of the articles can be joined to other articles in such a way so that their interrelatedness is measured against the integrity of the whole body of Christian truth. Some theologians would refer to the ensemble of revealed truth so arranged as manifesting a theological aesthetic. In a similar way, the Second Vatican Council affirms, "In Catholic doctrine there exists an order or 'hierarchy' of truths."[42]

A further issue concerns the relation of the articles to the broader range of truths and doctrines, which either are strictly and intimately connected with the articles or further explicitate them. Since they order the human person to possess eternal life, the articles stand on their own; they are proposed for their own sake, if you will. The other things pro-

---

the tutelage of a (spurious) definition attributed to Richard of St. Victor (d. 1173). In the work of his maturity, Aquinas appeals to the usage of the term in grammar and rhetoric (e.g., *Summa theologiae* IIa-IIae q. 1, a. 6): "the name 'article' seems to be derived from the Greek. *Arthron* in Greek, which is called *articulus* in Latin, signifies a certain coadaptation of distinct parts. And so the small parts of the body coadapted to each other are called the 'articles' of the members. And similarly in grammar the Greeks named 'articles' certain parts of speech coadapted to other locutions in order to express their genus, number, or case."

42. The Decree on Ecumenism, *Unitatis redintegratio*, no. 11.

posed for our acceptance somehow manifest the articles.[43] For example, the final purification of the elect that the Church calls purgatory elucidates the article of the Creed that expresses the Christian belief in life everlasting: In order to enter the joy of heaven, one must be holy. In the *Summa theologiae*, however, Aquinas seems principally to have in mind certain historical incidents related in Scripture. The articles include all those things proposed for our belief directly, whereas other things "of which the Scriptures speak"—to quote Aquinas—are proposed for our belief but in order to illuminate the articles.[44] But surely this principle can support broader conclusions. In this way, the theoretical groundwork is laid for the notion of the development of doctrine as well as for the exercise of the living magisterium of the Church.

There is, finally, the issue of a formal account of the relation among the articles. Aquinas conceived of this relationship along the lines of science according to the canon of Aristotle's *Prior Analytics*. Here the operative model relates the principal articles to the secondary articles and other things to be believed in the same way that *per se nota* principles stand in relation to conclusions in a teaching that natural reason elaborates.[45] This analogy with Aristotelian science also illumines Aquinas's theology of the gifts, although in both instances he will decidedly soften the harsh intellectualism that Aristotle's *Analytics* imply.[46] For the

43. For example, *Summa theologiae* IIa-IIae q. 1, a. 6 ad 1, trans. O'Brien: "Among its objects there are those that faith regards for their own sake; there are others that faith regards not for themselves but only for their relationship to other objects. This is like the case where the sciences propose some matters for their own sake, others simply for their explanatory value." For a development of this principle, see Congregation for the Doctrine of the Faith, "Instruction on the Ecclesial Vocation of the Theologian" (1990), no. 23.

44. Using the language of *Summa theologiae* IIa-IIae q. 1, a. 6 ad 1: *articuli : alia credenda (de quibus Scriptura)* :: *quae proponuntur ut per se intenta : quaedam proponuntur ad manifestationem aliorum.* The examples that Aquinas uses, moreover, indicate that he is thinking about the various miracles recounted in both the Old and the New Testaments that witness to the Godhead or Christ's coming among men.

45. See for example, *Summa theologiae* IIa-IIae, q. 1, a. 7; *In III Sent.* d. 25, q. 1, a. 1, sol. 1; *In Tit.* 1. 1. The actual terms of the analogy run like this: *articuli principales : articuli secundarii et alia credenda* :: *principia per se nota : conclusiones in doctrina quae per rationem naturalem habetur.*

46. R.-A. Gauthier claims that during the second Parisian regency, Aquinas was induced to "mitigate the excessive intellectualism that he had earlier displayed." See his "La date du Commentaire de saint Thomas sur l'Ethique à Nicomaque," *Recherches de Théologie ancienne et médiévale* 18 (1951): 103, n. 91. Santiago Ramirez, *De hominis beatitudine* III

knowledge of faith belongs preeminently to those who are in love with a personal God and who therefore rely on his truthfulness. So, while Aquinas considers that the Aristotelian notion of science helps to clarify the notion of a deposit of faith insofar as deposit suggests an ordered body of truth, those who live in charity best understand the interrelationships among the articles of the Creed.

The new Aristotelian learning of the thirteenth century had its impact upon describing the nature of Christian belief. It helped theologians clarify the true nature of Christian faith. By instrumentally using symbolic religious language, the one who exercises the virtue of faith really achieves a true knowledge of divine realities. The Christian believer transcends the limits of human concepts and communication and lays hold of the mysteries of the Kingdom that God reveals in Christ. We now turn to examine how Aquinas explains the function of the articles in a cognitive view of faith.

The Articles of Faith as Truth-Bearing

Aquinas's greatest achievement in explaining the articles of faith is the account that he gives of them as truth-bearing. This contribution merits attention not merely because of Aquinas's historical achievement in overcoming certain dialectically opposed school positions of his time, but for what this account implies for relating the doctrines of faith to the personal condition of the believer and, ultimately, to the gifts of knowledge and understanding. Aquinas's comprehension of the articles of faith exhibits none of the rigidity that certain critics claim characterizes the "received" modern understanding of dogma. Still, his concern to relativize and subordinate the articles of faith along a number of different lines always respects the permanence of divine Truth in the world.

We need to recall the larger context into which Aquinas inserts the articles of faith. The horizon of his analysis might be described as a universal outpouring of doctrine in which many share. The best illustration is that Truth which stands at the summit of the human vocation, namely, the beatific vision. In the joy of heaven, many persons share in

---

(Madrid, 1947), p. 192, observes something similar precisely with respect to Aquinas's teaching on faith and the gifts of the Holy Spirit.

a single community of beatifying truth. How does this happen? A generally agreed-upon explanation runs as follows: The formal influence of the divine Essence itself combines with what the tradition calls the light of glory *(lumen gloriae)*, so that the higher doctrine, God's own knowledge of himself, can redound to its lower expressions in the saints.[47] Something similar happens in the Church: From God and the blessed to the angels, to the prophets, to Christ and his apostles, to the prelates and teachers and preachers of the Church, Aquinas claims a formal community in those who are taught, the things taught, and one universal causal ordering that moves from principal through instrumental or ministerial teachers. Of course, Christ himself stands at the center of this entire process. For it is Christ who teaches both angels and men, and who alone fully communicates divine Truth to the world. The articles of faith serve as instruments of this universal outpouring of doctrine from God, which culminates in the offer of truth and friendship that Jesus extends as a free gift.

Various theological factors concretize this grand and imposing scheme. For one thing, the ordering easily combines an immediate and vertical doctrine with an ongoing and "horizontal" progress of doctrine in the historical economy of salvation. This development is guided by the Church's living magisterium, which ensures that the things God had once revealed for the salvation of all peoples remain in their entirety. The outpouring is manifest in the external word and illumination of the preacher or teacher, but it also requires in the hearer an interior locution, a direct divine touch of faith that moves the believer to accept whatever is proposed for belief.[48] No matter how many come to a knowl-

47. Kevin F. O'Shea, C.Ss.R., "Divinization: A Study in Theological Analogy," *The Thomist* 29 (1965): 1–45, explains: "The blessed in heaven see the divine essence with an intuitive, face-to-face vision, without the interposition of any creature in the function of object seen. The divine essence immediately manifests itself to them, plainly, openly, clearly. To see God in this way the soul needs a supernatural elevation called the light of glory" (p. 5). The author cites Benedict XII's *Benedictus Deus* as the ecclesiastical witness for the teaching on the *lumen gloriae* (*DS* 1000).

48. "Sed fides est duplex secundum duplicem auditum et duplicem locutionem; est enim *fides ex auditu* ut dicitur Rom. X, 17: est enim quaedam locutio exterior qua nobis Deus per praedicatores loquitur, quaedam autem interior locutio qua nobis loquitur per internam inspirationem. . . . Ab utroque autem auditu fides in cordibus fidelium oritur: per auditum quidem interiorem in his qui primo fidem acceperunt et docuerunt sicut in apostolis et prophetis . . . ; per secundum vero auditum fides oritur in cordibus aliorum fidelium

edge of the truth, within this organic structure constituted by participation in one community of Truth and one causal order, whose center is Christ, there exists a single, analogously uniform teaching that springs from God himself. This divine teaching conforms both to the evangelical doctrine *(doctrina evangelica)* and the doctrine of the Church *(doctrina Ecclesiae)*, even if the criteriology of this doctrine develops in a significant way only with the Catholic Reform of the sixteenth century.[49]

Two further factors influence the way in which the articles of faith exist within this overarching scheme of divine instruction. The first of these factors forms a decisive and central element of the treatise on theological faith. Aquinas subordinates the articles of faith, that is, the subsidiary material objects, to God, who as First Truth alone constitutes faith's formal object.[50] This means that the mind adheres to the truth-character of the articles solely and precisely inasmuch as it adheres to God himself, First Truth in Being and Speaking.[51] This adhering can take place only on the basis of a gracious, foregoing, divine address whereby God joins himself to the human mind as a proper formal object of the knowing capacity. This same address also elicits the first stirrings of love in the will. Catholic theology accordingly interprets the articles as subordinate to God's own speaking; through the gift of the Holy Spirit, the Church enjoys a participation in God's own infallibility. In other words, First Truth manifests itself instrumentally in the words of Christ and of the Church, guaranteeing the consistency and coherence of the articles.

A second factor that characterizes the Catholic treatment of the articles of faith arises in the context of an issue debated by early medieval

---

qui per alios homines cognitionem fidei accipiunt" *(De veritate* q. 18, a. 3, Leonine edition, 46–52 and 61–68, p. 538).

49. Motivated in large measure by the particular challenges of the Reform, Catholic theologians in the sixteenth century seriously undertook the task of sorting out the specifications of Christian doctrine. For example, Melchior Cano (1509–60) wrote his *De locis theologicis* (Salamanca, 1563) to establish standards for evaluating theological *sententiae.*

50. *Summa theologiae* IIa-IIae q. 1, a. 1; q. 5, a. 3.

51. Cardinal Cajetan introduces this helpful distinction in *In IIa-IIam* q. 1, a. 1: "And since truth is found in God in a twofold way, even as in any intellectual nature, namely, in being and in speaking. . . ." ["Et cum dupliciter veritas inveniatur in Deo, sicut et in quolibet intellectuali natura, scilicet in essendo et in dicendo. . . ."]

theologians. Aquinas formulates the question as follows: "Whether the object of faith is something complex in the way that a truth-bearing statement is?"[52] The question is whether the propositions of faith can actually mediate First Truth, or do they only point to a truth that remains essentially unknowable. Aquinas holds that propositions can serve as true objects of faith, even though the act of faith finds its ultimate term in the divine reality. For Catholic theology, the act of faith reaches beyond the formal content of doctrines and attains the very referent—"*res ipsa*"—of theological faith. This strong view of Christian doctrine develops partly as a result of the conviction that belief involves a specific kind of theological judgment.[53] While this interpretation of belief warrants a much fuller exposition, at this point we can only recapitulate its principal features.[54]

Faith as an act of judgment attains the uncreated Being of God—in scholastic shorthand, the *res*; thus, the oft-quoted adage of Aquinas: "*Actus autem credentis non terminatur ad enuntiabile, sed ad rem*" ["the act of the believer does not reach its end in a statement, but in the thing"]. He continues: "We do not form statements except so that we may have apprehension of things through them. As it is in knowledge, so also in faith."[55] The "things" refers to all of the mysteries of the Christian religion, but, in an ultimate and foundational way, to God himself, as the object of theological faith. Since human creatures can perform human but not divine actions, the attaining of the Uncreated, of God himself, is a human activity. This points to the fascinating and perplexing mystery of divinization that faith inaugurates, in which a finite gift enables a creature to share in the proper Truth of the uncreated God. For while faith, operating within the human cognitional structure, truly at-

52. For example, in *Summa theologiae* IIa-IIae q. 1, a. 2: "Utrum objectum fidei sit aliquid complexum per modum enuntiabilis?"

53. For a good explanation of this teaching and its relevance to contemporary issues in theology, see Colman E. O'Neill, O.P., "The Rule Theory of Doctrine and Propositional Truth," *The Thomist* 49 (1985): 417–42.

54. For a full discussion of this important point in a realist cognitive theory, see the two articles by Ambrose McNicholl, O.P., "On Judging," *The Thomist* 38 (1974): 768–825, and "On Judging Existence," *The Thomist* 43 (1979): 507–80.

55. *Summa theologiae* IIa-IIae q. 1, a. 2, ad 2: "non enim formamus enuntiabilia nisi ut per ea de rebus cognitionem habeamus, sicut in scientia, ita et in fide."

tains God, it does so mediately, through the instrumentality of the proposition or *enuntiabile*. The mediation of propositions, however, does not impede but achieves the attainment of the real Truth.

A brief mention of the pertinent elements of realist cognitional theory may serve a helpful purpose at this juncture.[56] There exists an isomorphism between thinking and reality, a parallelism in structure. The model, however, does not imply an exact correspondence, as if thinking produces a "picture" of being. Rather, it stresses the mind's capacity to lay hold of the real world.[57] Joseph Owens recapitulates the important point as follows: "One knows a thing when one's judgments about it is in conformity with what exists in the thing itself, and one knows that

56. For a helpful resumé of this theory, see Joseph Owens, C.Ss.R., *Cognition. An Epistemological Inquiry* (Houston: Center for Thomistic Studies, 1992), especially chaps. 5–6.

57. There are two moments in the structure of cognition. The first moment is simple apprehension. Apprehension comprises an abstractive act by the agent intellect, whereby individualizing characteristics are left aside and the material thing known is "translated" into the immateriality of the intellect. Simple apprehension also involves a conceptualizing act by the possible intellect, whereby the thing rendered knowable by the agent intellect comes to be known precisely as the actuality of the knower—the concept. The expressions agent and possible intellect refer to different functions of the one human intellective power. In terms of the structure of the real, this apprehensive moment is directed to the essence of things. The other component of the real—its *esse* or act of existence—is only obliquely available to this moment, as a presupposition of the essence's being-there to be apprehended at all. For there can be no direct abstractive concept of *esse* (see Owens, *Cognition*, pp. 174–77).

The second moment is judgment. Judgment itself comprises two distinct submoments. First, a synthetic submoment. At this point, the knower formulates a proposition and compares the relationship of the subject-class to the predicate-class. Take the example of an analytic proposition, a definition, e.g., "Man is an animal." The "is" of the proposition in this moment merely signifies class-conjunction. Notice that at this level the knower is still dealing with concepts, even though comparatively, and thus remains at the corresponding level of essence in real things. Secondly, the knower moves to a moment of existential assent. This is the root of the "complexity" of the proposition of which Aquinas is speaking when he asks whether the object of faith is something complex in the way that a truth-bearing statement is (see his discussion in *Summa theologiae* IIa-IIae q. 1, a. 2). At this moment in judgment, true composition occurs with the introduction of an intelligibility distinct from that of the concept or of class-conjunction. For, "is" is spoken in an existential and no longer merely conjunctive sense. The isomorphism of thought and reality is verified inasmuch as the real distinction in creatures between essence and *esse* is paralleled in cognition by distinct cognitive moments attaining each member of the distinction. In this moment of assent, *esse* does not come merely obliquely into view as in the case of the apprehensive/conceptual moment. Rather, the act of existence as it is extramentally, really exercised is attained in judgmental cognition.

the judgment is true when one sees the conformity between the judgment and the reality."[58]

In order to grasp the full importance that the Catholic tradition attaches to the meaning of doctrine, one must carefully note how different the cognition of *esse* is from the cognitive processes directed toward essences. In the cognition of *esse* there is no "token" signifying reality. Rather, the act of judgment joins the act of existing. The signification is dynamic and operational in kind. If *esse* can be compared to a great flood coursing by "out there," judgmental cognition of *esse* is attained not by "picturing" it but by flowing into it after the fashion of a tributary. Furthermore, inasmuch as *esse* is the radical actuality of the being-ness and actuality and intelligibility of a thing, it is the thing itself that is attained. It is the judgmental act itself that transforms the purely conceptual and conjunctive elements of the proposition. Then, as Owens again explains, "[Truth] is a relation set up by reason between a mental representation and an existent on the ground that the two are seen to be equated insofar as the one represents statically the dynamic synthesis exercised by the other."[59]

This grasp at the truth of being, attained in the act of knowledge, stands at the heart of Aquinas's doctrine about theological faith. "Thus," he states, "the object of faith can be explained in two ways: In one way, on the part of the thing believed itself, and thus the object of faith is something not complex, namely the thing itself about which faith is had. In another way, [it can be considered] on the part of the believer, and in this way the object of faith is something complex in the manner of a truth-bearing statement."[60]

How does this way of looking at the object of faith provide practical benefits for the person who wishes to enter more deeply into the life of Christian faith? Consider the example of Mary's Immaculate Conception as an article of faith. Because the universal Church confesses the doctrine of the Immaculate Conception, each of the faithful must give assent to the proposition that Mary *is* immaculately conceived. In the terms of Aquinas's cognitional theory, the "is-ness" thus seized by the

58. Owens, *Cognition*, p. 209.
59. Ibid., p. 201.
60. *Summa theologiae* IIa-IIae q. 1, a. 2.

act of belief is identical with the very "is-ness" of the *res*—in this case, the very grace of the Immaculate Conception—though as mediated through the proposition. Accordingly, the article of faith (in this example, as set down in the 1854 papal Bull, *Ineffabilis Deus)* serves as an instrument for an action that surpasses the limits of language. Just as knowledge implies intentional identity between the knower and the essence—or some formal aspect—of what is known, so faith's judgment transcends the conceptual content of the proposition *(enuntiabile)* and lays hold of the very realities that the articles express and mediate.[61] The Christian assenting to belief in the Immaculate Conception enters into the reality of Mary's spiritual motherhood and her "existing" as the first person to have benefited from the salvation wrought by her Son.[62]

Because the dynamic of faith itself includes an affective component, the believer attains to such a penetration of the mysteries of the faith. Unlike ordinary knowing, which depends on sense contact with the object known, acceptance of the articles of faith as true can come only upon surrender to a God who both exists as Truth and speaks the Truth. Volitional union of the believer with "that which is believed" subsequently begets an even greater love of the revealed truth. Within the Thomist tradition, one easily affirms a continuity between living by faith here below and seeing by vision in heaven. The underlying unity of the life of the wayfarer and the beholder exists only because of that special outpouring of divine love that results in the Incarnation of the eternal Word. Christ lived his human life as simultaneously *viator* and *comprehensor*, so he both communicates and grounds the propositions of faith. The First Letter of John explictly equates union with Christ and the fulness of life: "Whoever has the Son has life; whoever does not have the Son of God does not have life" (1 John 5:12).

---

61. For further information, T. C. O'Brien, "Faith and the Truth about God," appendix 3 of *Faith*, vol. 31 of the *Summa theologiae* (New York: McGraw-Hill, 1975), pp. 195–201.

62. The Bull explicitly refers to the saving work of Christ as instrumental in the preservation of the blessed Virgin Mary from every stain of original sin: "intuito meritorum Christi Iesu Salvatoris humani generis . . ." (*DS* 2803).

Summary

The Catholic tradition affirms that, from the point of view of the divine reality believed, the truths of faith remain simple and one, but from the point of view of the believer's act, the divine realities are given human shape in knowledge and affirmation. The propositions of faith adapt divine truth to the limitations of our intellects. Truth-bearing statements about divine realities are complex, because these mysteries are known according to the normal structure of human knowing, which unites a knowing subject with the object known. As Christ's human nature provides a visible form for the eternal Logos, so does theological faith assume the dipolar structure of human knowing.

The Catholic understanding holds theological faith and its material objects to be more than just an orthodox formulation of the articles of faith. Realist epistemology asserts that a knower does not fix on the being that the known has in the knower, but on the being the known is in itself. Analogically, this holds good for faith knowledge and its relationship to truth-bearing statements. Faith fixes on the being that the known is in itself. Otherwise the saints would not echo Aquinas's conviction about faith's unitive power: "Through faith the soul is joined to God, for through faith the Christian soul enters as it were into a marriage with God; 'I will espouse thee to me in faith' (Hos. 2:20)."[63] Like the humanity of Christ, faith's conceptual apparatus, especially as it bears on the truth-bearing statements which today are called dogmas, remains an instrument for our salvation.

Since the object of faith is complex in the way that a truth-bearing statement is, and since the act of the believer does not terminate in the propositional terms but in the reality itself, believing entails a judgmental act. Theological faith, therefore, possesses the complexifying and proposition-transcending character of all human judgment-acts. Faith differs from other acts of judgment not as regards the judgmental structure and attainment itself, but solely because faith's speaking of the judgmental existential "is" relies not on evidential apprehension but

---

63. *In symbolum Apostolorum Expositio*, prol. Aquinas of course is using the Vulgate. The *New Revised Standard Version* gives the Hosea text as "I will take you for my wife in faithfulness"; however, the Hebrew word is the same here and in Habakuk 2:4, which is translated as "but the righteous live by their *faith.*"

on the command of the will moved by grace. That which sets faith's assent in motion remains peculiar to faith; but once set in motion, that motion or operation proceeds according to the cognitional structure of judgment. "Two things are required for faith: one is the willingness of the heart to believe, and this comes not by hearing, but by the gift of grace; the other is a determination of what is to be believed, and this comes by hearing."[64]

Finally, to state that "propositional elements" are transcended in the direction of *esse* or the divine realities as they actually exist does not render them superfluous or expendable. For the existence *(esse)* signified in judgment is always the existence *(esse)* of the essence signified by the propositional terms. There is no "occasionalism" implied here—as if the propositional terms were merely the "occasion" for attaining what transcends them. There is genuine composition as intimate as that between existence *(esse)* and essence in the real order. The propositional terms are the real medium of existential assent: judgment always says both "*this* is" and "this *is*."[65] For this reason, the Church rightly exercises a proper surveillance so that the statements about divine realities properly express the truth of the Catholic faith, for all that the Church "proposes for belief, as being divinely revealed, is drawn from the one deposit of faith."[66] God alone as First Truth in Being and Speaking continues to guarantee the truthfulness of that deposit.

Faith's Object: The Light of Faith *(lumen fidei)*

A consideration of faith's objects as comparable to objects of human knowing points up the immediacy that theological faith establishes between the believer and God. As Aquinas insists, faith really joins the human mind to the divine knowing.[67] The immediacy of faith knowledge, however, does not undermine the fundamental character of Christian belief, for as St. Paul expresses it, "For now we see in a mirror, dimly" (1 Cor. 13:12). Aquinas too emphasizes the limitations of faith's

---

64. St. Thomas Aquinas, *Expositio in Romanos* lect. 10, no. 3.

65. See Lindbeck, *The Nature of Doctrine*, chap. 2.

66. The Second Vatican Council's Dogmatic Constitution on Revelation, *Dei Verbum*, no. 10.

67. See *De veritate* q. 14, a. 8.

knowledge when he cautions that "by faith, we do not gaze upon the
first Truth as he is in himself."[68] This quality of faith explains the say-
ings of the mystics who encourage us in many different ways to sustain
the darkness that authentic Christian experience brings. Like the Word
of God itself, theological faith is a "light that shines in the dark" (John
1:5). Thus, St. John of the Cross describes the journey of faith as one
undertaken "In the serene night / With a flame that is consuming and
painless."[69]

The metaphor of darkness, however, conceals a more basic truth
about the relationship of faith to its object. The dynamic of theological
faith involves both the intellect and the will. Aristotle describes four
ways in which an individual can be moved to assent to a given truth.
The first two derive from the apprehension of the object either directly,
as happens with the first principles of speculative reasoning, or mediately, as when one arrives at conclusions on the basis of premises. The
second two ways of assent rely on the power of the will. Aristotle names
these opinion and belief. In these instances, the will chooses to assent,
with hesitation and doubt in the case of opinion or with certainty in the
case of belief, because the will discovers some reason, such as the word
of a friend, to assent to a conclusion.

Theological faith attains its object through belief. Since we will discuss the act of belief in the next chapter, our present concern lies only
in the formal reason for credibility.[70] Because faith is about what is not
seen—what we cannot directly apprehend by our intellectual capacities—the theologian needs to explain how the human mind can achieve
a real knowledge of divine mysteries. For the Catholic tradition, the
answer remains simple: "The light of faith makes one see the things
that are believed."[71] On the one hand, faith is an intentional knowing.
God reveals himself to us through sense-perceptible signs. First Truth
is delivered to us in a finite and obscure mode, through the medium of
created screens (the scriptural images), which filter the blinding divine

68. *Summa theologiae* IIa-IIae q. 1, a. 2, ad 3.
69. *The Spiritual Canticle*, stanza 39.
70. The scholastics called this the *ratio formalis credibilium ex patre nostri*. See *Summa theologiae* IIa-IIae q. 1, a. 6, ad 2.
71. *Summa theologiae* IIa-IIae q. 1, a. 4, ad 3: "Lumen fidei facit videre ea quae cre-
duntur."

light. On the other hand, supernatural assistance is required to supply for the lack of evidence of faith's truths and to seize the concepts of faith and the divine meaning revealed there. We call this help a ray of the divine intellect: the *lumen fidei*. The meeting of these two participations of the same divine truth (looked at from the part of the object and from the part of the subject) gives birth to the knowledge of faith. Because the human person is a unity of the material and the immaterial, of body and soul, faith requires the unity of these two elements.[72] To suppress one of the two is to destroy the very notion of our Catholic faith. Because the light of faith enables the believer to judge the credibility of the Christian mysteries only in correlation with the virtue of faith itself, the *lumen fidei* belongs entirely to the order of habitual or sanctifying grace.

In the early part of the twentieth century, the French Jesuit Pierre Rousselot sparked considerable debate about the nature of apologetical argument by affirming that faith itself is required to seize even the rational credibility of the faith. He rejected any purely natural grounds for making a judgment of credibility about what is to be believed. Because of the harmonies that Catholic theology likes to sound between the order of creation and the order of grace, this attempt to inject divine grace into the natural motives for credibility struck the Catholic world as problematical.[73] It can, after all, be incumbent on theologians to discuss the human motives of credibility for divine faith. During certain periods of the Church's history, theologians especially sought to unearth convincing arguments for the reasonableness of Christian faith. Moreover, the undertaking enjoys a long tradition within the Church (to which no one can take reasonable exception) and still continues in the field of philosophical theology.[74] Aquinas, as we have seen, stresses

72. For this analysis of the "*lumen fidei,*" I am indebted to the account given by Pierre Boisselot, O.P., "La lumière de la foi," *La Vie spirituelle* 41 (1934): [34]-[45].

73. For a presentation of this interesting chapter in the history of modern theology, see John M. McDermott's introduction to Pierre Rousselot, S.J., *The Eyes of Faith,* trans. Joseph Donceel, S.J., and Avery Dulles, S.J. (New York: Fordham University Press, 1990). But for a critical assessment of Rousselot's contribution, see Avery Dulles, S.J., *The Assurance of Things Hoped For. A Theology of Christian Faith* (New York: Oxford University Press, 1994), pp. 110–12.

74. For example, see the collected works of Robert M. Adams, *The Virtue of Faith and Other Essays in Philosophical Theology* (New York: Oxford University Press, 1987).

that these persuasions remain invitations to belief and not formal reasons for assent. Even Christ's miracles or other supernatural phenomena fall short of providing proportionate evidence for the judgmental assent of faith. The same holds true for the persuasiveness of the preacher. The preached word never convinces one to accept what faith holds; it can only urge that we give assent as commanded by the will.[75] In one place, Aquinas writes that the "light of faith works less by way of knowledge than by way of inclination."[76] We can compare this inclination to a virtuous *habitus* that inclines the affective powers to follow the lead of prudence. In the case of theological faith, the "light of faith" conditions the intellect to give its assent to what the human heart delights in adhering to. Recall that John of the Cross emphasizes that "faith affirms what cannot be understood by the intellect."[77]

The special character of knowing in faith leads to the question whether the objects of faith can serve, in any way, as the goals of scientific inquiry. Is there a sense in which "natural" knowledge, following its own inherent processes, can actually discover truths that are to be believed? At face value, this would seem odd, for faith initiates in the believer a personal communion with the blessed Trinity, and human intelligence cannot penetrate the mystery of the divine life.

There is a category of truths that, even if some individuals may learn them only through the assent of theological faith, do cede to scientific demonstration. Aquinas sets forth this distinction as follows: "Things proved demonstratively can be counted among the things to be believed, but not in the sense that all should simply have faith about them. Since they are prerequisites to the things that are of faith, they ought to be presupposed all at once in faith by those who cannot demonstrate them."[78] In order to grasp the meaning of this text, we need to consider

75. See *Summa theologiae* IIa-IIae q. 1, a. 2, ad 2, where Aquinas discusses the role of miracles in the announcement of the faith.

76. *Expositio super librum Boethii De trinitate* q. 3, a. 1, ad 4. Aquinas developed his understanding of this aspect of faith's dynamic. In the *Scriptum super Sententias*, he held the view that the *lumen fidei* could discriminate between truth and falsity (see *In III Sententias* d. 23, q. 2, a. 2, quaes. 1 solutio). In *Summa theologiae* IIa-IIae q. 1, a. 2, ad 3, he shows a softer, less intellectualistic approach when he speaks about a "virtuous disposition." Faith remains an affective knowing.

77. *The Ascent of Mount Carmel* chap. 6, no. 2.

78. *Summa theologiae* IIa-IIae q. 1, a. 5, ad 3.

two suppositions: first, the distinction between something revealed *(revelatum)* and something able to be revealed *(revelabile)* and, second, the mutual exclusivity of scientific knowledge and faith in the same subject at the same time.

First, the distinction between what is revealed *(revelatum)* and what is able to be revealed *(revelabile)*. In his introductory preface on the nature of theology, Aquinas observes the difference between these two categories of divine instruction.[79] *Revelatum* refers to a mystery of faith in the strict sense of the term, namely, truths that entirely surpass the capacity of natural reason to grasp. Accordingly, only divine revelation can communicate these mysteries—the blessed Trinity, the divinity of Christ, the efficacy of the sacraments, the primacy of the Roman Pontiff, the assumption of the blessed Virgin Mary into heaven, and still others.[80] *Revelabile*, on the other hand, designates a category of truths that serve as the preambles or prerequisites of faith. These truths, such as the existence of God or the fact of a divine providence or government, do not surpass the capacity of natural reason in itself.[81] Still, it may happen that one or another individual cannot, for whatever cause, figure out these fundamental tenets. In order that everyone may come to a knowledge of these basic truths, revelation extends to the category of truths that fall within the capacity of natural reason but still are able-to-be-revealed.

79. See *Summa theologiae* Ia q. 1, a. 1 and the large suite of commentary available. See, for example, Victor White, O.P., "Holy Teaching, The Idea of Theology according to St Thomas Aquinas," *Aquinas Papers* 33 (London: Blackfriars Publications, 1958), who makes a strong case for interpreting the *sacra doctrina* mainly as an instrument of the divine pedagogy.

80. Cajetan described this category of truths as *supernaturale quoad modum et quoad substantiam* (supernatural with respect to their mode and their substance). In this description, he made it clear that not only does the mode, i.e., Christian revelation, by which these truths are known exceed the human capacity for learning, but the very substance of what these truths contain also surpasses our abilities. These truths reveal God in his very Godness—*sub ratione ipsa Deitatis*.

81. Cajetan described this category of truths as *supernaturale quoad modum tantum* (supernatural only in their mode of transmission). In this case, human reason possesses the ability to grasp the substance of the truth, for example, God as the first cause and end of the created order—*sub ratione causae entis communis et finis ultimi*. Still, God *de facto* reveals these conclusions in a way that does not conform to the ordinary way in which we acquire knowledge. In short, revelation always provides a cultural shock for the human being.

Second, knowledge in the unqualified sense of the term satisfies one of our deepest yearnings. Aristotle made this point clearly at the beginning of his *Metaphysics*. Proceeding on the basis of self-evident first principles, scientific knowledge develops a body of knowledge by understanding the causes at work in each field. This kind of developed and organized knowledge perfects the human capacity for intelligent life. Faith, as we have seen, proceeds on the basis of an assent to God's witness. Assent implies the inevident. In itself, the category of knowledge represents the fullest expression of human cognition. As a general cognitive phenomenon, however, belief is less intellectually complete. Yet, the Church holds that theological faith surpasses in excellence scientific knowledge, even though the requirements of faith works a certain violence on our intellectual capacities.[82] A more complete understanding of this seeming paradox of faith—that an act less complete intellectually is said to be more certain than scientific knowledge itself—calls for an analysis of the act of faith from the perspective of the believing subject.

On the basis of these aforementioned distinctions, the difference between a revealed truth *(revelatum)* and a truth able-to-be-revealed *(revelabile)*, and the difference between a subject who knows in the unqualified sense and one who assents, the following observations may be made. First, the strict mysteries of the faith do not allow for scientific demonstration or knowledge. By definition, these objects surpass our native capacity to learn about them. Second, we can attain naturally knowable truths that are *de facto* revealed either through scientific investigation or through the assent of belief. However, belief and scientific knowledge of these sorts of truths remain mutually exclusive in the same person, at the same time, and under the same respect.[83] In other words, we cannot believe what we already know, although we can first believe

---

82. Anthony Kenny goes so far as to affirm that "faith is not, as theologians have claimed, a virtue, but a vice, unless a number of conditions can be fulfilled. One of them is that the existence of God can be rationally justified outside of faith." See his *What Is Faith?* (Oxford: Oxford University Press, 1992), p. 57.

83. The scholastic apologists argued that one might come to a scientific knowledge that God is simple but also believe that the three divine Persons of the blessed Trinity subsist in the one divine nature.

a truth and later come to grasp the intrinsic evidence for its truthfulness.[84]

Faith begins the personal communion with God that we call the theological life. As the beginning of eternal life, faith surpasses all creaturely expectations. Christ himself insists on the utter gratuity of the divine call to faith: "No one can come to me unless drawn by the Father who

84. It is characteristic of Catholic theology to express the complementarity of faith and reason, not to isolate one from the other. So the Church cannot accept the distinction/ separation of the historical Jesus and the Christ of faith, which turns out to be the liberal Protestant correlative to the separation of faith and reason of the Reformers. The remote roots of the distinction are nominalism and the conviction of nominalism that the only way to know the real is through sense data. The mind merely gives us ideas, and ideas are less real than the material objects that impinge on our senses. Enlightenment thinkers furthered the isolation of faith from reason. In his *Theological Political Treatise*, Spinoza sought to privatize faith and show how the Scriptures were to be empirically studied, as nature is: "I may sum up the matter by saying that the method of interpreting Scripture does not widely differ from the method of interpreting nature—in fact, it is almost the same" (p. 99). Such an interpretative study of the Scripture restricts itself to the texts alone. No appeal can be made to faith, for that is private and personal, sharply separated from reason. Spinoza makes clear that biblical interpretation does not concern itself with the truth of the texts, but only with perceptible meanings. Thus the birth of the historical-critical methods is to treat the Bible as any other text. As Newton's mechanics sought only three-dimensional perceptible motions, so Spinoza's canons of interpretation recognize only those perceptible textual meanings found in the Scriptures as a perceptible book. Again, Spinoza: "We are to work not on the truth of passages, but solely on their meaning. We must take especial care, when we are in search of the meaning of a text, not to be led away by our reason insofar as it is founded on principles of natural knowledge (to say nothing of prejudices): in order not to confound the meaning of a passage with its truth, we must examine it solely by means of the signification of the words, or by a reason acknowledging no foundation but the Scriptures themselves" (p. 100). The deconstructionist insistence upon severe restriction to intertextuality, "all we have is texts," is here anticipated by Spinoza. Little wonder, then, that in Spinoza's view that the assent of faith is only obedience, an act of will, not an intellectual act. Theology is founded on obedience to revelation and has no power ever to oppose reason. While philosophy and reason are concerned only with knowledge and truth, theology is totally separate, concerned only with obedience and piety. The teachings of the Scriptures, as Spinoza cynically remarks, need not be true, they need only promote pious and obedient acts. But the dichotomy between teaching and action, between doctrinal content and text, between witnessing to the truth and confessing in word and deed, is impossible to maintain once one has taken seriously the constitutive meaning and truth of confessing the faith. Contemporary exegetes fail insofar as they adopt the separation of reason and faith: To introduce a distinction between the historical Jesus and the Christ of faith makes it impossible to establish the unity of faith that the virtue's formal object gives it. Historical-critical method reduces to sense alone, and fails to take into account that the truths of faith put the believer in touch with the sacred realities, with the *res*. This "method" destroys the theological life and makes preaching an act of political or ideological rhetoric. I am indebted to Professor Matthew Lamb of Boston College for helping with this note.

sent me" (John 6:44). Nothing other than what God provides adequately prepares the human person for what faith reveals, and so, strictly speaking, there is no human solution for unbelief. To say, however, that only divine grace can account for the act of faith does not mean that theological faith intrudes into the life of the believer. The *Catechism of the Catholic Church* clearly makes this point: "Believing is possible only by grace and the interior helps of the Holy Spirit. But it is no less true that believing is an authentically human act."[85] If a human action, then faith is also a free action. Aquinas explains the freedom of belief by appeal to the judgment of assent: "Believing itself is an act of understanding assenting to divine truth by command of the will, moved by God in grace, and so it lies under a free decision as ordered to God."[86] And because no one is coerced to believe, the grace of faith, like every other good work, is meritorious. In God's gracious plan, the Christian believer makes bold to claim the riches of God's glorious inheritance.

85. The *Catechism of the Catholic Church*, no. 154
86. See *Summa theologiae* IIa-IIae, q. 2, a. 9.

ℬ Chapter 3

The Eyes of Your Heart Enlightened

When St. Paul challenged the false contention of the Galatian Judaizers that Christian believers needed to observe the ritual prescriptions of the Mosaic law, he also expounded the true nature of Christian life. "For in Christ Jesus," Paul insisted, "neither circumcision nor uncircumcision is of any avail, but faith working through love" (Gal. 5:6). The rituals of the old dispensation established the grounds for an outward relationship between the human person and God, whereas the Gospel and its new law of grace communicate an entirely unexpected kind of interiority, one that initiates a personal communion with God. St. Augustine sought to explain the true nature of this interiority, and to fathom the Christian conviction that just "as the law of works was written on tables of stone, so the law of faith is written in the hearts of the faithful."[1]

Because it communicates divine Truth to us in a dynamic way, theological faith effects an authentic interior transformation of the human person in Christ: "Through him justification from all sins which the Law of Moses was unable to justify is offered to every believer" (Acts 13:38, 39). This is the case because theological faith involves believing

---

1. St. Augustine, *De spiritu et littera*, no. 24 (PL 44, 225). In his important work *The Sources of Christian Ethics* (Washington, DC: The Catholic University of America Press, 1995), esp. pp. 141–63, the Dominican theologian Servais Pinckaers provides a lengthy analysis of the Augustinian teaching about Christian interiority and its importance for moral instruction.

in a Person as well as believing that something is true.[2] We believe that, in the Church, the forgiveness of sins is available and we discover, in faith, a mercifully loving Father, who welcomes back the sinner into the communion of divine friendship. The Council of Trent put it succinctly: "Justification is not only the remission of sins, but also the sanctification and renewal of the interior man."[3] Christian interiority describes the highest form of personal communion that the human creature can experience in this life. For in the offer of divine grace, God draws without partiality every human being into a personal relationship with himself and remedies the moral deformity in the human person that results from sinful behavior. Interiority, then, is a predominant trait of the theological life. And so St. Paul describes those who believe the message of the Gospel as "justified by faith in Christ" (Gal. 2:16), enjoying a rectitude that leads straight to God.

On the plain evidence of the New Testament, theologians customarily distinguish between the Incarnation as the visible sending of the eternal Son and the coming of the Holy Spirit as an invisible sending or mission of the third divine Person of the Trinity. The biblical images of a hovering dove and of fire and wind symbolically represent God's invisible action in the world; the Incarnation—the humanity of Jesus Christ personally united to the second divine Person—is God's visible involvement in human history. As the Irish theologian Colman O'Neill explains, "The humanity of Christ in all its reality, physical as well as spiritual, has become the instrument through which the grace-giving Spirit is sent into the world."[4] Although the Christian believer enjoys a personal communion equally with each one of the three divine Persons,

2. For a development of this theme, see P. T. Geach, *The Virtues* (Cambridge: Cambridge University Press, 1977), pp. 36f.

3. Council of Trent, Decree on Justification (13 January 1547) (*DS* 1528), also cited in *Catechism of the Catholic Church*, no. 1989. The full sentence reads: "This disposition and preparation [described in the previous section] precede the actual justification, which consists not only in the forgiveness of sins but also in the sanctification and renewal of the inward man by a willing acceptance of the grace and gifts whereby a man from being unjust becomes just, from being an enemy becomes a friend, so that he is an heir in *hope of eternal life* (Titus 3:7)." I have slightly modified the translation found in *Decrees of the Ecumenical Councils*, ed. Norman P. Tanner, S.J., vol. 2, *Trent to Vatican II* (Washington, DC: Georgetown University Press, 1990), p. 673.

4. Colman E. O'Neill, O.P., *Meeting Christ in the Sacraments*, revised edition by Romanus Cessario, O.P. (New York: Alba House, 1991), p. 24.

the theological tradition attributes the work of our justification to the Holy Spirit. This practice emphasizes the inwardness of Christian justification, that "the law of faith is written in the hearts of the faithful," and reminds us that Christ's mission reaches its consummation only when "God has sent the Spirit of his Son into our hearts crying, 'Abba! Father!'" (Gal. 4:6). Faith inaugurates our union with Christ, but the Church teaches us to recognize in this union the Trinitarian contours of God's love.

The historical outpouring of the grace that justifies us comes through Christ and, according to the divine plan that Christ himself reveals, within the Church of faith and sacraments.[5] As a permanent witness of Gospel teaching in the world, the Christian Church encourages the believer to pursue the two great commandments of love of God and love of neighbor: "Pursue peace with everyone, and the holiness without which no one will see the Lord" (Heb. 12:14). To the Church alone belongs the charge of authentically communicating God's saving doctrine. And only the New Being of grace that each member of the Church receives from and in Christ enables a person to accept this doctrine as coming from God himself. It is a radically interior act that leads the man or woman of faith to engage in a life of public witness centered around the confession of the Christian creed. Indeed, because of the public character of Christian faith and witness, Christian belief can never remain a matter of purely private concern.

From a theological perspective, the proximate origin of this communion and unity in faith lies in what the Thomistic tradition calls the capital grace of Christ. As Head of the Body, Christ constitutes the Church as an assembly of the elect and bestows on it an apostolic mission. Moreover, as the concrescence of hierarchical communion in the world, the Church marks out the place where God's word is authentically spoken and understood. The dogmatic constitutions of both the

---

5. This claim of course raises the question of the salvation of those who are not members of Christ's Body. In his encyclical on missionary activity, *Redemptoris Missio*, Pope John Paul II explains *extra ecclesiam, nulla salus* (outside of the Church, there is no salvation) in this way: "For such people [who do not have an opportunity to come to know or accept the Gospel revelation or to enter the Church], salvation in Christ is accessible by virtue of a grace which, while having a mysterious relationship to the church, does not make them formally part of the church, but enlightens them in a way which is accommodated to their spiritual and material condition" (no. 10).

First and the Second Vatican Councils taken together offer a symmetric illustration of how the Church and its structures serve the life of Christian faith. The Second Vatican Council explicitly joins the kingdom of God, an image for the Church, with God's plan to reveal a definite doctrine, a saving teaching about the divine mysteries: "Christ, to carry out the will of the Father, has inaugurated the kingdom of heaven on earth and has revealed the mystery to us, and through his obedience has brought about the redemption."[6] The First Vatican Council definitively taught that the members of this same Church, who constitute historically the full dimensions of Christ's Body, are assembled "by unity with the Roman pontiff in communion and in profession of the same faith."[7] The Catholic Church is the icon of that new and heavenly Jerusalem where the saints gaze upon the glory of the Lord. In her life and teaching the Church continues to realize the mission that God entrusted once and for all to Jesus of Nazareth.

Through the Incarnation of the eternal Son, transcendent divine Truth adapts itself to our human way of knowing. "Indeed, God's words, expressed through human language, have taken on the likeness of human speech, just as the Word of the eternal Father, when he assumed the flesh of human weakness, took on the likeness of human beings."[8] The human nature of Christ, so the Fathers tell us, serves as an instrument of his divinity. The Church proposes for belief propositions, or truth-bearing statements, of faith that are likewise conceived of as instruments, since through them the members of the Church give their assent to divine Truth. Without these specific propositions of faith expressed through meaningful human language, we would have no way to ensure that our believing in fact unites us to the True God, the God who is our happiness and salvation. The view that individuals or com-

6. The Second Vatican Council's Dogmatic Constitution on the Church, *Lumen gentium*, chap. 1, no. 3.

7. See its 1870 Dogmatic Constitution, *Pastor aeternus*, chap. 3 (*DS* 3060). *Lumen gentium*, chap. 1, no. 8, again states that the unique Church of Christ, "set up and organized in this world as a society, subsists [*subsistit*] in the Catholic Church, governed by the successor of Peter and the bishops in communion with him."

8. The Dogmatic Constitution on Divine Revelation, *Dei Filius*, chap. 3, no. 13. Aquinas summarizes the relationship of divine faith to the missions of the blessed Trinity when he writes: "So before all else, the new law is the very grace of the Holy Spirit, given to those who believe in Christ" (*Summa theologiae* Ia-IIae q. 106, a. 1).

munities enjoy the prerogative to alter or to choose among the propositions of faith leads to a Docetist outlook on faith. The Docetist argues that since Christ could have accomplished his saving work by simply *appearing* to be like us in all things but sin, whether or not Christ possesses a real and concrete human nature is a matter of little consequence. As a sin against faith, heresy manifests a similar nonchalance concerning the form that the articles of faith take on. By claiming the authority to choose some faith-propositions and reject others, the heretic in effect denies any real dependence on the instrumentality of the human statements that express divine revelation, just as the Docetist denies that believers have any real dependence upon the human nature of Christ. But the Christian religion brooks no such indifference either about Christ's real human nature or about the human language that expresses his teaching. For the Christian believer accepts the teaching of Christ as the definitive historical revelation of the God whom all men and women without exception need to approach in faith.

In the preaching of the Christian Gospel, God initiates the call to belief. But to call is not to coerce. The theological life does not neutralize personal freedom, rendering the human person wholly passive in the face of divine initiatives. On the contrary, by making a personal commitment to divine Truth-Speaking, the Christian believer initiates and energizes the most active of all human activities, namely, believing, hoping in, and loving God. Still, the innate capacities of the human creature without grace would fall entirely short of being able to achieve any operations that lead straight to God himself. Faith makes it possible for us to embrace freely the important truths of our salvation.

St. Augustine gives a candid appraisal of the hereditary condition that marks each member of the human race born into the world and shows how humankind's utter dependence on the divine goodness fits accurately into the context of God's historical plan for our salvation:

But since the mind itself, though naturally capable of reason and intelligence, is disabled by befuddling and inveterate vices, not merely from delighting in and clinging to them, but even from preferring them to the unchangeable light, until it has been gradually restored and healed and so made capable of such felicity, the mind had, in the first place, to be impregnated with faith, and so purified. And that in this faith it might advance the more confidently toward the truth, the truth itself, God, God's Son, assuming humanity without destroying his divinity, established and founded this faith, that there might be a way for human-kind to its God through a God-man.[9]

As the sole mediator between God and humankind, Christ alone es-tablishes the conditions that allow the theological life to flourish in the world. Through the practice of theological faith, the Incarnate Son shows us the way to happiness.

The patristic tradition associates the sixth beatitude, "Blessed are the pure in heart, for they will see God" (Matt. 5:8), with theological faith.[10] For theological faith both purges our emotions of inordinate affections and dismisses from our minds fanciful and erroneous rep-resentations of what is to be believed. But this takes place only because God, the First Truth, shapes our intelligence through the *habitus* of theological faith and, through minds renewed by a living faith, effects a radical change in the whole person. The Church celebrates this purity of heart in her saints, but especially in the Blessed Virgin Mary who, as St. Irenaeus writes, "became by her obedience the cause of salvation for herself and for the whole human race." In an effort to suggest the depth of involvement that our blessed Lady enjoys in the plan of sal-vation, and therefore in the Church's pilgrim journey of faith, Irenaeus goes on to develop a theological comparison between Eve, the first woman, and Mary, the first person to conceive the Word of God in her heart. "The knot of Eve's disobedience was untied through the obe-dience of the virgin Mary; what the virgin Eve had bound up through her lack of faith, the virgin Mary untied by her faith."[11]

9. *De civitate Dei*, Bk. 11, chap. 2 (PL 41, 318; NPNF 2, 206): "Sed quia ipsa mens, cui ratio et intellegentia naturaliter inest, uitiis quibusdam tenebrosis et ueteribus inualida est, non solum ad inhaerendum tenebrosis et ueteribus inualida est, non solum ad in-haerendum fruendo, uerum etiam ad perferendum incommutabile lumen, donec de die in diem renouata atque sanata fiat tantae felicitatis capax, fide primum fuerat inbuenda atque purganda. In qua ut fidentius ambularet ad ueritatem, ipsa ueritas, Deus Dei filius, homine adsumpto, non Deo consumpto, eandem constituit et fundauit fidem, ut ad hominis Deum iter esset homini per hominem Deum" (CCSL 48, p. 322).

10. See St. Augustine, *De sermone Domini in monte*, Bk. 1, chap. 4 (PL 34, 1235): "To the pure of heart—as to those who keep the eye cleansed for discerning eternal realities—the power to see God is rewarded."

11. St. Irenaeus, *Adversus Haeresis*, Bk. 3, chap. 22, 4 (PG 7: 959), as cited in *Catechism of the Catholic Church*, no. 494. When speaking of Eve, Irenaeus employs the term "faith" to describe an attitude of confident trust in God that should have characterized and grounded the first woman's obedience to God. While the Church holds that Adam was constituted in sanctity and justice, it is silent about the means God used to communicate

The object of theological faith is God as First Truth. As an operative *habitus*, the virtue of faith enables the human person to reach out and lay hold of First Truth. Through the gift of the Holy Spirit, God allows the Church to participate in his own infallibility. It belongs to the Church, therefore, both to ensure that the articles of faith remain in their entirety for all generations and to propose for our belief whatever is required for Christians to discover full truth and authentic freedom. We now turn to examine the act of faith which is belief, or to borrow St. Paul's expression, to see how it is that faith works through love (see Gal. 5:6).

The Inward Act of Faith: Belief

Two Classical Definitions of Belief

Theologians usually distinguish between the principal inward act of faith, which they call belief, and the outward profession of faith, for which they reserve the technical term *confession*. Among the significant legacies that the Augustinian theological heritage has bequeathed to Western theology, two classical definitions of belief clearly hold a prominent place. The first is found in St. Augustine's *De Trinitate*: to believe means to think or to ponder with assent—"*cogitare cum assensione*.[12] When in the thirteenth century Aquinas comes to consider this definition (which by that time had become normative in theological circles), he lifts the Augustinian formulation from its original setting within an illuminationist theory of knowledge in order to interpret it within his own intentional model of realist knowing.[13] As we have seen, Aquinas uses the categories of a realist epistemology to analyze belief. So the

this original justice. Therefore, theological faith is usually associated with the Christian dispensation, including its anticipatory stages during the old Covenant.

12. See *De Trinitate* Bk. 15, chap. 16. For the history of this formula in the schools, see M.-D. Chenu, "Psychologie de la foi dans la théologie du 13ème siècle," *Etudes d'histoire littéraire et doctrinale du 13ème siècle* (Paris: J. Vrin, 1932), pp. 187–88.

13. While the elements for this interpretation are to be found in the Aristotelian texts themselves, notably Aristotle's treatise *On the Soul*, the arrangement of materials likewise reflects Aquinas's familiarity with the commentatorial tradition as well as his own *expositio* on the text, the *Sententia super De anima* (English translation: *Aristotle's De Anima with the Commentary of St. Thomas Aquinas*, trans. K. Foster and S. Humphries [New Haven, CT: Yale University Press, 1951]).

Thomistic analysis of faith manifests an orientation markedly different from those theories that retain elements of the Augustinian epistemology of divine illumination.[14] The intentional approach that developed within the Thomist tradition interprets belief more explicitly as an active and public engagement with the mysteries of the Christian religion. Aquinas turns the articles of the Creed into real objects of cognition; for him, they are not outer symbolic expressions of divine truth communicated to the person by means of an inner illumination.

Since the Catholic tradition continues to speak about faith in terms of human cognition, as a "cogitare," we would do well to review certain relevant points in epistemology. What *kind* of knowing is faith? The background to this question involves the epistemological principle that specific kinds of objects really distinguish the actions that engage them. By matching the appropriate cognitive act with a given knowable object, philosophers can distinguish one activity of the human mind from another. Thus, for example, one can distinguish between conjecturing about something contingent, such as the future of the stock market, and forms of scientific knowing about such things as the principles of astrophysics.[15] The development of this method of distinguishing owes much to Aristotle's remark that "mind must be related to what is thinkable, as sense is to what is sensible."[16]

On Aristotle's account, knowable objects, "what is thinkable," include two major categories: necessary realities and contingent realities. Because the human mind possesses both intuitive and demonstrative capacities, philosophers customarily distinguish two classes of mental

14. Apropos of realist epistemology, Father Lonergan has remarked that "the *quod quid est* is at the very center of Aristotelian and Thomist thought. . . . The *quod quid est* is the key idea not only in all logic and methodology, but also in all metaphysics." See Bernard J. Lonergan, S.J., *Verbum. Word and Idea in Aquinas* (Notre Dame, IN: University of Notre Dame Press, 1970). For a comparison of Aquinas and St. Augustine on the act of faith, see Peter Riga, "The Act of Faith in Augustine and Aquinas," *The Thomist* 35 (1971): 143–74. For an earlier study, see Tad W. Guzie, S.J., "The Act of Faith according to St. Thomas: A Study in Theological Methodology," *The Thomist* 29 (1965): 239–80.

15. One school of Thomist realism holds that human reason can achieve true philosophical demonstration in natural science, even if such demonstrated conclusions remain limited in any field of inquiry. For a fuller treatment of the Thomist-Aristotelian conception of knowledge and more on demonstration in natural philosophy, see William A. Wallace, *From a Realist Point of View: Essays on the Philosophy of Science* (Lanham, MD: University Press of America, 1979), pp. 39–63.

16. Aristotle, *On the Soul*, Bk. 3, chap. 4 (429a17–18).

acts that deal with necessary realities. The first category includes those intuitions into reality that Aristotle calls *nous*, such as the immediate understanding of first principles. The second category embraces all forms of intelligent reasoning that Aristotle calls *epistēmē*, such as the reasoned demonstration of any true proposition. Though each kind of knowing achieves its objective in quite different ways, both intuitive understanding and reasoned demonstration aim at sure and reliable knowledge of extramental reality.

Contingent realities, on the other hand, are able to generate knowledge in us only in a limited way, through refined opinion, or what Aristotle calls *doxa*.[17] When this opinion becomes intensified by one factor or another, such as the high credibility that attaches to the person who expresses a certain conviction, then opinion becomes what Aristotle calls *pistis*, or (human) faith. We should also distinguish *pistis* from the counsel that a moral agent normally seeks from a well-informed person, whose advice shapes the formation of a moral judgment in the practical intellect. Rather, *pistis* contains a developed assertion about some truth to be accepted, one whose soundness extends beyond the here-and-now of contingent ethical judgments.[18] Because *pistis* can stand on its own, so to speak, theologians recognize in the structure of philosophical belief something useful for the Christian understanding of faith. The fact that many philosophers dispute Aristotle's assertion about necessary realities need not cause concern for the theologian who recognizes the dispensability of historically conditioned examples.[19]

The epistemological dynamics of purely human belief shed some light on the psychology of theological faith as a mode of adherence to trustworthy testimony. Yet Christian belief is never just a specific instance of Aristotelian *pistis*, but is rather a uniquely Christian activity that unites the person with God. Inasmuch as faith really attains uncreated First Truth, the act of faith which is belief does not depend on

17. See Aristotle's discussion of opinion in *On the Soul* Bk. 2, chap. 3 (428a20–428b8).

18. See Aristotle's *Nicomachean Ethics* Bk. 6, chap. 9 (1142b13–16).

19. The very category of necessary beings itself implies a sort of perfection quite foreign to the contemporary empirical mentality. Moreover, because of the direct empirical contact with the heavenly bodies unavailable to the natural scientists of the pre-modern period, philosophers and scientists today easily repudiate the classical view that the heavenly bodies in fact represent a class of necessary beings.

a contingent reality. On the contrary, Christian belief is specified by the most necessary truth; as Aquinas explains it, "Not only is truth in God but he is the supreme and First Truth."[20] Since God, through the Holy Spirit, bestowed upon his Church a participation in his own infallibility,[21] everything that the Church proposes for belief shares in the necessary truthfulness that belongs to God alone. We are reminded in the Gospel of John that those who believe in the word that Jesus speaks receive an initiation into the mysteries of the Trinitarian life.[22] In this sense, believing requires the Christian to think about a wide range of salvific truths. Because faith unites us to the One who is supreme and First Truth itself, the believer gains an unimpeachable certitude about God and the things related to God. First Truth rescues Christian belief from being a deficient form of human knowing (the lot of belief in the Aristotelian schema), and makes of the very human disposition to give credence to another person a means of attaining the highest and most necessary Truth that is God himself.[23]

Christian belief supplies surety about divine Truth, but not by making an immediate vision of divine Truth accessible to the human intellect. That grace belongs only to the blessed in heaven, who already possess the vision of God's glory. As a thinking that requires assent to the word of another person, belief observes the affective structures that govern all interpersonal relationships. And although firm adherence or assent to First Truth-Speaking surmounts the liabilities inherent in trusting the word of another person, it does so without removing the obscurity that even a confident trust in God involves. "The intellect of

20. "Unde sequitur quod no solum in ipso [Deo] sit veritas, sed quod ipse sit summa et prima veritas." For this and further discussion of what divine Truth means, see *Summa theologiae* Ia q. 16, a. 5. In the same article, Aquinas's realist view of knowing truth parallels how God "has" truth, namely, as one for whom truth remains identical with his very being: "One finds truth in the mind when it apprehends the thing as it is, and truth in the thing when it possesses being conformable to mind. This is verified most of all in God."

21. The Dogmatic Constitution on Revelation *Dei verbum*, no. 7, as cited in *Instruction on the Ecclesial Vocation of the Theologian*, no. 13.

22. For example, see John 14:20–31, and for more on the role that intelligence plays in the life of Christian faith, see Ceslaus Spicq, O.P., *Connaissance et morale dans la Bible* (Paris: Editions du Cerf, 1985), pp. 25–27.

23. See Aquinas's discussion on whether truth is eternal in *Summa theologiae* Ia q. 16, a. 7: "quia veritas intellectus divini est ipse Deus . . ."

the believer," explains Aquinas, "is called 'captive' in that it is bound by principles foreign to it rather than its own."[24] In other words, since assent rests on principles unlike those that govern the natural operations of the intellect in science or art, assent itself contributes to faith's obscurity. Within this darkness of faith, however, the assent of faith generates a distinctive consolation insofar as the believer treasures the personal word of another.

Theological faith requires that we completely rely on First Truth-Speaking, with the result that authentic belief leads us to a contemplative beholding of divine Truth. In fact, the affective element in assent directs the believer more to a true pondering of the Christian mysteries than to a thinking about particular propositions. Furthermore, as a thoroughly ecclesial reality, belief flourishes within the context of friendship. Jesus tells his disciples, "I have called you friends, for all that I have heard from my Father I have made known to you" (John 15:15). The friendship based on shared belief establishes the foundation for the Christian communion that we call the Church, the People of God guided on pilgrimage by their adherence to God's Word. "Whoever says 'I believe,'" explains the *Catechism*, "says 'I pledge myself to what *we* believe.'"[25] The loving pondering of the mysteries of the Christian religion belongs to the very structure of theological faith; this explains why faith leads the believer toward a religious self-commitment to God.

In order to emphasize that the believer receives God's own self-communication, some theologians avoid using terms associated with ordinary human knowing (terms such as apprehension, pondering, arguments, understanding, certitude, judgment, or wisdom) to describe belief. By drawing upon the glossary of biblical expressions that describe personal relationships rather than from philosophical categories that explain knowledge, these authors aim, one assumes, to underscore the affective element of faith. Instead of describing faith as an apprehension and a cognition of divine Truth, faith is presented in terms used to describe interpersonal encounter or dialogue. Within this perspective, the stress upon the unseen character of Christian faith tends to displace the role of cognition in Christian belief. The challenge

24. See his *De veritate* q. 14, a. 1.
25. *The Catechism of the Catholic Church*, no. 185.

for the Christian theologian remains to acknowledge that faith qualifies as a proper kind of knowing, and at the same time to give full weight to the affective element ingredient in Christian belief.[26]

A formula of Augustinian provenance provides a helpful way to present a balanced account of the inward act of faith. The formula developed as a gloss on a parochial sermon of St. Augustine in which he states, "But it makes a great deal of difference whether someone believes that Jesus is the Christ, or whether he believes in Christ."[27] Aquinas takes up the formula in a modified version: "Whether the act of faith is appropriately distinguished into 'believing about God' (credere Deum), 'believing God' (credere Deo), and 'believing for the sake of God' (credere in Deum)."[28] This adapted formulary permits him to illustrate the objective or intentional objects of faith and the subjective or affective elements that nourish the act of faith. When the formulary speaks about credere Deum, "believing about God," it broadly points to faith's material object, though more specifically as designated by its terminative formal object, God as First Truth-in-Being. Second, when the formulary describes faith as credere Deo, "believing God," it signifies the formal mediating object of faith, God as First Truth-Speaking. Finally, the formulary distinguishes faith as credere in Deum, which we can translate "believing for the sake of God," or "unto God." Since belief presents First Truth as something that the whole person seeks after so as fully to possess it, this third formulation points to the directional or dynamic aspect of faith, its eschatological movement.

The Augustinian formulary as a whole, especially the clauses "believing God" (credere Deo) and "believing for the sake of God" (credere in Deum), clearly points out the role that human affect or will plays in

26. For a detailed textual analysis of Aquinas's entire teaching on this important matter, see Benoit Duroux, O.P., La psychologie de la Foi chez S. Thomas d'Aquin (Tournai: Descleé, 1963).

27. St. Augustine, Sermones ad populos 144, no. 2 (PL 38, 788), trans. Edmund Hill, O.P., in Sermons (Brooklyn: New City Press, 1990).

28. See Summa theologiae IIa-IIae q. 2, a. 2. The phrase as Aquinas uses it comes from a medieval amalgam of materials from various patristic authors, the Sermo de Symbolo I. Because so much depends on the grammatical nuances of the Latin tongue, translators dispute the exact rendering of the formulary into English. In any event, the original formula, "credere Christum, credere Christo, credere in Christum," surely better reflects St. Augustine's theological cast of mind; see for example, In Johannis Evangelium 29, 7, 17 (PL 35, 1631).

commanding the intellect's assent to divine Truth. When a person is drawn toward God's promises as announced, for example, through the preaching of the Gospel or through other proclamations of doctrine in the Church, such a movement toward divine Truth clearly signifies that grace is moving the human will. But since the full dimensions of divine Truth always remain hidden from the eyes of faith, faith's affective movement generates a sense of anticipation in the believer, for, as Aquinas remarks, "we hope to be made blessed, that we might see with plain vision the truth to which we adhere by faith."[29] Recall that, in St. Augustine's text, the *"credere"* formulary actually speaks about believing Christ, and this reminds us that only strong adherence to Christ can overcome the inherent darkness of belief. It is Christ who is the "true light" (John 1:9) that enlightens every person who comes into the world. And this evangelical doctrine gives the believer reason for great confidence, as St. Paul makes clear at the beginning of the Letter to the Romans: "For I am not ashamed of the Good News: it is the power of God saving all who have faith" (Rom. 1:16).

Faith's Restlessness

The present shape of the treatise on theological faith owes much to the interplay between the affective categories for belief that derived from Augustinian "language of the heart" and the conceptual categories that derived from thirteenth-century realist epistemology. Both the Augustinian and the realist categories, however, raise pertinent questions about the obedience of faith. Faith prompts a personal commitment in the believer to truths that are neither seen nor demonstrated. To believe God involves a loving pondering of God's Truth as it is embodied in the mysteries of the Christian religion. Because of this pondering, Christian belief by its nature engenders a restless movement within the human spirit, for the act of faith initiates a process of development that always reaches out toward a more complete embrace of divine Truth. This tension at the very heart of our faith-knowing serves a highly constructive purpose. As a matter of practical experience, the saints accept this restlessness as proof that Christian belief reaches its perfection only in the vision of divine Truth that awaits us in heaven. When the First

29. See *Summa theologiae* q. 4, a. 1.

Letter of John reminds its readers that even now they have a claim on eternal life, it points out the eschatological dimension of faith: "I write this to you who believe in the name of the Son of God, that you may know that you have eternal life" (1 John 5:13).

As long as the Christian remains united with God through belief, he or she is bent toward seeing God "face to face" (1 Cor. 13:12) in beatific communion. Belief never stops at a simple acceptance of divine Truth, so that the believer can carry on the ordinary routines of life—as if subscribing to a body of doctrines serves only to distinguish the adherents of one religious group from those of another. Moreover, inasmuch as an entirely tranquil and tensionless attainment of God occurs only within the state of bliss, Christian belief pushes the members of the pilgrim Church beyond the familiar and the expected into what the mystical authors rightly compare to a dark night. In fact, even in the peak moments of mystical experiences, faith's fundamental inquietude perdures, with the result that the same spiritual writers often testify to the expected but still terrifying darkness that envelops even the most deeply felt experiences of divine Truth. A page from the writings of the nineteenth-century Carmelite Thérèse of Lisieux speaks to this point with unusual simplicity. In a letter to her religious superior, the austere and aristocratic Mother Marie de Gonzague, the Little Flower tells us about her own personal experience of faith's darkness:

At this time I was enjoying such a living faith, such a clear *faith*, that the thought of heaven made up all my happiness, and I was unable to believe there were really impious people who had no faith. I believed they were actually speaking against their own inner convictions when they denied the existence of heaven, that beautiful heaven where God himself wanted to be their Eternal Reward. During those very joyful days of the Easter season, Jesus made me feel that there were really souls who have no faith, and who, through the abuse of grace, lost the precious treasure, the source of the only real and pure joys. He permitted my soul to be invaded by the thickest darkness, and that the thought of heaven, up until then so sweet to me, be no longer anything but the cause of struggle and torment. This trial was to last not a few days or a few weeks, it was not to be extinguished until the hour set by God himself and this hour has not yet come.[30]

30. *Story of a Soul. The Autobiography of St. Therese of Lisieux.* A New Translation from the Original Manuscript by John Clarke, O.C.D. (Washington, D.C.: ICS Publications, 1975), Manuscript C, pp. 211–12.

Although not every soul undergoes the same ordeal that Thérèse describes here, the tension that affective knowledge generates as it matures in the darkness of faith underlies the faith experiences of every believer.

The element of inquietude in the Christian act of belief can be explained from three different vantage points. The first approach considers the difference that exists between a concept and the reality that it represents. For there is a difference between what a person cognitively apprehends in the act of knowing and what he or she really possesses in the act of love. Like its Trinitarian exemplar, human knowledge is ordered to break forth in love. This breaking forth initiates in the knower a special kind of movement, one that follows upon a particular act of judgment. The act of judgment—the speaking of the existential "is"—by which a knower affirms the relationship between the intelligible concept and the actual reality that it represents, psychologically bridges the hiatus between the image and the reality. Even though a believer can never express any of the mysteries of faith in an adequate or fully representational manner, the assent exercised in the *judgment* of faith lays hold of divine Truth. In other words, when Christian believers assent to the truth that Jesus is their Savior, they are united at that moment to the very mystery of Christ's salvific life and glorious resurrection, not simply to a notional account of them. For in addition to affirming the existential character of the predicate *(copula)*, the judgment of faith affirms the *verum*, or the true.

Theological faith employs concepts, but only so that the believer can instrumentally reach out through the concepts to First Truth-in-Being. But in order for this dynamic movement to occur, the concepts that the faith employs must represent accurately the object known. Take an example: the proposition that God is the highest good excludes any assertion that God actively causes evil in the world. Again, to believe that our blessed Lady is the Mother of the Church excludes the assertion that Mary remains on a par with the saints. Concepts are important for expressing what we believe. But because divine Truth is infinitely more profound than its conceptual expressions, belief incessantly tugs the believer toward a deeper penetration of the divine mysteries. Only the act of love ultimately bridges the gap between concept and reality. The celebrated monastic author Dom Marmion records the example of a holy Benedictine nun who testifies to the power that contemplating the mysteries of salvation can exercise in those who piously cultivate the practice. "At Christmastide," the nun recorded, "during all those solemnities of our Savior's birth, I received great favors; his Majesty often gave me a vivid light so that I knew these divine mysteries as if they were then really taking place."[31] To sum up, God draws the believer into a participation of the living, divine mysteries that transcends the level of both their propositional and their conceptual representation. The communal celebration of liturgical prayer offers an appropriate setting for believers to pass beyond the concepts of faith to an experience of divine Truth.

A second reason for faith's inquietude lies in the fact that the Christian mysteries supply no adequate evidence to win the assent of belief. Christian belief at every stage requires an act of will. Aquinas distinguishes the two different ways that will is involved in the assent of theological faith by noting that, though an act of the will is prerequisite for faith, it need not be an act of the will informed by charity. At the same time, Aquinas affirms that every act of charity "presupposes faith, since the will cannot tend to God with complete love unless the understanding has right faith about him."[32] Following the Second Council of Orange, we call the initial act of the will the pious affect of credibility *(pius credulitatis affectus)*.[33] Through this initial assent of faith, the one who effectively hears God's word recognizes, in the promises that the Gospel makes, a humanly attractive offer—for example, the security that an expression of paternal love offers, or the relief from guilt that the remission of one's sins achieves. With the infusion of theological charity, this initial movement of preliminary assent flourishes in fully formed belief. Then, as St. Paul insists is the norm, we have "faith working through love."

31. See his *Christ the Ideal of the Monk* (St. Louis: Herder, 1926), p. 318.

32. See *Summa theologiae* IIa-IIae q. 4, a. 7, ad 5. O'Brien, *Faith*, p. 142, note h, provides a helpful commentary: "In the final act of an adult's complete conversion from nonbelief and sin to belief and grace, the infusion of grace, including charity, and the active turning to God in belief and love are simultaneous; yet there is a pattern of priority in meaning among the various elements—thus knowing before loving."

33. The fifth canon of the Second Council of Orange, held in 529, anathematized the view that there exists even in the very initial moment of faith a natural inclination in the will, so that grace at this point would seem a needless intervention of the Holy Spirit: "ita enim initium fidei ipsumque credulitatis affectum, quo in eum credimus . . . per gratiae donum, id est per inspirationem Spiritus Sancti" *(DS* 375).

The role of human affectivity in the virtue of faith can be compared with the way a behavioral virtue steadies and perfects the work of prudence. Just as the intellectual virtue of prudence requires the exercise of a moral virtue in order to determine its mean, so does belief require some kind of affective movement in order to achieve its status. In other words, in the unfolding of theological faith there exists a synergy of intellect and affectivity that resembles the unity of the intellectual and moral virtues in the development of the Christian life. In any case, the intellect grasps the truths of faith, not on the basis of its ability to discover their inner intelligibility, but on the basis of the will's commitment to God as First Truth-Speaking that we call the assent of faith.

This synergy between intelligence and affectivity, however, is not without inquietude and restlessness. For a difference exists between the way that the intellect relates to what it knows and the way that the will relates to what it loves. In one of his philosophical works, Aquinas explains this difference in the following manner: "A difference exists between the knowing capacity and the appetitive capacity. The act of a knowing capacity aspires to know things as they come to exist in the knower; on the other hand, the appetitive capacity gives birth to an inclination for the reality in its own right."[34] Since the capacity for love itself generates an impetus for union with the beloved, there exists a certain tension between the personal union with God that only charity brings about and the mediate, conceptual attainment of divine Truth that Christian belief achieves. Even in the case of human loving, two lovers can never adequately express through words and concepts what they hope to achieve in a loving union. Consider, for example, the deep disappointment that would beset a suitor who discovers upon arriving for a long-awaited rendezvous that his cherished fiancée has decided to leave a photograph and note instead of being there in person. In the same way, at the center of Christian belief there exists a tension between the dynamics of knowing and loving that can find its resolution only in the personal union of the believer with God that charity brings. From

---

34. *In de divinis nominibus* IV, c. 10. See also, *In II Sententias* d. 39, q. 1, a. 1: "By its own proper act the will tends towards its object as it exists in its own right ... while the intellect tends towards its object insofar as it comes to exist in the soul." Again, in the *De veritate* q. 1, a. 2: "The process of the knowing power terminates within the soul itself, while that of the appetitive power terminates at the reality."

this point of view, even theological faith remains radically incomplete with respect to the final fulfillment that God ordains for all those whom he calls to holiness.

A third reason why belief introduces a tension into Christian existence involves the unrealized eschatological dimension of Christian faith. Our personal union with God reaches its full and final completion only in the light of glory that accompanies the possession of beatitude. In heaven, the divine essence itself mediates the vision of God. But faith, says Aquinas, "is the beginning of eternal life in us."[35] During the period of our journey on earth, the believer remains necessarily restricted by the concepts that the mind requires in order to think adequately about God, to ponder the mysteries. This struggle with imperfect images and concepts, even of the most theologically precise variety, generates a yearning for a more perfect mode of being in love with God. At the same time, theological faith sets us on the road to meeting God face to face.[36] "For now we see in a mirror, dimly, but then we will see face to face. Now I know only in part, then I will know fully, even as I have been fully known" (1 Cor. 13:12).

The Christian tradition of course recognizes that knowledge without the clarity of vision signals an imperfection, but it also affirms that to be cognitively imperfect belongs to the very nature of knowledge of faith.[37] At this point, we should remark how little Aristotle's analysis of *pistis* in fact controls a Christian theology of faith, in which the restlessness of faith arises out of a desire for unchangeable Truth, rather than from a forced reliance on the mercurial opinions of another human being. Thus the saints teach that theological faith always abides as a light glowing in the darkness, a true *fides quaerens intellectum*. The seventeenth-century French reformer St. John Eudes (1601–80) gave poetic expression to this "pulling forth" that accompanies Christian belief.

Faith is a divine and celestial light, a participation in the eternal, inaccessible light, a beam radiating from the face of God. Although it is true that faith is

---

35. *De veritate* q. 14, a. 2.

36. For further information on the eschatological dimension of Christian faith, see R. Bellemare, "Credere. Note sur la définition thomiste," *Revue de l'Université d'Ottawa* 30 (1960): 37*-47*.

37. See this remark in the context of *Summa theologiae* Ia-IIae q. 67, a. 3.

accompanied by obscurity and permits you to behold God, not clearly as he is seen in heaven, but as through a cloud, dimly, nevertheless faith does not debase God's supreme greatness to fit the captivity of your mind, as does science.[38]

In its act of belief, theological faith illustrates a hybrid instance of attaining sure knowledge through absolute confidence. Since the will motivates the mind to accept those truths that it can seize neither immediately nor mediately, Christian belief shares in the surety of *epistēmē* or scientific knowledge. On the other hand, since the real cause of divine Truth remains hidden from us, faith likewise shares the obscurity of *doxa* or opinion, though it suffers from none of the perplexing uncertainties that ordinarily accompany our reliance on merely human opinion.[39]

The Necessity of Christian Belief

Commenting on the definition of faith found in Hebrews 11:1, "Only faith can guarantee the blessings that we hope for, or prove the existence of the realities that at present remain unseen," St. John of the Cross writes:

Faith is the substance of things to be hoped for, and these things are not manifest to the intellect, even though its consent to them is firm and certain. If they were manifest, there would be no faith. For though faith brings certitude to the intellect, it does not produce clarity, but only darkness.[40]

It is true, the things that one believes are not manifest to the intellect; still, there remains a sense in which faith satisfies human intelligence even as the believer reaches conclusions that human intelligence naturally would never reach. Faith makes it possible for human reason to explore—according to its own inherent methods of inquiry—matters that are strictly supernatural.

---

38. St. John Eudes as quoted in Jill Haak Adels, *The Wisdom of the Saints. An Anthology* (New York: Oxford University Press, 1987), pp. 49–50.

39. See *De veritate* q. 14, a. 1, ad 8.

40. See his *Ascent to Mount Carmel* Bk. 2, chap. 6. Authors such as Aquinas and John of the Cross read this verse of Scripture in the Latin of the Vulgate version: "Est autem fides sperandarum substantia rerum, augumentum non apparentium."

Faith and Reason

The grace-inspired assent that lies at the heart of belief distinguishes the Christian understanding of knowledge in faith from other views about the nature of rationality. If we consider efforts to account for reasonableness, there are at least three major philosophical alternatives to Christian belief: secular humanism, radical empiricism, and natural religion. First, the secular humanist argues that the innate resources and capacities in human nature can provide everything that humankind requires in order to achieve its full perfection and happiness in this life. An unbridled confidence in what human reason can accomplish often leads to utopian visions of human society, such as schemes for promoting model human communities. For utopian projects to succeed, however, the human spirit would have to embody a sufficient cause for its own perfection. Inasmuch as utopian authors hold that "man himself remains man's well-being and consolation," their notion of virtue urges the individual to rely on his or her own efforts, and to love others on account of a common "humanity."[41] When they veer toward the moral and metaphysical optimism that characterizes the varieties of secular humanism, certain kinds of "Christian humanism" tend to eclipse the significance of First Truth as the uniquely specifying object of theological faith. But the upbuilding of the global village can never substitute for the Christian *beatitudo* that subsists only in the communion of Church and that God alone can bestow. Secular forms of humanism fall short of the mark precisely at the point where they deny that the human capacity for transcendence ranks among the noblest endowments of the human spirit, and that only an authentic union with the true God can fulfill this *pondus naturae*.

A second attitude that frequently shows itself inimical to Christian belief is the sweeping rationalism that develops in an age dominated by the spirit of philosophical hubris. A through-and-through rationalist frame of mind bases its final judgment about truth or falsity solely on the basis of evidence available either from the human senses—the em-

---

41. Thomas More's *Utopia*, p. 104: ". . . et id laudandum humanitatis censeat, hominem homini salus et solatio." I am following the pagination of the Froben edition produced at Basle in 1518, reproduced by André Prévost.

piricist version—or from rational argument. For both rationalist and empiricist, the obscurity that results from faith's inability to explore the first principles of divine Truth constitutes an affront to the dignity of the human spirit and to the supremacy of its investigative powers. In the modern period, the "siècle des Lumières" best illustrates this mentality. British Enlightenment authors, for instance, did more than react to exaggerated and debased versions of Christian doctrines. They challenged the Church to uphold only those tenets that rational analysis or scientific experimentation could verify. Given this pragmatic frame of mind, everything that cannot be shown to be reasonable falls under the heading of superstition. The "reasonable" religion of John Locke provides a good example of this religiously deficient *esprit*, but the more radical treatises such as John Toland's *Christianity Not Mysterious* (1696) and Matthew Tindal's *Christianity as Old as the Creation* (1730) supply the best examples of what happens when ideological presuppositions require that one trim Christian faith to fit the contours of the human mind.

The third challenge to Christian belief comes from the proponents of natural religion. This nonconfessional view asserts that religious experience represents nothing more than a heightened expression of experiences or processes that in the final analysis remain thoroughly natural. In other terms, brute human nature establishes the parameters for religious experience. In his *Supplément au voyage de Bougainville,* the French author Diderot gives a good example of the radical reductionism that the eighteenth-century Encyclopedia tradition fosters. Consider the complaint of Orou, an imaginary Tahitian, for whom Nature itself seems to cry out against all repressive morality, especially the kind that blinds one to the significance that Nature has conferred on the sensual life of men and women. When a visiting European priest politely declines to accept his host's offer to enjoy the sexual favors of his wife and daughters, Orou voices a reproach with which all natural religionists could agree:

> I don't know what this thing is you call religion, but I can only think badly of it, since it prevents you from tasting an innocent pleasure, to which Nature, the sovereign mistress, invites us all; to give existence to one like you; . . . to do your duty toward a host who has given you a good welcome, and to enrich a nation, by bestowing upon it one subject more.[42]

---

42. "Je ne sais ce que c'est que la chose que tu appelles religion; mais je ne puis qu'en

The bent of some French intellectuals to poke fun at Christian moral norms ironically coincides with a period of enthusiasm in France for imposing other rational strictures on nature, such as universalizing French etiquette in the nineteenth century, the better to regulate public human mores, or perfecting formal gardening in the eighteenth, the more effectively to control the forms and figures of plants and trees.

When we emphasize the distinction between what faith teaches and what reason discovers, we do not of course imply a radical discontinuity between the two paths to knowledge about God. True enough, Aquinas remarks that "our knowing is so feeble that no philosopher could ever completely explore the nature even of a single fly."[43] Still, natural reason can discover certain truths that illumine the reality of the divine nature under certain aspects. In a succinct summary of both the biblical witness and the Church's interpretative tradition, the Second Vatican Council affirms this teaching on faith and reason:

"God, the first principle and last end of all things, can be known with certainty from the created order by the natural light of human reason" (See Rom. 1:20). Further, this teaching is to be held about revelation: in the present condition of the human race, even those truths about God which are not beyond the reach of human reason, require revelation for them to be known by all without great effort, with firm certainty and without error entering in.[44]

In a similar way, Aquinas warns that "many things must be known before those that natural reason can discover about God, since the speculations of almost all of philosophy are directed toward a knowledge of God. Thus metaphysics, which treats of the divine, is the last of the philosophical disciplines to be learned."[45] In other words, natural knowledge

---

penser mal, puisqu'elle t'empêche de goûter un plaisir innocent, auquel nature, la souveraine maîtresse, nous invite tous; de donner l'existence à un de tes semblables; . . . de t'acquitter envers un hôte qui t'a fait un bon accueil, et d'enrichir une nation, en l'accroissant d'un sujet de plus" (Diderot, *Supplément au voyage de Bougainville*, in *Oeuvres philosophiques* [Paris: Garnier, 1964], p. 476). I am indebted to Charles Taylor, *Sources of the Self. The Making of the Modern Identity* (Cambridge, MA: Harvard University Press, 1989), pp. 328–29, for this reference.

43. *In Symbolum Apostolorum expositio*, prol.

44. *Dei verbum*, chap. 1, no. 6. This conciliar text cites Vatican I's *Dei Filius*, chap. 2 (*DS* 3004 and 3005).

45. See *Summa contra gentiles* Bk. 1, chap. 4. Also, see Aquinas's remarks in *In De trinitate* 5, 1 where he makes the well-known distinction between the subject of a science

about the divine nature should not be confused with innate sentiments or natural intuitions about divinity, for natural knowledge comes only after a rigorous exercise of human reasoning powers.

As the conciliar text suggests, few persons actually complete the course of philosophical studies required in order to acquire naturally knowable truths about God. Thus, Aquinas advances at least three reasons for the suitableness in proposing to humankind for belief even those truths about God that unaided natural reason can attain. These arguments resemble those that explain the necessity for the human race to receive a revealed holy teaching. The first argument observes that different persons possess varying degrees of native intelligence, that most people lack sufficient leisure for intellectual pursuits, that many others are compelled to set aside higher studies in order to provide the necessities of life, and that still others lack the proper moral disposition to engage in intellectual pursuits. These circumstances constitute such a severe handicap for so many people that, were it not for revelation, very few people indeed would possess any knowledge about God. Next, Aquinas reminds us that even those who possess the talents necessary to do metaphysics attain their goal only after a long period of time. Moreover, the passions and preoccupation of youth, Aquinas notes, frequently delay even beginning the process. This means that such men and women would come to God only late in life, with all the inconveniences that such tardiness would entail. Thirdly, individual efforts at philosophical inquiry and dialectic can lack precision and surety. Witness the contradictory opinions held by thinkers even about such things so apparently self-evident as human nature itself. If philosophical ingenuity alone were left to discover those truths that reasoning admittedly can attain, it is likely that disagreements among thinkers would continually frustrate human efforts to uncover truths about God.

To sum up, theological faith guarantees that truths, which are indispensable for salvation, are more quickly accessible to all men and women and with a certitude and surety otherwise unattainable. Since First Truth-Speaking guarantees them, faith provides a proper way to accept even those truths that reason can demonstrate. Of course, the

---

(e.g., *ens commune* as the subject of metaphysics) and its principle (e.g., God as the universal cause of being and object of metaphysics).

human sciences include many knowable truths not directly related to our beatitude, but the Church does not propose such truths for our belief.[46] Faith, as the Letter to the Hebrews says, concerns "the blessings that we hope for."

Because humankind is made in God's image, each human being remains *capax Dei*—that is, a person who is capable of reaching unto God. This prerogative belongs only to human and angelic persons, for, as St. Augustine reminds us, "the grace of God through Jesus Christ is not given to stones or stumps or beasts of the field."[47] Our ultimate beatitude consists in a vision of God that definitively surpasses the natural order of things.[48] Because "the last blessedness of man lies in a certain supernatural vision of God," Aquinas argues that all men and women need to learn from God as pupils from a teacher.[49] For no one can attain to this vision of God except by being a true learner, that is, one who loves having God as a teacher. The Johannine Gospel instructs us: "It is written in the prophets, 'And they shall all be taught by God.' Every one who has heard and learned from the Father comes to me" (John 6:45).

Faith is necessary for salvation. The theological tradition jealously guards the supernatural character of divine faith. Why? "God is the end of faith," answers Aquinas, "in that he is the unique good who by his eminence transcends human capacities, but who by his liberality offers us a share in the very goodness which he is."[50] Aquinas further elaborates on this, linking God's gratuitous revelation of himself to his being "teacher" in a unique sense: "In order that a person come to the full,

46. See *Summa theologiae* IIa-IIae q. 2, a. 4, ad 3: "Even if all scientific matters were as one in their knowability, they are not as one in being equal guides to blessedness. They are not, therefore, all proposed for belief."

47. See his *Contra Julianum* IV, 3 (PL 44, 744).

48. Although the Scholastic theologians disputed concerning the proper way to interpret St. Augustine's affirmation that "the soul has a natural capacity for grace" (*De trinitate* 14, 8 [PL 42, 1044], they did agree on two basic premises. First, that the supernatural order remains utterly gratuitous, so that nothing that any man or woman achieves by means of their natural capacities can attain God. Second, the divine plan for creation involves neither futility nor frustration. Given the reality of human sin having entered our corporate and personal histories, only one concrete way to God remains open and that is the incarnate Son of God. "For as the Father raises the dead and gives them life, so also the Son gives life to whom he will" (John 5:21).

49. *Summa theologiae* IIa-IIae q. 2, a. 3.

50. *In III Sententias* d. 23, q. 2, a. 1.

beatific vision, the first requisite is that he believe God, as a learner believing the master teaching him."[51] And his sixteenth-century commentator Cajetan remarks apropos of this: "Such was that love divine come down to us . . . that [God] should have communicated by grace what was incommunicable by nature."[52] All efforts to attenuate the strictly supernatural character of theological faith ultimately thwart the sheer gratuity of the Incarnation and, thereby, God's true plan for our salvation. Because our fulfillment lies in something beyond the reach of our natural capacities, and because grace proceeds from God's free initiative, it is absolutely essential that God teach us, even about in what our own happiness consists.

The Explicitness of Faith.   The Danish religious thinker Søren Kierkegaard portrays the uniqueness of Christian faith as a disposition in the subject that survives even in the face of obscurity and paradox.[53] For this nineteenth-century prefigurer of existentialist philosophy, true belief represents a passion for challenging the established institutions of state-controlled religious institutions and a pursuit of human existence and communion that Kierkegaard calls authenticity. And though authors like Kierkegaard do concede some role for credal propositions in maintaining the Christian Gospel, they prefer to emphasize the subjective meanings and psychological outgrowths of belief.[54] While it is true

51. "Unde ad hoc quod homo perveniat ad perfectam visionem beatitudinis præexigitur quod credat Deo tanquam disciplus magistro docenti" (*Summa theologiae* IIa-IIae q. 2, a. 3).

52. Cajetan, *in loco* n. VII. This view reflects Cajetan's solution to the question of how an obediential potency in man operates within salvation history. He argued that the natural desire for God could achieve its fullest naturalness only through the intervention of divine grace. Otherwise, the *potentia obedientialis* would remain more a vacuum capacity than a positive calling out for divine fulfillment. Cajetan, of course, understood how easily humanist values can substitute for the reality of Christian grace. Recall that Thomas More's *Utopia*, a model of sage folly, argued that human reason itself can practically attain to the paradoxical wisdom of Christ's little ones. More showed how Utopian society, still incomplete despite its crimped and limited perfection, actually awaits the proclamation of the Gospel in order to realize its own proper plenitude. More undoubtedly intended a sort of metaphor here for the Kingdom of God, for the spiritual homeland, for the City of God; Cajetan, though, emphasized the chasm that exists between the metaphor and the reality.

53. For further reading on this aspect of Kierkegaard's thought, see Louis Dupré, "L'acte de foi chez Kierkegaard," *Revue Philosophique de Louvain* 54 (1958): 418–55, and Robert M. Adams, "Kierkegaard's Arguments againt Objective Reasoning in Religion," in *The Virtue of Faith*, pp. 25–41.

54. See Alastair McKinnon, "Søren Kierkegaard," in *Nineteenth Century Religious*

that belief engages our hearts as well as our minds, Christian faith nevertheless remains about *something*. And even though certain biblical narratives lend themselves to interpreting faith as a simple disposition in the human person toward trust and confidence, the true theological virtue of faith revolves around the representation of explicit truths about God and the things that pertain to God. This is another way of affirming that faith achieves its explicit character from the "divine objects" that it knows.

The explicit content of theological faith centers exclusively on those things that God himself proposes for our salvation. "By divine revelation God has chosen to manifest and communicate both himself and the eternal decrees of his will for the salvation of humankind, 'so as to share those divine treasures which totally surpass human understanding.'"[55] Because the knowledge of these "divine treasures" involves many different truths, First Truth undergoes what Aquinas describes as a "plurification." In this process, divine Truth breaks down into a number of distinct conceptual truths, such as those formulated in the articles of the Creeds.[56] The Church holds this about the historical transmission of the doctrine of salvation: "Tradition and scripture together form a single sacred deposit of the word of God, entrusted to the Church. . . . All that is proposed for belief, as being divinely revealed, is drawn from the one deposit of faith."[57] The metaphor of "divine treasures" preserved in a "deposit" is intended to point up the explicit and determined character of the divine Truth that is entrusted for safekeeping to the Church.

As historical circumstances warrant, the bishop of Rome, Church councils, and recognized creeds give structure in various ways to the tenets of faith. "The task of authentically interpreting the word of God," declares the Second Vatican Council, "whether in its written form or in that of tradition, has been entrusted only to those charged

---

Thought in the West, ed. Ninian Smart, John Clayton, Patrick Sherry, and Steven T. Katz, vol. 1 (Cambridge: Cambridge University Press, 1985), pp. 188–200.

55. *Dei verbum*, chap. 1, no. 6; this text makes reference to the First Vatican Council's Dogmatic Constitution on the Catholic Faith, *Dei Filius*, chap. 2 (*DS* 3005).

56. See Aquinas's disputed question *De veritate* q. 14, a. 12, where he says that Truth is made manifold through different propositions: "pluificatur per diversa enuntiabilia."

57. See *Dei verbum*, chap. 2, no. 10.

with the Church's ongoing teaching function, whose authority is exercised in the name of Christ."[58] Medieval theologians like Aquinas, even before the formal definition of papal infallibility, fully recognized the legitimate place and authority of the Roman see within the communion of the Church. Their understanding of magisterium developed within a vision of the formal continuity that exists among those who, in different ways, are responsible for imparting sacred truth. The teaching of Christ, the preaching of the apostles, the pronouncements of popes and councils, and even the work of theologians are all ministerial instruments of one Truth and contribute variously and variously to the elucidation of the deposit of faith. Within this historical unfolding of divine truth in the world, the bishop of Rome, the successor of Peter, guarantees the unity of the Church in matters of faith. St. Paul expressed to the church at Corinth that unity of faith ensures that "you all speak the same thing, and that there be no schisms among you" (1 Cor. 1:10).[59] As part of the Church's living magisterium, the Petrine office serves as a special instrument for the communication of the highest Truth, insofar as only bishops in communion with the bishop of Rome possess the charge to interpret with authority the Word of God. Theologians who today appreciate the special ministry of the Roman pontiff with respect to instruction in the faith avoid the unhappy reductionism that construes the virtue of faith as a mere disposition to respect ecclesiastical declarations.[60]

At the beginning of the nineteenth century, the Tübingen school instituted one of the first serious efforts on the part of Catholic theology to confront modernity. Since that time, theologians have discussed questions related to the teaching mission of the Church in a separate discipline called *ecclesiology*, which is the special study of Church structures and practices. But a theological inquiry into the act of faith ought also to address some of these same questions from the distinctive perspective of theological faith—for example, whether the propositions of

58. *Dei verbum*, chap. 2, no. 10.

59. See *Summa theologiae* IIa-IIae q. 1, a. 10. See also, *Dei verbum*, no. 10.

60. See *Instruction on the Ecclesial Vocation of the Theologian*: "When the Magisterium of the Church makes an infallible pronouncement and solemnly declares that a teaching is found in Revelation, the assent called for is that of theological faith. . . . This kind of response cannot be simply exterior or disciplinary but must be understood within the logic of faith and under the impulse of obedience to the faith" (no. 23).

faith are to be formulated in an explicit way or whether the Roman pontiff enjoys special jurisdiction over the articles of faith. In dealing with the explicitness of faith's content, for example, Aquinas proposes the following theological criteria:

> There is something of faith that all men in every age are bound to believe explicitly; however, there are other things that must be believed explicitly in every age, but not by all; still other things that must be believed by all, but not in every age; and finally, other things that need not be believed either by all or in every age.[61]

This analysis assumes that the primary and proper cause of faith's explicitation is the historical revelation, culminating in Jesus Christ, that God makes throughout the "ages" of salvation history. Those who are drawn into the stream of illuminating and explicating the faith participate as instruments, though in various ways, in the announcement of what is to be believed.[62] In any event, the recognition that the Church encompasses both a "learning" dimension and a "teaching" dimension—an *ecclesia docens* and an *ecclesia discens*—implies that we can expect to discover diverse degrees of explicitness in what the faithful actually believe. The *Catechism* says: "Even if Revelation is already complete, it has not been made completely explicit; it remains for Christian faith gradually to develop its full significance over the course of the centuries."[63]

To start with the central and fundamental mysteries of the Christian religion, the Trinity and the Incarnation both occupy an indispensable place at the heart of the Church's faith. Thus, everyone, whether teacher or learner, is held to believe explicitly these mysteries. Why? In accord with the doctrinal declaration of the Council of Nicaea, belief in the Trinity requires the Church to profess that the incarnate Logos

---

61. See *De veritate*, q. 14, a. 11.

62. In this discussion, theologians attempt to distinguish the different moments and significances of God's historical revelation. See *Dei verbum*, chaps. 5 and 6, for the way the Council fathers distinguished revelation on the basis of its proximity to the mystery of Christ. This view assumes that there have existed and do exist among believers those who are *maiores* or the elders and leaders and those who are *minores*, who are the beneficiaries of instruction about divine things. In other words, both the old and the new dispensations include those who are held to a greater and clearer awareness of what the Church believes and those who occupy a more passive position insofar as they receive instruction about divine truth.

63. *Catechism of the Catholic Church*, no. 66.

remains a distinct Person in the Trinity of divine Persons. Indeed, the Trinitarian God that Christ alone reveals to us establishes all Christian belief, insofar as the missions of the divine Persons, both the visible mission of the Son and the invisible mission of the Holy Spirit, draw believers into the inheritance that faith promises.[64] No blessedness exists outside living the theological life, and without Christ and the Trinity there is no theological life. And so the Church orders the articles of faith as they stand in relation to these two mysteries, namely, the Trinity and the Incarnation.[65]

As long as the Church remains a pilgrim Church, there will exist many people who have not heard the evangelical preaching concerning the relationship of Christ and the blessed Trinity. Even in their own day, the medieval theologians recognized this phenomenon. But they found no difficulty insisting that salvation requires some kind of faith in the mediation of Christ. Does such a position necessarily lead one to uphold rigid conclusions concerning salvation outside the Church? It would seem not. For the theologian can still assert, as Aquinas in fact does, that the essential truth of the Christian faith exists in the claim

64. Aquinas saw this truth clearly: "Et iterum ipsa missio personarum divinarum perducit nos in beatitudinem" (*Summa theologiae* IIa-IIae q. 2, a. 8, ad 3). For further reflection on the Trinity as a mystery of salvation, see also Ia q. 43.

65. When one considers the preoccupations of the early ecumenical councils, the logical claim that the Trinity and Incarnation remain at the heart of Christian belief seems easy enough to accept. However, Aquinas addresses the more difficult question of how these truths were believed during the various theological moments of human history, the ages of salvation. Aquinas thus reflects the medieval preference to view salvation history as a single expression of God's providential action toward creation. Accordingly, Aquinas speculates that before original sin, man had foreknowledge of the Incarnation under the aspect of its final and predominant objective, namely, the consummation of glory. This position need not contradict what Aquinas says in IIIa q. 1, a. 3 about the redemptive purpose of the Incarnation; here the author is looking back from the vantage point of the Incarnation, and concludes, on the basis of ecclesial symbolism of marriage, that it would have been untoward for Adam not to have had some foreknowledge of so great a mystery. After the sin of Adam, however, believers gradually came to recognize that the perfection of the Godly image in men and women required the full paschal mystery, i.e., Christ's passion and resurrection, though for Aquinas, only the *maiores*—the leaders of the Jewish people—grasped the full significance of the various sacrifices that prefigured Christ's own. Once the dawn of redeeming grace appeared in the world, all men and women without distinction of rank have access to the saving Truths concerning the meaning of Christ's life and death. "This belief," Aquinas asserts, "mainly regards those points that are universally celebrated and publicly taught in the Church" (*Summa theologiae* IIa-IIae q. 2, a. 7).

that God alone delivers us from our sins and their destruction, and that God accomplishes this deliverance in ways of his own choosing. Aquinas's text on whether explicitly believing the mystery of Christ is necessary for salvation among all reads as follows:

> If some were saved to whom a revelation was not made, they were still not saved without faith in a mediator. So that even if they did not have explicit faith, they nonetheless had implicit faith in divine providence, believing that God would be the liberator of men, in ways pleasing to him and according as he would reveal the truth to some who would know it, according to Job 35, "Who teaches us above the beasts of the earth."[66]

This assertion, that even those who have never heard revelation must have some expressed, explicit faith (at least in the reality of divine salvific providence) in order to be saved, goes against certain contemporary views that seem to overlook the necessity for some specific content in Christian faith. Aquinas helps the theologian avoid the relativism that easily surfaces in some contemporary Catholic speculation about the status of the unevangelized. At the same time, it is clear that Aquinas's position permits a wide latitude. Thus, the neo-scholastic commentator Reginald Garrigou-Lagrange concludes that "if one considers those who enjoy supernatural faith, the majority [of these] have an explicit faith in Christ the Savior. In what *de facto* it consists, God alone knows!"[67]

Belief and Human Endeavors

For Christian theology, there exists a real sense in which human endeavors achieve a meritorious status before God. But this state of affairs exists only because God himself has ordained that certain exercises of human initiative would lay claim to a divine reward. In other words, "human merit" from an omnipotent God is possible only in a world of

---

66. *Summa theologiae* IIa-IIae q. 2, a. 7, ad 3: "Quia etsi non habuerunt fidem explicitam, habuerunt tamen fidem implicitam in divina providentia, credentes Deum esse liberatorem hominum secundum modos sibi placitos et secundum quod aliquibus veritatem cognoscentibus Spiritus revelasset. . . ."

67. See Reginald Garrigou-Lagrange, *Faith*, p. 160. For an interesting application of this insight, see J. A. DiNoia, O.P., "Implicit Faith, General Revelation and the State of Non-Christians," *The Thomist* 47 (1983): 209–41. Father DiNoia has further developed this proposal in his *The Diversity of Religions. A Christian Perspective* (Washington, D.C.: The Catholic University of America Press, 1992).

absolutely prior divine initiative and self-giving. In the present order of salvation, Jesus Christ alone remains the principle for meritorious good acts; as God's personal gift to the human race, Christ himself embodies every grace and merit that exists in the Church. Christ is therefore the source of the merit associated with the act of faith. This does not mean, however, that faith is any less a *free* act of the created person.[68] To be sure, God alone remains the effective agent cause of belief, but like any authentically virtuous action the act of belief gains merit only to the extent that it proceeds, under the impulse of divine grace, from a free personal choice. The exercise of human freedom serves as a condition for faith's meritoriousness, and also leads the believer to take up other activities that depend on faith and in one way or another flow from Christian belief.

The merit involved in Christian believing does not result simply from the fact that faith is accompanied by obscurity. Faith's merit is not founded on its being *difficult* for the human intellect. The mind's discovery of "reasons" that facilitate belief is entirely legitimate and consonant with faith's meritorious character. As Aquinas observes, "When anyone has a ready will to believe, he loves the truth he believes, he dwells upon it and treasures any supportive arguments he may discover."[69] The fundamental charter for all Christian theology lies in the injunction that we find in the First Letter of Peter: "Always be prepared to make a defense to any one who calls you to account for the hope that is in you, yet do it with gentleness and reverence" (1 Pet. 3:15). The Second Vatican Council draws no fewer than three times on this text in those places where Christian mission in the world is under discussion.[70] The vocation to holiness embraces the states both of the theologian and

---

68. Only in bliss can the human will make no other choice than God. In *Summa theologiae* Ia q. 82, a. 2, Aquinas explains that "other things have a necessary connection with happiness, those namely that join man to God in whom alone true happiness consists. Yet, before the certitude enjoyed through seeing God proves the necessity of this link, the will clings by necessity neither to God nor to the things of God. But the will of one who sees God's essence necessarily clings to God, because then we cannot help willing to be happy."

69. *Summa theologiae* IIa-IIae q. 2, a. 10: "Cum enim homo habet promptam voluntatem ad credendum, diligit veritatem creditam et supra ea excogitavit et amplectitur si quas rationes ad hoc invenire potest."

70. In *Lumen gentium*, chap. 2, no. 10, on the common priesthood of the faithful; in *Gravissimum educationis*, no. 2, on the importance of the Christian education of youth; and in *Presbyterorum ordinis*, chap. 1, no. 2, on the nature of the ministerial priesthood.

of the contemplative. The contemplative and the theologian search out in different ways "the assurance of things hoped for, the conviction of things not seen" (Heb. 11:1), even when the same person pursues both callings. The practice of the Eastern Church to recognize only saints as theologians reflects this fundamental principle of Christian faith and the theological life.

Faith, Theology, and Contemplation.   We know that belief brings one to the knowledge of a real object, even though it remains an affective knowing. Because belief brings knowledge, we can think about our knowledge in faith. This constitutes the simplest definition of theology: to think about what we know in faith. On Aquinas's view, theology can achieve a scientific status because it remains a participation in God's universal saving doctrine. Even by contemporary standards, one expects to discover in theological writings a body of knowledge that is critically justified, methodically conducted, and systematically planned. So, according to its own proper character, theology promotes a rational enquiry that, among other tasks, aims to expound the inner intelligibility of the Christian mysteries.[71] In an early essay, the Flemish theologian Edward Schillebeeckx summarized the four principal functions of speculative theology: to develop and maintain a penetrating knowledge of faith through the search for the mutual connections among the mysteries of faith; to achieve a profound insight into the intelligibility of the separate truths of faith by analogy from the things that reason knows by natural means; to derive theological intelligibility from the saving value of the content of revelation; and finally, to promote a deeper knowledge of faith through the theological study of the natural approaches to faith *(praeambula fidei).*[72] In the judgment of the American theologian Avery Dulles, these objectives continue to characterize the project of the theologian in the present postcritical period.[73]

Since, in the strict sense of the term, theology means dealing with the propositions of faith, it is possible at least to conceive of a person doing theology without faith, as a kind of logical exercise involving faith-

71. See *Dei Filius,* chap. 4 *(DS* 3016).

72. See his "What Is Theology?" in *Revelation and Theology,* vol. 1, trans. N. D. Smith (New York: Sheed and Ward, 1967), pp. 130–60.

73. See his *The Craft of Theology. From Symbol to System* (New York: Crossroad, 1992), esp. chaps. 2, 4, 8, 9.

statements. The scholastic theologians raised the question whether one who did not assent to divine truth could indeed properly engage in theology and, as one might expect, they reached diverse conclusions. Some agreement, however, did emerge from their exchanges: no one can successfully continue to do theology and remain entirely outside the real world of Christian faith and sacramental practice. But today, when theology has been forced into the narrow confinement created by professional circles of religious studies, a non-committed approach to theological topics has gained widespread acceptance, and in some places has even become normative. Whatever benefits this arrangement offers for the academic study of religion, it cannot substitute for the work of theology as a science of faith. Theology represents Christian faith working through human reflection, and in order for theology to maintain its unique identity, both members of the equation—faith and human reflection—must receive adequate attention.[74] To put it differently, the theologian can never forget that she or he is also a disciple. The practice of theology flows from the theological life, even if not everyone who lives the theological life is a theologian.

Authentic Christian theology develops in the person who ponders divine truth and lovingly commits the entire self to the same divine truth. When this self-committal develops in an authentic way, the dynamism of belief motivates a sort of rational activity that harmonizes with revealed Truth. One recalls the axiom of St. Anselm, *credo ut intelligam*, that is, I believe in order that I might [better] understand. About this familiar feature of Catholic teaching, the Second Vatican Council remarks: "Sacred theology takes its stand on the written word of God, together with tradition, as its permanent foundation. By this word it is made firm and strong, and constantly renews its youth, as it investigates, by the light of faith, all the truth that is stored up in the mystery of Christ."[75] Again, in the classical perspective of the Eastern churches, the title "theologian" implies the actual living out of a holy life, and not simply a professorial rank. Western Christianity at this time badly needs to learn from the Eastern tradition. The talent for speculative thought

---

74. On the relation of faith to religion in Aquinas's thought, see his *Expositio super librum Boethii De trinitate* q. 3, a. 2. Also, q. 5, a. 4, ad 8: "Fides est quasi habitus theologiae."

75. *Dei verbum*, chap. 6, no. 24.

(so much emphasized in the Western approach) must rediscover its roots and its vital context in a genuine sanctity. The work of the Swiss theologian Hans Urs von Balthasar points in this direction. The *Communio* model for theological discussion and writing that von Balthasar and other *ressourcement* theologians were instrumental in establishing is one example of what a "balanced theology" looks like. In a phrase that von Balthasar takes from the seventeenth-century French Jesuit Claude de la Colombière, a balanced vision means "doing theology on one's knees."[76]

As the account of the act of faith shows, belief sires different legitimate versions of scientific theology, but the practice of Christian faith also develops the affective dimension of belief. We distinguish acquired contemplation from theological reflection because contemplation arises from a prolonged and devoted beholding of the truths to which faith assents. And this beholding impels the Christian believer toward expressions of worship and praise—to kneeling before God in adoration. The contemplative consequently relies less on the discursive structures of the human mind than does one dedicated to the development of theology. In contemplation, God draws the person into a union with divine truth that progressively eludes the limitations established by concepts and argumentation. The tradition distinguishes between acquired and infused contemplation. Acquired contemplation occurs when the believer actively fosters the means that favor this sort of prayerful beholding. Infused contemplation, on the other hand, results from the sheer power of the Holy Spirit working in those whom God wishes to instruct. There is nothing that a person can do to prepare for the full gift of infused contemplation, "for it is not by measure that he gives the Spirit" (John 3:34).[77]

Arguments for Faith—the praeambula fidei. The hybrid character of Christian belief as both a knowing and a loving raises questions con-

76. Von Balthasar's German expression is "Kniende Theologie." For the English version, see his "Theology and Sanctity," in *Explorations in Theology* I: *The Word Made Flesh* (San Francisco: Ignatius Press, 1989), pp. 181–209, at 208.

77. In the Middle Ages, the glosses on this text gave rise to diverse views concerning the infinite character of Christ's grace and knowledge. The text supports a long tradition in theology that affirms the plenitude of Christ's wisdom. Because he alone perfectly beholds the Father, Christ remains the model for all contemplatives: "The Father loves the Son, and has given all things into his hand" (John 3:35).

cerning the role that rational arguments can play in promoting Christian faith. The whole question of a rational apology for Christian belief generates much less interest today than it did some decades ago.[78] Indeed, the mood of contemporary apologetics seems generally willing to rest content with St. Ambrose's view concerning the order of faith and reason: "It is good for faith to precede reason, lest we seem to require reason not only from man but from God our Lord as well. For how unworthy it would be that we should believe human testimonies of another, and yet not believe the utterances of God."[79] One reason for this attitude stems from the optimism of many post-conciliar theologians regarding a "correlation" between Christian truth and human experience. On the other hand, the Church has always recognized both the necessity and the challenge of an authentic cultural outreach. Those persons whom we call apologists seek to develop cogent ways of making the Gospel appealing to human intelligence, while still guarding against the temptation to trim faith's objective content to fit better the limits of human understanding or the experiences of a particular time or place.[80]

Historically, the effort on the part of Christian believers to develop an apologetic gained new momentum in the wake of the First Vatican Council's Dogmatic Constitution on the Catholic Faith, *Dei Filius*, which makes the following declaration:

> Not only can faith and reason never be at odds with one another but they mutually support each other, for on the one hand right reason established the foundations of faith and, illuminated by its light, develops the science of divine things; on the other hand, faith delivers reason from errors and protects it and furnishes it with knowledge of many kinds.[81]

Because they hoped to counterbalance the ravages of an uncritical and destructive rationalism, certain of the neo-scholastic theologians expended much energy and research in an effort to discover new ways to

78. For a penetrating comment on "the vaunted rationality" of the preambles to faith, see Anscombe, "Faith," pp. 113–20.

79. *On Abraham*, Bk. 1, chap. 3 (PL 14, 428) in *The Teachings of the Church Fathers*, ed. ohn R. Willis, S.J. (New York: Herder and Herder, 1966), p. 31.

80. For an invigorating analysis of the benefits that derive from confidence in conceptualization, see Kenneth Schmitz, "St. Thomas and the Appeal to Experience," *CTSA Proceedings* 47 (1992): 1–20.

81. *Dei Filius*, chap. 4.

describe the rational foundations and structure of Christian faith.[82] The First Vatican Council, it should be recalled, also anathematized the view that divine revelation cannot be made credible by external signs.[83] And so Catholic intellectuals enthusiastically developed various philosophical approaches to issues such as the existence of God, a discernible order in creation, the sanctions that result from wrongdoing, and the rewards that follow upon good behavior. This enthusiasm eventually was given a definite shape when, in his 1879 encyclical *Aeterni Patris*, Pope Leo XIII mandated a return to the study of Aquinas.

In the middle of the twentieth century, a group of European theologians reacted against some overstated attempts to provide clear-cut and self-evident preambles for Christian belief. The logical clarity of such arguments, it was said, marginalized the aesthetic element that is a trait of Christian faith. In an earnest effort to make revealed truth more attractive to modern spirits, theologians associated with *La nouvelle théologie* school drew upon a wide range of patristic and literary sources. These theologians professed concern lest overly rational arguments for both the credibility and the development of revealed truths should obscure the greatness and beauty of the Christian faith itself. In other terms, while human reason can discourse about God, only faith, they would contend, announces the God of Abraham, Isaac, and Jacob; again, while reason can assert that there exists an order in the universe, only faith can instruct us about a personal providence that observes each inch of a person's height (see Luke 12:25); and finally, while reason can elaborate an ethical code, even one that includes sanctions for bad behavior, only faith reveals the life of Christian virtue that hope and love infuse with specifically divine energies. Again, the work of Hans Urs von Balthasar represents one of the best efforts to develop this kind of new faith apologetic. On von Balthasar's account, faith creates its own experience, and so can easily establish the basis for its own credibility and make a judgment about its own credentity.[84] Although von Bal-

---

82. Specialists will find the new edition of articles by Pierre Rousselot, S.J., *The Eyes of Faith*, trans. Joseph Donceel, S.J., and Avery Dulles, S.J. (New York: Fordham University Press, 1990), a good introduction to an alternative way in which theologians responded to the Modernist crisis.

83. *Dei Filius*, Third Canon on Faith (*DS* 3033).

84. For an analysis of his approach, see Louis Dupré, "The Glory of the Lord. Hans

thasar's theory exhibits an attractively inclusivist view of the relationship between faith and human experience, his theological "aesthetic" must complement what the First Vatican Council describes as a "most fruitful" *(fructuosissimam)* intelligibility of divine truths that, by analogy, human reason discovers in human experience.[85]

In addition to the arguments that reason can develop, the First Vatican Council affirms the view that the public actions of Jesus as recorded in the canonical Scriptures, especially his miracles and the fulfillment of the Messianic prophecies, and the reality of the Church remain convincing signs of credibility for the act of faith. In the mid-twentieth century, the Second Vatican Council reaffirmed this way to belief:

> Jesus Christ, the Word made flesh, sent as a human being among humans, "speaks the words of God" (John 3:34) and accomplishes the work of salvation which the Father gave him to do. . . . This is why Jesus completes the work of revelation and confirms it by divine testimony. He did this by the total reality of his presence and self-manifestation—by his words and works, his symbolic acts and miracles, but above all by his death and his glorious resurrection from the dead.[86]

Whatever doubts subsequent historical-critical studies of the New Testament have raised in the minds of some about the validity of an apologetic appeal to the miracles of Christ, the logic of the Incarnation obliges us to recognize that the Father intends that Christ manifest the glory they share from all eternity. "Father," Jesus exclaims, "I want those you have given me to be with me where I am, so that they may always see the glory you have given me because you loved me before the foundation of the world" (John 17:24). The life and action of Jesus

Urs von Balthasar's Theological Aesthetic," in *Hans Urs von Balthasar. His Life and Work*, ed. David L. Schindler (San Francisco: Ignatius Press, 1992), pp. 183–206: "As von Balthasar presents it, that faith, far from standing opposed to experience (as past theology frequently implied), creates its own experience. . . . If experience does not belong to the essence of faith itself, the form construed on the basis of that experience possesses no theological standing whatever" (p. 198).

85. For the text of the First Vatican Council, see *DS* 3016. Like von Balthasar, Avery Dulles, in *The Craft of Theology*, p. 56, attempts "to pierce the supposedly impermeable wall between reason and faith." He submits that "to persons untouched by a grace-filled Christian experience . . . Christian faith can only appear as exorbitant and irrational. At best, it would be dismissed as an overcommitment."

86. *Dei verbum*, chap. 1, no. 4.

of Nazareth remain not only a credible sign but also the means through which we receive our faith, the revelation of the glory of the Trinity. And because Jesus wants all persons to live the theological life, to be one in him, and to share his life of love with the Father, the interior act of faith must attain public expression in the Church.

The Exterior Act of Faith: Confession

Christian belief means to *think* with assent, and so belief necessarily remains an inward action in the person who hears God's word. However, given the public witness that Christ himself gives to the world, the Christian faith that unites his disciples can never remain strictly a matter of private or inward activity. A complete treatment of the theological virtue requires that we consider another dimension of theological faith—its outward act—which the tradition of the Church refers to as confession, or the public proclamation and profession of our faith.

Since the Church exists only by virtue of the capital grace and headship of Christ, the Word of God remains absolutely prior to the establishment of the Church. The Second Vatican Council says: "The Church, the 'spouse of the incarnate Word,' taught by the Holy Spirit, strives to attain, day by day, to an ever deeper understanding of holy scripture, so that she may never fail to nourish her children with God's utterances."[87] As a visible society in the world, the Church marks off the place where one authentically and efficaciously hears this word. To borrow the expression of Martin Luther, the members of the Church remain "captive to the word of God." And as a result of this captivity, the Church forms a communion of those whose charity urges them to announce to others the rich truths about God and Christ. This created charity forms as it were the very soul of the Church, the created breath of the Holy Spirit, who in the Trinity personally represents the unifying bond of Love between the Father and the Son. "Through Christ, God's Word made flesh, and in his Holy Spirit, human beings can draw near to the Father and become sharers in the divine nature (see Eph. 2:18 and 2 Pet. 1:4)."[88] The Trinitarian dimension of the Church establishes

---

87. *Dei verbum*, chap. 6, no. 23.
88. *Dei verbum*, chap. 1, no. 2.

the formal relationship between faith's inward act and its outward or public manifestation, between the belief in the heart that leads to justification and confession on the lips that leads to salvation.[89]

The act of faith is a response to God's gift of himself, and as such depends entirely on his testimony. While nothing human commands the interior witnessing of God, the Church composed of those who hear God's word and receive his grace is a Church that must bear witness. In this sense, the Church "extends" the relationships of the blessed Trinity in the world. Just as the Father and the Son "send forth" the Spirit within the life of the Trinity, so also the person in whom faith is generated is impelled toward an outward expression. As Aquinas explains it, "Outward speech is ordered to signifying what is conceived in the heart."[90] In this work of realizing the Trinitarian life in both the members and the structures of the Church, the human person instrumentally joins her or his voice to that of First Truth-Speaking. For this reason, each member of the Church who accepts the testimony of Christ is held bound within the limits of prudence to proclaim God's Truth to the world. Confession, then, signals a flowering of the grace of faith, a personal proclamation (through the mediation of the Church) of the divine activity that has moved the person to faith.

In the Church's proclamation of divine Truth, there exists one causal order between the principal divine witnessing in the Trinity and the instrumental witnessing of the believer. As head of the Church, Christ enjoys the principal place in this mediation, and for that reason witnesses directly through vision to the divine Truth, which he himself speaks as God, but the members of Christ also are joined to him in their confession by theological faith. The Second Vatican Council makes this point explicitly:

Christ, the great prophet, who by the witness of his life and the power of his word proclaimed the Father's kingdom, continues to carry out his prophetic task,

89. The Dogmatic Constitution on the Church, *Lumen gentium*, chap. 4, no. 35, applies this point to the apostolate: "Just as the sacraments of the new law, by which the life and apostolate of the faithful are nourished, foreshadow the new heaven and the new earth (see Rev. 21:1), so the laity become effective heralds of faith in the things we hope for (see Heb. 11:1) if they firmly combine the profession of faith to a life of faith."

90. *Summa theologiae* IIa-IIae q. 3, a. 1.

until the full manifestation of his glory, not only through the hierarchy who teach in his name and by his power, but also through the laity whom he constitutes his witnesses and equips with an understanding of the faith and a grace of speech (see Acts 2:17–18; Apoc. 19:10) precisely so that the power of the Gospel may shine forth in the daily life of family and society.[91]

Von Balthasar made a point of identifying St. Peter as one of the four main representational figures that direct the Church's life. The "confession" of Peter (see Matt. 16:13–23; Mark 8:27; Luke 9:18–22) concretizes and symbolizes the whole Church's external profession of faith, namely, that Jesus is "the Christ, the Son of the living God." Moreover, in this work of mediating and proclaiming the divine action in human history, our blessed Lady holds a preeminent place.[92] For she, before all others, confesses and proclaims the greatness of the Lord. In her, the Church teaches us, we behold the most perfect realization of what St. Paul calls "the obedience of faith" (Rom. 1:5).

In the New Testament, the Greek word *homologein* refers to a comprehensive recital of praise and thanksgiving that the Church utters as a response to God's mighty and merciful deeds toward sinners.[93] Aquinas distinguishes two elements of *homologein* and relates each to its proper virtue. "Confession" of the truths of faith first entails the proclamation of thanks and praise, which the Church traditionally associates with the virtue of justice or *latria*;[94] second, it involves the confession of sins, which forms part of the virtue of penitence.[95] The dynamic toward exteriorization that belongs to theological faith perfectly expresses itself in love. The Church announces to all men and women "a life of faith and charity," offering to God a sacrifice of praise, the

---

91. *Lumen gentium*, chap. 4, no. 35.

92. See *Lumen gentium*, chap. 8, no. 53: "Therefore [Mary] is also acknowledged as the supereminent and uniquely special member of the church as well as its model in faith and love and its most outstanding exemplar; and the catholic church, instructed by the Holy Spirit, with the affection of filial piety, treats her as its most loving mother."

93. For the Second Vatican Council's teaching on how the entire Church participates in the prophetic role of Christ, see *Lumen gentium*, chap. 2, no. 12.

94. *Latria* relates to the adoration of the true God. In the schema of the moral virtues that Aquinas develops in the *secunda pars* of his *Summa Theologiae*, this action belongs to the virtue of religion, which is a subjective part of cardinal justice (see IIa-IIae q. 81; q. 103, a. 3).

95. See *Summa theologiae* IIa-IIae q. 3, a. 2, ad 1.

tribute of lips that give honor to his name (see Heb. 13:15). The life of charity forms the heart of both witness and preaching, and in this sense, even the outward word of proclamation and confession imitates the Trinitarian model as *Verbum spirans Amorem,* a "Word breathing forth love."[96]

96. The reference comes from Aquinas's discussion of the Trinitarian missions: "The Son in turn is the Word; not, however, just any word, but the Word breathing Love; as St. Augustine says, 'The Word as I want the meaning understood is a knowledge accompanied by love.' Consequently not just any enhancing of the mind indicates the Son's being sent, but only that sort of enlightening that bursts forth into love . . ." (*Summa theologiae* Ia q. 43, a. 5 ad 2).

β Chapter 4

The Harvest of Your Faith, the Salvation of Your Souls

To illustrate what the gift of justification by faith accomplishes in a person, the Church's preachers and teachers have over time employed a variety of metaphors. For example, in one of his biblical commentaries, St. Augustine takes up the image of consecration: "We have received an anointing by the Holy One," he writes, "that teaches us inwardly more than our tongue can speak." Inasmuch as all baptized persons benefit from this received gift, St. Augustine encourages Christians to pursue the ultimate vocation: "So let us turn to this source of knowledge, and since at present you cannot see, make it your business to desire the divine vision."[1] He can make this appeal because the grace of justification causes the sanctification and renewal of the interior man, enabling one to walk in newness of life.

As the ancient biblical practice of consecrating monarchs illustrates, anointing signifies the bestowal on someone of a permanent capacity to fulfill a specific office or responsibility. The Second Vatican Council alludes to the gravity of this responsibility when it teaches that "the whole body of the faithful who have an anointing that comes from the holy one (cf. 1 John 2:20, 27) cannot err in matters of belief."[2] In the context of the theological life, the anointing of faith makes us super-

1. St. Augustine, *Tractates on the First Letter of John*, 4, 6 (PL 35, 2008–2009), trans. International Committee on English in the Liturgy in *The Liturgy of the Hours*, vol. 3 (New York: Catholic Book Publishing Company, 1975), p. 220.
2. The Dogmatic Constitution on the Church, *Lumen gentium*, chap. 2, no. 12.

natural knowers of God. The virtue of faith is like a spiritual seal, says St. Ambrose, since the Creed both imprints a meditation on our hearts and serves as a safeguard that is always present.[3] The seventeenth-century English poet George Herbert captures the difference the seal of faith makes: "That which before was darkned clean / With bushie groves, pricking the lookers eie, / Vanisht away, when Faith did change the scene: / And then appear'd a glorious skie."[4]

Faith cognitively informs Christian believers about God and the things of God—Herbert's image of the "glorious skie." Theological faith, however, remains the virtue of the wayfarer, since living by faith means seeing as in a mirror, dimly (see 1 Cor. 13:12). In this dimness, belief nonetheless unites us to divine Truth and consecrates us for the harvest of faith, the salvation of our souls. It remains for us to examine the "supernatural sense of faith" as it exists in the person who shares in Christ's kingly and prophetic offices. This inquiry requires two steps: first, to consider faith precisely as a virtuous qualification of the human person and, second, to look at the steps involved in a person's coming to faith.

The Virtuousness of Faith

The Christian tradition appeals to certain philosophical concepts to help explain the permanent character of Christian virtue. We have seen that certain authors in the theological schools have developed Aristotle's account of *hexis*, especially as this concept appears in the *Nicomachean Ethics*, his long essay on moral philosophy.[5] There, *hexis* represents a definite ability for growth through activity. The Latin commentators on Aristotle translated the Greek term *hexis* as *habitus*, and moral philosophers continue to describe virtue as a habit—*habitus*. Recall that the

---

3. See his *Explanatio symboli ad initiandos* no. 1 (PL 17, 1155), trans. R. H. Connolly (Cambridge: Cambridge University Press, 1952).

4. "Faith" in *The English Poems of George Herbert*, ed. C. A. Patrides (London: Dent, 1974), p. 70.

5. See *Nicomachean Ethics* Bk. 2, chap. 6 (1106b36), but also Aristotle's smaller work, the *Eudemian Ethics* Bk. 1, chap. 10 (1227b8). Cf. above, chapter 1, "Grace: Form and Dynamism of the Theological Life." For applications to theological issues, see especially, Walter Farrell, O.P., and Dominic Hughes, O.P., *Swift Victory* (New York: Sheed and Ward, 1955).

development of *habitus* means that the moral agent develops and enjoys a particular "state of character" formed by his or her voluntary acts.[6] Thus, we can identify a person according to the patterns of activity represented by *habitus*. To draw upon examples of praiseworthy conduct only, we call the individual who acts with courage a brave person, the one who acts with moderation a temperate person, the one who acts with equity and fairmindedness a just person, and so forth. Because the scholastic theologians especially understood the important role that *habitus* play in shaping human conduct, they described these *habitus* as holding a middle position between potency, or the radical capacity for action, and full actuality, that is, the condition of actually doing something.[7] So, as instances of voluntary activity, human actions ordinarily embody the realization of one or another *habitus*. Since a person without these *habitus* lacks what is required for sure comportment, any kind of purposeful activity would be difficult and burdensome for one who lacks virtue. Moreover, as long as a person's psychological capacities persist in such an underdeveloped state, his or her human potential goes unrealized.

Because possessing a *habitus* implies that the human person remains open to development and modification from a variety of natural causes, the notion of *habitus* effectively points up the difference between what derives from authentically personal activity and what remains rooted in the biological givens of temperament or personality type.[8] Each human

6. St. Thomas develops his views on *habitus* in a small, well-crafted treatise in the *prima secundae*, qq. 49–54. Anthony Kenny, *Dispositions for Human Acts* (1a2ae. 49–54), vol. 22 (New York: McGraw-Hill, 1964), chooses to translate the Latin term *habitus* as "disposition." Although he offers reasons for his choice (pp. xix–xxxiv), it seems preferable simply to accept the original Latin term *habitus* as serviceable for English usage. For a recent exposition of how the notion of *habitus* presently suits theological ethics, see my *The Moral Virtues and Theological Ethics* (Notre Dame/London: University of Notre Dame Press, 1991), chap. 2.

7. For example, the scholastic adage, "*habitus medio modo se habet inter potentiam et actum purum.*" D. W. Hamlyn, "Behavior," *Philosophy* 28 (1953), pp. 132–145 makes the same point. Movement, he writes, "arises out of a potentiality and may lead to a *hēxis* (a state or disposition). The activity is the realization of that *hēxis*. Perfect activity would be quite independent of any potentiality but human activities only approximate to this state of affairs which is characteristic of the divine" (p. 132).

8. For example, Vernon Bourke, "The Role of Habitus in the Thomistic Metaphysics of Potency and Act," in *Essays in Thomism*, ed. R. E. Brennan, O.P. (New York, 1942), pp. 103–9, offers a magisterial lecture presentation on this subject. In addition, Bourke's

person possesses certain natural endowments, as distinct from those that are developed through *habitus*; and these establish, within the limits set by common nature, the range of expression achievable by personal effort. To take a simple example, the capacity for maintaining the healthy nutrition required for basic well-being develops one way in the *gourmand* and another way in the person who must observe, for reasons such as bodily metabolism, a simple, even frugal diet. Barring biological defect, every human being possesses the capacity for developing the major *habitus* of human action and comportment. In fact, *habitus* development can even compensate for natural imbalances in a person, as happens when the *gourmand*, upon discovering the benefits that observing a moderate diet brings, begins to develop a taste for simpler victuals. Even though individuals develop their gifts in different ways, the native excellence of the human person lies precisely in the common inbred capacities proper to the species. At the same time, since this potential originally exists in a pure state of indeterminacy, each person also experiences a certain poverty with respect to human development, such that the moral life in large measure remains for everyone an educative and developmental process. Indeed, a person's progress in virtue or growth in vice mainly depends upon how successfully the individual can modify these indeterminacies into developed qualities of excellence.

Philosophers locate *habitus* within the predicamental category of quality, the second of nine basic types of reality that embody the ways that any substance is constituted as a special, predicable kind of thing.[9] As a real property of being, quality amounts to more than a classification of things, and achieves more than a simple modification of its subject. Rather, as a category of being, quality describes the actual internal ordering or arrangement of the various parts that make up a substance. For example, quality accounts for why a Bach organ prelude differs so much from popular folk tunes, a cultivated English Tea rose from the wild New England rambling rose, and French *haute cuisine* from Amer-

---

unpublished doctoral dissertation, *Habitus as a Perfectant of Potency in the Philosophy of St. Thomas Aquinas* (University of Toronto, 1938), provides the textual study that supports his conclusions.

9. Aquinas considered the categories to be irreducible kinds of being. Even though they have yet to add another modality, the English analysts, including Gilbert Ryle, have consistently challenged the absolute character of Aristotle's predicamental table.

ican fast food. As distinct substances, these things are easily identified as musical composition, rose flowers, and foodstuffs respectively. But the difference in the music, roses, and food lies precisely in the particular substance's unique qualities.

In the human person, virtuous *habitus* describe a state of self-possession. Some commentators point out that the Latin *se habere* more clearly indicates the reflexive sense of having ("having oneself") than does the usual transitive meaning of "to have," as when a person is said to have or to possess something. Vicious *habitus* account for why someone develops into a vicious individual, whereas virtuous *habitus* explain a virtuous person.

The notion of *habitus* also provides, as we have seen, a way to illustrate how grace transforms the principal psychological capacities of human nature. In fact, one philosopher even describes *habitus* as "a metaphysical perfectant."[10] For such a perfection heightens our human capacities to such an extent that those who act with a "habituated" intellect, will, and appetites approach the optimum performance of the strongest and most perfect human being. To look at the theological life in this way does not rob Christian virtue of its spontaneity and human creativity. For *habitus* do not establish obsessive routine. Instead of inhibiting the exercise of human autonomy, *habitus* actually provide the indispensable condition for the realization of authentically free and responsible Christian behavior. The encyclical letter *Veritatis splendor* calls this the state of theonomy.[11]

The most appropriate use of the category of *habitus* in Christian anthropology lies in the realm of the theological and infused virtues. Though theologians refer to sanctifying grace as an "entitative" *habitus* of the soul, this way of speaking constitutes an extended use of the

10. Bourke, "Role of Habitus": "It is a metaphysical perfectant, heightening man's rational capacities to such an extent that he who acts with a habituated intellect and will, approaches the optimum performance of the strongest and most perfect human being" (106, 107).

11. See *Veritatis splendor*, no. 41: Theonomy describes the state in which man's free obedience to God's law discloses that human reason and human will participate in God's wisdom and providence. Virtuous *habitus* develop this state of self-possession. Aquinas stresses that the radical source or principle of human action, and consequently freedom, remains the human potencies/capacities. See *Summa theologiae* Ia-IIae q. 49, a. 4: "But it is obvious that the nature and notion of a capacity is to be a source of action. And so every *habitus* whose possessor is a capacity is connected primarily with action."

concept.[12] The theological virtues, however, are *habitus* in the precise sense. They shape the capacities or powers of the human soul that form the basis for knowledge and love, namely, the intellect for faith and the rational appetite, or will, for the virtues of theological love (hope and charity). Only sanctifying grace can simultaneously elevate and perfect these powers, so that a person can live fully the theological life. To consider theological faith as a *habitus* proper to the Christian reflects a long-standing theological intuition about how God bestows the gift of faith. In his treatise entitled *The Divine Names*, the fifth-century Christian author known as Dionysius the Areopagite writes: "Faith is the permanent Ground of the faithful, which builds them in the Truth and builds the Truth in them by an unwavering firmness, through which they possess a simple knowledge of the Truth of those things which they believe."[13] A judicious and creative use of the Aristotelian category of *habitus* aids the affirmation that this "unwavering firmness" abides as a personal quality or trait in everyone who is "justified by faith in Christ" (Gal. 2:17).

Thus the definition of the virtue *(habitus)* of faith stands in the same relationship to belief as faith's proper act does to its object. For just as objects specify human actions, so actions specify the capacity or power from which they flow. Since God as First Truth in Being and Speaking formally specifies and causes faith's acts of belief and confession to be particular kinds of actions, these same actions, especially the inward act of belief, also specify the nature of faith principally as a *habitus* of our minds. For the *habitus* of theological faith enables a person to grasp whatever First Truth utters—in the language of the First Vatican Council, to accept something as true "on account of the authority of God, who makes the revelation and can neither deceive nor be deceived."[14]

In order to emphasize that the theological virtue of faith distinctively shapes the character and life of the believer, theological ethics must consider faith precisely as a virtuous *habitus*. Whatever their value in exciting the imaginations of believers may be, descriptive narratives of

12. See *Summa theologiae* Ia-IIae q. 50, a. 2.

13. Dionysius the Areopagite, *The Divine Names and The Mystical Theology*, trans. C. E. Rolt (London: SPCK, 1979), chap. 7, no. 4 (p. 153).

14. First Vatican Council, Dogmatic Constitution on the Catholic Faith, *Dei Filius*, chap. 3 (*DS* 3008).

personal experiences and testimonies do not adequately substitute for an account of what causes and institutes the human person's access to the "One who lives in unapproachable light" (1 Tim. 6:16). For the New Testament's own description of Christian belief warrants a substantial account of the virtue of faith. To point out the proper sentiments that a person should have on religious issues or ethical values, or to render a merely descriptive account of how a believer ought to think or react in particular circumstances, falls short of saying fully what Christian faith is about. Rather, an adequate theological account of the virtue must consider faith as a true modification of the believer's "state of character."

The Definition in Hebrews 11

Since the patristic era, theologians who recognize that the virtue of faith both constitutes an authentic form of knowing and initiates a real beginning of eternal life have fixed their attention on a verse from the Letter to the Hebrews: "Now faith is the substance of things hoped for, the evidence of things that appear not" (Heb. 11:1).[15] The theological exegesis of this one biblical text has supplied the Catholic tradition with a rich suite of glosses and commentaries. During the late Medieval period, however, theologians who developed an overly intellectual approach to faith began to neglect the indispensable role that human affect plays in the act of Christian belief. Authors such as these let the Latin term *substantia* dominate their exegesis of Hebrews 11:1, with the unfortunate result that they failed to emphasize faith as the beginning of a true interpersonal relationship with God. During the fourteenth and fifteenth centuries Nominalist theology, with its insistence on syllogistic deduction and its logical separation of acquired from infused faith, made it seem even more that faith is about propositions, that is, faith's

---

15. This rendering in English is based on a literal translation of the Vulgate version, namely, "Est autem fides sperandarum substantia rerum, augumentum non apparentium" (Ad Heb. 11:1). The *Jerusalem Bible* renders the original Greek "Only faith can guarantee the blessings that we hope for, or prove the existence of the realities that at present remain unseen," and the *Revised Standard Version* has "Now faith is the assurance of things hoped for, the conviction of things not seen." When it explains that the definition applies to Abraham, "our father in faith," the *Catechism of the Catholic Church* uses the latter translation (see no. 146).

"substance."[16] So we can appreciate that when the sixteenth-century Christian humanist Erasmus of Rotterdam came to comment on the Vulgate text of Hebrews, chapter 11, he quipped that "these words are a eulogy of faith, not a definition."[17] Erasmus, one assumes, perceived the grave mistake of separating Christian faith from the theological life. But in some subsequent traditions, Erasmus's criticism has been used to minimize the importance of faith's propositions for the salvation of souls.

In the Catholic theological view, faith's knowledge of God always remains dynamically ordered to love's perfect fulfillment in God, which is the harvest of faith. The second-century theologian and bishop Irenaeus of Lyons affirmed this truth when he explained the profound connection between faith in Christ and the attainment of beatitude: Since unbelievers "do not know him who from the Virgin is Emmanuel, they are deprived of his gift which is eternal life; and not receiving the incorruptible Word, they remain in mortal flesh, and are debtors to death, not obtaining the antidote of life."[18] The virtue of faith points to a living relationship between knowledge and everlasting life. In order to understand this relationship correctly, however, theology must grasp the connection between the knowledge of faith and the love of charity. When in the early sixteenth century, Martin Luther wanted to make a sharp contrast between what the Protestant Reform taught about justification and what the earlier scholastic period had developed, he declared: "Where they speak of love, we speak of faith."[19] For Aquinas, on the other hand, Christian life is never a matter of choosing between faith or love, but always of faith *and* love. Today, however, both Catholics and Lutherans recognize the inadequacy of this simple antithesis between faith and love.[20] In fact, faith can be understood only within the

16. The Dominican commentator John Capreolus argued against the Nominalists on infused faith. See the articles by Cessario and White in *Capreolus (1380–1444) en son temps*, ed. Guy Bedouelle, Romanus Cessario, and Kevin White. Mémoire dominicaine 1 (Paris: Cerf, 1997).

17. *In Epistolam ad Hebraeos*, cap. XI: "Hic quidam ridicule nugantur circa hanc definitionem, ut ipsi vocant, cum non sit finitio sed encomium fidei. . . ." in *Erasmus' Annotations on the New Testament. Galatians to the Apocalypse*, ed. Anne Reeve, vol. 52, Studies in the History of Christian Thought, ed. Heiko A. Overman (Leiden: E. J. Brill, 1993), 727.

18. Irenaeus of Lyons, *Against Heresies*, Bk. 3, chap. 19 (PG 7, 938; ANF 1, 448).

19. Martin Luther, *Commentary on Galatians* (1535) 2:16.

20. For a good example of the differences of perspectives, however, see the exchange

context of the three theological virtues. A responsible reading of Hebrews 11 suggests this integral understanding of faith.

In the last half of the thirteenth century, Aquinas took up the challenge to show that Hebrews 11 legitimately serves as source, a *locus
theologicus*, for a theological analysis of the virtue of faith. Moreover, his
exegesis of the Hebrews text reveals that he was sensitive to the language of Scripture. Aquinas concludes his treatment of the Latin Vulgate version of Hebrews 11:1, "Now faith is the substance of things
hoped for, the evidence of things that appear not," by translating the
scriptural text into propositional form: "If therefore someone wanted
to reduce words of this kind to the form of a definition, it could be said
that 'faith is a habit *[habitus]* of mind, by which eternal life begins in us,
making the understanding assent to what does not appear."[21] By developing the gloss on Hebrews 11 in this way, Aquinas puts the scriptural
language at the service of theological discussion, so as to bring out more
clearly the two principal elements of a Catholic understanding of justification: First, the human mind's native inability to fathom the reality
of divine beatitude and, second, the end-term of divine faith, which is
the believer's sure possession of eternal life.

What does it mean to say that theological faith enables a person to
gain knowledge of "things that do not appear"? Because faith's proper
object is uncreated and therefore remains unseen, belief necessarily entails the active involvement of both the mind and the will. (Recall that
Aquinas refuses to reify the capacities of the soul. It is not the intellect
that understands or the will that loves, but the person.) As long as human
intelligence can find no grounds on which to reason conclusively concerning the witness of First Truth-Speaking, a person who wishes to
assent to what God proposes for belief must rely on some other human
activity. Since emotion or sentiment remains inadequate to the task, only

---

between Frederick Crosson and Bruce Marshall, "Postliberal Thomism Again," *The Thomist* 56 (1992): 481–524.

21. The text comes from *Summa theologiae* IIa-IIae q. 4, a. 1: "Si quis ergo in formam
definitonis huismodi verba reducere velit, potrest dicere quod fides est habitu mentis, qua
inchoatur vita aeterna in nobis, faciens intellectum assentire non apparentibus," which
Mark D. Jordan, *On Faith. Summa theologiae, Part 2–2, Questions 1–16 of St. Thomas Aquinas*
(Notre Dame: University of Notre Dame Press, 1990), renders ". . . faith is a habit of
mind, by which eternal life begins in us, making the understanding assent to what does not
appear" (p. 104).

the rational appetite or will is left to give its assent, to choose to believe. On the other hand, the human appetitive powers, the reasons of the heart, cannot discern intellectual realities, still less divine truths. This means that only the goodness that the proclamation of divine truth embodies can effectively elicit the assent of the will.[22] To put it differently, while belief remains formally an act of the intellect, a person must hear something in the preaching of the Good News that is attractive. Just as the execution of any virtuous action involves the interrelatedness of mind and will, so the act of belief represents a psychological integration of volitional assent with the propositional structure of faith. In this way, the Catholic tradition upholds the virtue of faith as both a conceptual knowledge and an affective trust. Or to adapt the Protestant Reform's emphasis on *fiducia*, theological faith by definition remains fiduciary in character.[23] For the sureness and firmness of Christian belief ultimately rest on the believer's loving self-commitment to the Truth that is God.

If we accept the witness of Aquinas, the authentic theological tradition of the Church has never explained faith without reference to its fiducial component. In the definition of faith that the medieval theologians excavated from the first verse of Hebrews 11, the term "substance" refers in a seminal way to all that the Church hopes to receive from God.[24] Faith sets the members of Christ's Body on the road to beatitude, the full and joyful possession of God that the Christian Gospel both announces and promises to fulfill. When Aquinas expressly relates the role of faith to the life of grace, he emphasizes how faith inaugurates and sustains the promise of eternal life and beatitude, even though this virtue of the pilgrim Church can never fully attain the goal that here below it establishes: "God is the end of faith in that he is the

22. Realist epistemology maintains that the essential character of the intellect is ordained toward attaining clear knowledge of the truth; the will, on the other hand, remains blind and, therefore, is dependent on intelligence in order to discriminate the goods to which the will naturally inclines.

23. For some examples, see the sixteenth-century French Reformer John Calvin, *Commentary on Romans*, 4:14, and the Swiss Heinrich Bullinger, *Summa of the Christian Religion*, 6 introduction; 6.1.

24. Aquinas justifies this interpretation by comparing substance with the first principles of any science: "So we could say that first indemonstrable principles are the substance of a body of knowledge, because the first things that are in us of a body of knowledge are principles of this sort, and in them is virtually contained the whole body of knowledge" (*Summa theologiae* IIa- IIae q. 4, a. 1).

unique good, who by his eminence transcends the capacities of humankind, but by his liberality offers his very good to be shared in."[25] To put it differently, theological faith conduces to beatific fellowship with God, inchoatively here and now in the Church of faith and sacraments and definitively hereafter in the company of the blessed Virgin Mary and all the saints. St. Augustine underscores the same truth when he remarks, "We may go on speaking figuratively of honey, gold, or wine—but whatever we say we cannot express the reality we are to receive. The name of that reality is God. But who will claim that in that one syllable we utter the full expanse of our heart's desire?"[26]

The Letter to the Hebrews calls faith the evidence or argument for things unseen. But we know that the evidence of faith really belongs to the person who firmly adheres to First Truth-in-Being, namely, faith's formal terminative object, for no other argument or evidence is available or possible for God's truth than God himself. This means that the believer must learn to abide the obscurity that inescapably envelops those who undertake the journey of faith. Living the theological life entails facing darkness. Or we can borrow another metaphor from the fourteenth-century Dominican preacher and mystic John Tauler, who talks frequently in his sermons and elsewhere about the "nakedness of faith."[27] In the life of the Church, centered around the blessed Eucharist and fraternal charity, the dynamics of faith gently wrest the soul away from its native preference for its own measure of cognitive certitude, and they urge upon the believer a tranquil assent to divine truth on the sole basis of the divine truthfulness. Because it so manifestly offers neither argument nor evidence for the mystery that it is, the holy Eucharist itself serves as the preeminent sacrament of faith in the Church. For in the Eucharist we receive the body and blood of Christ under the sacramental signs of bread and wine, and so are drawn into his relationship with the Father (see John 6:44).

Faith remains, therefore, in some sense "light" and in some sense

25. *Scripta super libros Sententiarum* III, d. 23, q. 2, a. 1.

26. St. Augustine, *Tractates on the First Letter of John* 4 (PL 35, 2008–2009), trans. International Committee on English in the Liturgy in *The Liturgy of the Hours*, vol. 3 (New York: Catholic Book Publishing Company, 1975), p. 221.

27. See especially his sermons and also the compendium of thought his followers composed, the *Institutiones*.

"darkness."[28] In a certain way, the chiaroscuro technique developed by the artists of the Baroque period, both in Protestant Holland and in Catholic Italy, visually reflects the true character of Christian belief. The definition of faith culled from the text of Hebrews 11 strives to articulate this reality in a thematic way. In the scholastic exegesis, "substance" refers to faith's end term, the shining glory of eternal life, and "evidence" to faith's distinctively nonevidential way of knowing, which overcomes the darkness of concepts and propositions used to communicate First Truth.[29]

The Augustinian school developed its model of faith within an illuminationist epistemology, which fundamentally conceives human intelligence as a receptacle for truths that filter into it from one or a series of superior intelligences. For this reason, the standard Augustinian teaching on faith accepts as axiomatic certain perspectives about the psychology of Christian belief, for example, that the human mind remains essentially passive in the reception of divine truth. Adherents of this particular view of faith are therefore constrained to speak as if the rational appetite or will serves as the effective source of all human subjectivity and, therefore, as the psychological capacity in which the virtue of faith resides. In his *De praedestinatione sanctorum*, St. Augustine actually affirmed that "faith has its place in the will of the believer."[30] Aquinas's Aristotelian psychology provided him, on the other hand, with a deep appreciation of how intelligence always interacts with appetite whenever it is a case of producing authentic human action. As a result of this realist epistemological perspective, the common theological tradition came to recognize that the virtue of faith in fact pertains to the intellect.[31] To be sure, the synergy of intellect and will requires a right

28. See the Second Vatican Council's Dogmatic Constitution, *Lumen gentium*, chap. 1, no. 8: The Church "reveals [Christ's] mystery faithfully in the world—albeit amid shadows—until in the end it will be made manifest in the fullness of light."

29. See St. John of the Cross, *The Ascent of Mount Carmel*, Bk. 2, chap. 8, and *The Dark Night*, Bk. 2, chap. 2.

30. See chap. 5 (PL 44, 968).

31. See *Catechism of the Catholic Church*, no. 155, which quotes *Summa theologiae* IIa-IIae q. 2, art. 9: "Believing is an act of the intellect assenting to the divine truth by command of the will moved by God through grace." During the first half of the twentieth century, this position was strongly defended by the Thomists, who reacted to the claims of some Modernist theologians that the assent of faith can be accounted for on the basis of the natural tendency of the will for a transcendent good. For one example of the Thomist

disposition in both capacities of the human soul, for "it is not enough that the will be ready to obey, but the mind also must be rightly disposed to yield to the will's command."[32] But even though the intellect is moved to give its assent to divine truths under the impulse of the will, theological faith—as a distinctive *habitus* in the human person—shapes principally the mind of the believer.

Faith and the Religious Affect of Credence

During the first half of the sixth century, an important theological discussion took place on the hills overlooking the Rhone River valley in south central France. In a series of 25 *capitula* or canons that the Roman Pontiff Boniface II subsequently confirmed in 531, the Second Council of Orange (529) restated the significant points of St. Augustine's case against the Pelagian misconstruals of how divine grace envelops human nature. These canons, especially nos. 5, 6, and 7, determine certain features of the Church's understanding of the act of faith. They emphatically set forth as authentic Church teaching that theological faith develops in us only through a movement of divine grace, which initiates the beginning of faith and perdures throughout its development as a virtue. Canon 5 particularly underscores that "the beginning of faith and [the] affect of credence" depend on a gift of divine grace.[33] In other terms, human resources alone cannot "jumpstart" belief, though, as a necessary condition for its coming to be, faith always requires a genuinely free human act. The Council identifies this act as the "affect of

---

presentation of faith as cognitive, see Pietro Parente, "De munere rationis naturalis in actu fidei eliciendo," *Doctor Communis* 3 (1950): 10–21. For a brief overview of the period, see Avery Dulles's chapter on the "Early Twentieth Century" in *Assurance*, pp. 96–115.

32. See *Summa theologiae* IIa-IIae q. 4, a. 2, ad 2. However, in the presentation to the human mind of those things that are to be believed, God uses the instrumentality of other intelligent beings, for example, through various preachers of the word, but "primarily by the angels through whom the divine mysteries are revealed to us." See *Summa theologiae* Ia q. 111, a. 1, ad 1.

33. Canon 5: "Si quis, sicut augmentum, ita etiam initium fidei ipsumque credulitatis affectum, quo in eum credimus, qui iustificat impium, et ad [re]generationem sacri baptismatis pervenimus, non per gratiae donum, id est per inspirationem Spiritus Sancti corrigentem *voluntatem nostram* ab infideltiate ad fidem, ab impietate ad pietatem, sed naturaliter nobis inesse dicit . . ." (*DS* 375) [emphasis added]. The substance of this canon reflects the teaching that St. Augustine sets forth in his *De praedestinatione Sanctorum* (PL 44, 959–992).

credence." Even though this initial will-act does not result in the grace of justification, this first movement of the will toward belief depends on divine help, which theological usage identifies as an actual grace.[34]

In the course of subsequent discussions, teachers of Catholic doctrine sought to explain how the first affective movement of faith causally belongs to the supernatural order. This kind of will-act is not proportionate to our human resources, so it must proceed from "the inspiration of the Holy Spirit moving our will from infidelity to faith."[35] The synergy of human knowing and reliance on God's truthfulness remains so fundamental to the structure of belief that, even without the full weight of theological charity, some explanation is required to account for the fact that human appetite seeks those "things which appear not." Since it is a seeking that leads to salvation, even this leaning depends on the gratuity of God's mercy. In the nineteenth century, the First Vatican Council again took up this theme of Catholic doctrine: "And so faith in itself, even though it may not work through charity, is a gift of God, and its operation is a work belonging to the order of salvation, in that a person yields true obedience to God himself when he accepts and collaborates with God's grace which he could have rejected."[36] What Jesus says of Peter's confession holds true for every act of belief: "flesh and blood has not revealed this to you, but my Father in heaven" (Matt. 16:17). For even a "dead" faith—a faith "unformed" by the fullness of charity—requires an appetitive movement of the soul that reflects the workings of divine providence. Without divine charity, however, unformed faith cannot assure the obedience of faith which is the salvation of the Christian's soul. Thus even a believer, if he or she does not allow the gift of faith to "work through love," can fail to achieve the final goal of eternal life.

Christian theology takes seriously the intellectual content of divine faith and the sanctification of the intellect that the *habitus* of faith accomplishes. But Christian belief never amounts merely to a cool com-

---

34. See *Summa theologiae* IIa-IIae q. 4, a. 7 ad 5: "An act of the will is prerequisite for faith, but not an act of the will informed by charity. But this kind of act presupposes faith, since the will cannot tend to God with complete love unless the understanding has right faith about him."
35. The Council of Orange, Canon 5 (DS 375).
36. *Dei Filius*, chap. 3. (DS 3010).

munication of abstract verities. First Truth makes theological faith a distinct virtue, but God does not address his people simply by imparting information for the human mind to assimilate. The seventh-century Greek theologian and mystical writer Maximus the Confessor alludes to the integral nature of the Christian life when he relates the virtue of faith to the practice of the other virtues: "By itself faith accomplishes nothing. For even the devils believe and shudder. No, faith must be joined to an active love of God which is expressed in good works. The charitable person is distinguished by sincere and long-suffering service to other people; faith also means using things aright."[37] The Scriptures witness abundantly to God's wise creativity in drawing the human race to its authentic end. Theological faith initiates the work of salvation. But since faith belongs to the whole person, the divine gift by its very nature makes a person crave the perfection that only theological charity can impart. For only faith "formed" by charity realizes the goal of "faith working through love" (Gal. 5:6). Aquinas sums it up this way: "And so charity is called the form of faith, inasmuch as the act of faith is completed and formed by charity."[38] But as a particular kind of action, belief remains specified by its formal object, God as First Truth.

Catholic teaching states that the initial act of belief as an effective assent to God's word depends on a movement of divine grace, though in the adult this initial grace does not equal the full infusion of habitual or sanctifying grace that charity alone produces. In the adult convert, there is a logical sequence of steps whereby the virtue of faith attains the perfection of formed faith. As an analysis of the first step, Aquinas offers the following evaluation:

> The act of faith consists essentially in knowledge, and its perfection as to *form* or species is there, as is clear from its object. . . . But as to *end*, faith is perfected in the affective [part of the soul], inasmuch as the will determines the intellect to assent to those things which are of faith. But this willing is not an act either of charity or of hope, but a certain desire for the promised good.[39]

---

37. Maximus the Confessor (c. 580–662), "The Chapters on Charity," *Centuria* 1, chap. 1, 30- 40 (PG 90: 962–967), trans. International Committee on English in the Liturgy in *The Liturgy of the Hours*, vol. 3 (New York: Catholic Book Publishing Company, 1975), p. 230.

38. See his discussion in *Summa theologiae* IIa-IIae q. 4, a. 3.

39. *Quaestiones disputatae de veritate*, q. 14, a. 2, ad 10.

Catholic theologians, following the Council of Orange, have come to call this initial movement of the appetite for a "promised good" the *pius credulitatis affectus*, which we will translate as the religious affect of credence. The fundamental difference between the *pius credulitatis affectus* and the full movement of assent informed by charity lies in what causes the will to assent. The affect of credence commands the intellect to assent judgmentally to the truth of God's promises only on the basis of the *human good* contained in the divine promises, or as Aquinas phrases it, "a certain desire for the promised good." This happens, for example, when someone recognizes the human value in the promise of divine forgiveness or discovers the happiness that belonging to a communion of holy persons brings. But while the affect of credence in itself is sufficient to carry on intellectual assent, it cannot move the person to make a full self-commitment to what remains beyond the reach of his or her natural capacities.[40] God communicates his fully personal love to us only in the bestowal of theological charity. The movement of divine grace alone can ensure that a believer enters into the life-giving mysteries of faith. From that moment, the mysteries, as the articles of faith represent them, begin to shape the character of the one who believes.

Unformed Faith

As a result of the semi-Pelagian controversies that first took shape in response to the writings of the fifth-century French monk Cassian (c. 420), the Church was forced to clarify the distinction between the initial moments of belief and fully formed faith. In the sixth century, proponents of a compromise version of Pelagian naturalism contended that the initial movement of faith must lie within the powers of our human resources. Otherwise, they argued, there would be no grounds for assigning merit to the act of faith. In response to this specious claim, Caesarius of Arles (c. 470–542), who represented the ecclesiastical authority at the Second Council of Orange, maintained the Catholic view. Claiming the authority of the Apostle Paul, "What do you have that you did not receive?" (1 Cor. 4:7), Caesarius unwaveringly insisted that

---

40. Again, see *Summa theologiae* IIa-IIae q. 4, a. 7, ad 5: "An act of the will is prerequisite for faith, but not an act of the will informed by charity."

the first movement toward belief occurs as the result of supernatural grace.[41]

Throughout the history of the Church, versions of the semi-Pelagian reductionist argument have continued to reemerge under various guises. For example, in the seventeenth-century controversies concerning grace and freedom, some theologians contended that a person of good will can rationally establish the *motive* for rousing the initial yearning of faith. Today theologians sometimes speculate about a "response in faith," as if our initial self-commitment to God first of all consists in a deliberate decision on the part of the creature to enter into a beneficiary relationship with a Supreme Being. What is worse, preachers often gratuitously adopt this language as a way of encouraging their listeners to heed the Gospel message and to draw closer to God. Such theological and homiletic portrayals of faith unfortunately come close to compromising the utter gratuity of God's saving initiative in history. Moreover, because they introduce human motives into the act of belief, the same notions easily denigrate the genuinely theological character of divine faith. But there are even more serious consequences, for, to the extent that a person attempts to put such maxims into practice, much discouragement and disillusionment can result; as Jesus himself assures us, "No one can receive anything except what has been given from heaven" (John 3:27).

The Letter of James states in plain words: "Even the demons believe—and shudder" (James 2:19). To be sure, the demons do not assent because they are the beneficiaries of divine grace; rather they recognize the truth of divine revelation because of the acumen of their intuitive intelligences. For as Aquinas astutely observes, "They see many clear signs on the basis of which they perceive that the Church's teaching is from God."[42] Furthermore, since not even an angelic intellect can comprehend the causes of divine Truth, the demons themselves give the assent that lies at the heart of believing. They are, in other words, stirred to some form of affective credence. Sadly however, this

---

41. See *DS* 396, 397.

42. See *Summa theologiae* IIa-IIae q. 5, a. 2. The question is posed to theologians by the text from James 2:19: "Even the demons believe—and shudder."

credence only contributes further to the demons' torment. Why? Because the demons, whose wills are settled in a posture of hateful aversion from God, still perceive the truths that God reveals and, compelled by the power of their natural intelligence, are persuaded to assent to them.[43] So they abide in the paradox of sin, being drawn toward what they despise.

The example of the demons' predicament graphically illustrates the psychological torment that can accompany unformed faith. Their experience remains a salutary lesson for the Church. There are persons who recognize the goodness contained in the announcement of God's truth, but at the same time, on account of their state of sinful alienation from God, instead of singing about the mercies of the Lord, rail against them. As long as any believer is unrepentant of some serious sin, he or she experiences this state of internal alienation, a sort of spiritual schizophrenia. For such a person remains compelled to despise what he or she knows to be true, even the very saving truth that effectively heals the self-destructiveness of sin. In the case of the human creature, however, the powers of discursive intelligence allow for the possibility of conversion and the subsequent reordering of the affective powers—a circumstance that the psychological structure of intuitive cognition excludes for angelic spirits.

It is important to emphasize that even the person in a state of serious sin can still comprehend with genuine faith what First Truth communicates as necessary for salvation. Thus Aquinas holds the view that such unformed faith is "perfect with the kind of completeness sufficient to preserve the meaning of faith."[44] However, unformed faith seeks only representations of the promised good and not the full communication of divine Goodness itself. This means that the truths accepted but not fully loved remain practically inefficacious for salvation until such time as the sinner, moved by a sheerly operative grace, embraces divine Truth under the full weight of theological charity.

---

43. See *Summa theologiae* IIa-IIae q. 5, a. 2. The angelic mind can intuit the congruity of divine truth, but this cannot happen in the human person. Thus, Aquinas holds that "to believe is said equivocally of the Christian faithful and of demons" (*De veritate* q. 14, a. 9, ad 4). John of St. Thomas further explains that this affective movement is required in the demons, for otherwise their intellects would remain in a state of suspense—"*ne intellectus maneat suspensus.*"

44. *Summa theologiae* IIa-IIae q. 6, a. 2, ad 1.

Though every sinner must await from God the grace of conversion and repentance, the sinner who retains an unformed faith enjoys a better advantage for conversion than does a person who has outrightly rejected an article of faith. For example, consider the article of faith that the sacrament of reconciliation offers the ordinary means for the forgiveness of mortal sins committed after baptism. The person who assents to this truth with unformed faith remains better disposed to receive the grace of justification than the person who does not believe that Christ himself—in the human person of the priest—stands ready to welcome personally the contrite sinner. Here it should be noted that there is a difference between the person whose lack of faith is the result of unintentional ignorance and the person who consciously puts obstacles in the way of giving assent to divine truths. To oppose with one's will the traits of faith—whether they be about dogmatic matters, such as the Petrine office or the Marian doctrines, or about morals, such as the Church's social doctrine or teachings about human life, marriage, and family—creates a particularly grave situation. For now the sinner gradually becomes hardened and even rebellious toward accepting certain articles of faith as authentic expressions of what God has revealed for our salvation. This leaves the person who abides outside of the communication of both divine charity and faith less disposed to conversion. "The faith that justifies is no mere historical knowledge," Luther observed, "but the firm acceptance of God's offer promising forgiveness of sins and justification."[45] Although, as we have already noted, Luther misconstrued the character of theological faith, nevertheless his assertion here remains true, inasmuch as disbelief works effectively against the disposition to receive saving forgiveness. The medieval theologians sought to expound this same point when they associated the New Testament blasphemy against the Holy Spirit (see Matt. 12:31) with this kind of obstinate disbelief.[46]

There are many incidents in the New Testament that identify belief with the reception of salvation, as when Jesus comforts a person with the words that "your faith has made you well" (Matt. 9:22). But the canonical Scriptures also offer examples of something that approaches

---

45. See the *Apology of the Augsburg Confession* 4, 48, composed by Philipp Melanchthon.
46. *Summa theologiae* IIa-IIae q. 14, aa. 1–4.

what we have called unformed faith, when they mention people who intellectually seize divine truth "from hearing" the word of God, but then stop short before embracing the divine truth in full love. For some biblical personages, such as Nicodemus (John 3:1–21) and Zacchaeus (Luke 19:1–10), this initial seizure of truth apparently opens up the way of salvation, but for others, like King Herod, who was anxious to see Jesus work a miracle (Luke 23:8), or the men of the Areopagus, who circumvented St. Paul by telling him that they would hear him about Christ "on another occasion" (Acts 17:32), the same interest fails to bear fruit. For reasons hidden in the mysterious interface between divine providence and human freedom, this initial contact with the preached Word of God can fail to achieve the purpose that the New Testament announces as God's purpose for all men and women: "For this is the will of God, your sanctification" (1 Thess. 4:3).

In the course of the Reformation polemics on faith and justification, the Church had to give explicit attention to the question of unformed or dead faith. Responding to the simple alternatives of the Reformers, the Council of Trent anathematizes the views that "when grace is lost by sin, faith too is always lost; or the faith that remains is not true faith, even if it is not a living faith (see James 2:26); or that one who has faith without charity is not a Christian."[47] Even though Aquinas in one place remarks that "unformed faith is not a virtue," this Tridentine pronouncement conforms to the substance of his doctrine on faith.[48] For when Aquinas says that unformed faith is not a virtue, he means simply that "dead" faith, lacking the indwelling grace of the Holy Spirit that characterizes formed faith, does not possess the stability and perfection that the complete notion of a virtuous *habitus* requires. Nevertheless, unformed faith maintains the basic structure of a *habitus,* for by it the person who believes still gives assent to authentic divine truth. Moreover, this unformed faith provides a foundation for conversion and repentance that simply does not exist among those who either have never known that God freely forgives the sins of those who trust in his mercy, or who have stopped believing that the forgiveness of sins belongs to

---

47. The Council of Trent, Session 6 (13 January 1547), "Decree on Justification" (*DS* 1578; see also 1544).
48. *Summa theologiae* IIa-IIae q. 4, a. 5.

the spiritual patrimony of the Church. Therefore, those charged with the responsibility of teaching the faith ought to conserve the truths of the Catholic religion through good catechetical instruction, even in profoundly secularized cultures where the living practice of Christianity is widely rejected, and where the majority of believers habitually fail in their personal commitment to the faith. The tenuous attachment to divine truth represented by unformed faith is better than none at all; it ensures that the human mind remains the sort of arable land in which the seed of God's grace can take root.

Even if it falls radically short of perfecting the whole person with respect to eternal life, unformed faith represents a true excellence of the human intellect.[49] As a quality of the human mind, this *habitus*, albeit an imperfect one, still serves a highly useful purpose in sustaining the Christian life during periods of spiritual crisis and moral lapse. In other words, even the sinner needs to "remember the mercies of the past" and to hear again about the wonderful works of God. The Council of Trent affirms this Catholic intuition when it insists on the legitimacy of calling those Christians who possess only unformed faith. Such persons, in some sense, comprehend the truth about God and the divine mysteries of the Trinity, of the Incarnation, even of the entire sacramental economy of salvation, and this knowledge serves them in a way that eludes one who knows no saving truth about God. While relatively complete as to its own species, namely, as a virtue of the intellect, unformed faith engenders a spiritual gnawing in the person. For unformed faith characterizes the person with a divided heart, one who does not love completely what he or she knows to be true. For some people, the half-heartedness leads them to reject faith, to commit the sin of formal disbelief or infidelity.[50] But in the case of other persons, such as the venerable

49. See *Summa theologiae* IIa-IIae q. 4, a. 5 ad 1: "Truth is the good of the intellect, for it constitutes its perfection. Insofar, then, as the mind is settled upon truth through faith, faith has one sort of good as its end. Further than this, however, faith, insofar as it is informed by charity, has as its end the good that is the object of the will."

50. See *Summa theologiae* IIa-IIae q. 10, a. 3, where Aquinas declares that infidelity ranks foremost in the "perversion of morals." Although the other anti-theological vices wreak even greater harm in the spiritual life of the believer, disbelief undercuts the foundation of the Christian life, for as a result of this sin one "has no true knowledge about God." Timothy McDermott, *Summa Theologiae. A Concise Translation* (Westminster, MD: Christian Classics, 1989) supplies this helpful résumé of q. 10, a. 1: "Disbelief in the strict

Charles de Foucauld or the French poet and dramatist Paul Claudel, retaining the memory of divine truth about the heavenly Father, the Savior Jesus Christ, the Church and the communion of saints, the sacraments and the Church's sacramental piety can lead to the sort of full conversion experience that turns the nominal believer into an ardent Christian, and even a saint.

Summary

The notion of virtue implies a quasi-permanent resource or basis for activity; thus, even on the natural level, a person requires virtues in order to perform well the actions necessary for human existence. Strictly speaking, there are no counterparts for the theological virtues in the natural order, whereas there are acquired moral virtues. Since the theological virtues unite us immediately to God, these infused virtues come only from God. Justification establishes cooperation between God's grace and man's freedom. So even though theological faith is infused into us by God, it initiates a genuinely human project within the sphere of personal self-commitment.

Aquinas establishes the true virtuousness of faith on the grounds that faith ensures that a person achieves the supernatural goal to which human life is ordained: "Since believing is the act of the understanding assenting under the will's command, two things are required for completing this act. One is that the understanding infallibly tend to its good, which is the truth; the other is that it infallibly be ordered to the last end, because of which the will assents."[51] Christian belief directly touches the most important elements of human life, as we read in 1 John: "Who is it that conquers the world but the one who believes that

---

sense is an opposition to faith, resisting it and even despising listening to it; so it is a sin. But disbelief as sheer absence of belief because we haven't heard about it is not so much a sin as a penalty consequent on Adam's sin. And if men who lack faith in this sense are lost, that is because of other sins that cannot be forgiven without faith, rather than because their disbelief is sinful."

51. *Summa theologiae* IIa-IIae q. 4, a. 5: "Cum enim credere sit actus intellectus assentientis vero ex imperio voluntatis, ad hoc quod iste actus sit perfectus duo requiruntur. Quorum unum est ut infallibiliter intellectus tendat in suum bonum, quod est verum; aliud autem est ut infallibiliter ordinetur ad ultimum finem, propter quem voluntas assentit vero." This translation comes from Jordan, *Faith*, p. 114.

Jesus is the Son of God?" (1 John 5:4–5). And Aquinas expands: "Not only is the *habitus* of virtue and grace given to us, but we are renewed inwardly by the Holy Spirit with regard to acting rightly."[52] Because those without faith are bereft of the interior consolation that the Holy Spirit bestows, the Church encourages missionary efforts against every form of nonbelief. The infidelity that marks the person who is in contrary opposition to faith provides the strongest challenge. Here, as Thomas Gilby explains, "a distinction may be drawn between unbelief and disbelief, respectively a lack of assent and a dissent, or a refusal to accept and a rejection of what should be believed."[53] As a product of the Enlightenment, modernity unfortunately relegates the Christian faith to one among the several religious options available to choosing selves. But since the virtue of faith is the beginning of eternal life, the vicious *habitus* that incline a person away from faith constitute a grave threat to the happiness of the human person, both here and now and for all eternity.

The importance of maintaining a complete knowledge of the Highest Truth points up the tragic dimensions of one form of unfaithfulness, the *infidelitas* of heresy. Heretics choose not the things that are truly handed down by Christ but the things that their own minds suggest to them.[54] In other words, the heretic chooses not what the Church proposes for belief but whatever suits an individual's estimate, sentiment, wish, and sometimes even imagination. The hubris of the heretic leads not only to a relativization of the articles of faith but also to an enormous miscalculation about what constitutes the good and beatific life. Indeed, the heretic forgoes the authentic renewal of spirit that the Holy Spirit promises to those who abide in the Church of Christ, in Christian communion. In addition to heresy, the sins against the virtue of faith include apostasy and blasphemy. Apostasy, Aquinas tells us, "implies a retreating from God."[55] As a species of unfaithfulness or infidelity, apostasy adds the additional note of falling away from the faith in a public man-

---

52. See *In Ephesios*, chap. 2, lect. 3.
53. Thomas Gilby, O.P. *Consequences of Faith*, vol. 32 (New York: McGraw-Hill Book Company, 1975), pp. 38–39, note a.
54. See *Summa theologiae* IIa-IIae q. 11, a. 1.
55. *Summa theologiae* IIa-IIae q. 12, a. 1.

ner, and so the Church regards apostates as guilty of a spiritual treachery. Blasphemy embodies "a kind of detracting from the divine good."[56] As a sin against faith's inward act of belief, blasphemy of the heart remains within a person, but when the blasphemy breaks forth into speech, then the sin is opposed to the outward act of confession.

Because faith consists in the "substance of things hoped for," it comes first among the theological and infused moral virtues in the pattern of priority. "Since in things that can be done the end is the principle," says Aquinas, "it is necessary that the theological virtues, of which the object is the last end, be prior to the other virtues."[57] For the one who understands that an end must first be present in the human mind before the will can move toward it, there is no difficulty in recognizing that theological faith forms the first sure moment in the life of a person on the way to beatitude. Other human virtues, however, can dispose a person to make an act of faith. For example, fortitude can take away a fear that inhibits belief, or humility can temper an intellectual arrogance that resists submission to the truth. The acquired virtues do not concretely express the Christian life, since they lack the grounding in divine charity that would make them virtues in the complete and perfect sense of the term. Only theological charity perfects human life, and so it remains, simply speaking, the most excellent of the theological virtues. Moreover, the fact that certain virtues can dispose one to make an act of faith does not imply that a purely rational "motive" for believing God is possible. What Christ reveals to us about the blessed life of the Three-Personed God surpasses the capacity of the human mind to investigate and disclose.[58] In the final analysis, the holy person teaches us best about what it means to possess the *habitus* of theological faith. Nicholas of Flüe, the fifteenth-century Swiss who spent the last nine-

---

56. *Summa theologiae* IIa-IIae q. 13, a. 1.

57. *Summa theologiae* IIa-IIae q. 4, a. 7. Again, T. C. O'Brien, *Faith*, p. 142, note h, provides a helpful commentary: "In the final act of an adult's complete conversion from non-belief and sin to belief and grace, the infusion of grace, including charity, and the active turning to God in belief and love are simultaneous; yet there is a pattern of priority in meaning among the various elements—thus knowing before loving."

58. To affirm that we believe God's Speaking ("*credere Deum*") because we believe God as First Truth-Speaking ("*credere Deo*") does not make for a circular argument. As we pointed out in chapter one, Aquinas holds that the real motive for belief is at once the object of belief, namely the First Truth.

teen years of his life in prayer and contemplation, encouraged those who sought his advice: "Believe in God with all your might, for hope rests on faith, love on hope, and victory on love; the reward will follow victory, the crown of life the reward, but the crown is the essence of things eternal."[59]

What Draws a Person to Believe the Gospel Preaching

The tradition of the Church clearly witnesses to the truth that, even in its initial moments, the *habitus* of theological faith is a free and gracious gift that the person who hears the preaching of the Gospel receives from God. Moreover, theological reflection can identify—at least in a general, schematic fashion—the various stages of the process whereby men and women come to believe in Jesus Christ. Such a scheme, of course, simply provides a kind of grid upon which to map out concrete conversion experiences; it is not meant to substitute for the personal stories of each believer. God demonstrates remarkable ingenuity in the ways in which he calls people to faith. No theological analysis can capture the mystery of how a person comes to believe. Nevertheless, to put conceptual clarity and simplicity in a theology of conversion can shed light on the dynamics of grace that underlie the diverse historical circumstances of those who come to believe.[60] Indeed, some conceptualization of the steps in conversion is surely desirable, for as Kenneth Schmitz explains, "Conceptualization issuing in judgment and insight permits us to re-situate the concrete particularities and the historical situation within a larger horizon of understanding and of discourse."[61] The conceptualization of conversion and justification that Christian theology develops centers on the interplay of human intelligence and will in response to a twofold grace: first, the external preaching of the Gospel

59. Cited by Jill Haak Adels in *The Wisdom of the Saints. An Anthology* (Oxford: Oxford University Press, 1987), p. 49.

60. Certainly, specific expressions of religious experience, especially in the forms of narrative and personal witness, contribute significantly to the theologian's appreciation of the ordinary ways that divine providence works in drawing people to faith. But however important the personal testimonies of believers may prove to be, a truly theological account of Christian conversion needs to attain some measure of universal understanding of the discreet moments involved in justification.

61. Schmitz, "Experience," p. 14.

and, second, the internal instinct *(instinctus)* of divine grace, which moves a person to adhere fully to First Truth.

In theological idiom, to inquire into the causes of faith means to examine the efficient causes of faith's coming-to-be in the human person. In the course of his commentary on the vocational call that Christ extends to Matthew the tax collector, the eighth-century English doctor Bede the Venerable grasps the essential elements that lie at the heart of conversion. We should not wonder, says Bede, that Matthew, upon hearing the words of the Lord, left his secular occupation and immediately joined the ranks of the disciples:

> For that Lord who called him by a word from outside also taught him within by an invisible instinct [*instinctu*] that he should follow him, infusing his mind with the light of a spiritual grace by which he would understand that the one who called him from temporal concerns on earth was able to bestow on him an incorruptible treasure in heaven.[62]

St. Bede pictures Christ himself as drawing Matthew to the "incorruptible treasure in heaven," which, in the terms of the present discussion, symbolizes the faith's formal specifying object, or God as First Truth. In the biblical narrative, Christ himself embodies both the principal and the instrumental cause of Matthew's conversion. As a human being, Christ can speak the human words that bid the tax collector to come follow him; and as God, Christ can supply the interior instruction and grace that effectively make of Matthew a true disciple.

In the life of the Church, the ordinary instrumental causes operative in the call to faith are other human persons who themselves are joined to Christ by faith and the sacraments. But these instruments who speak the external word of proclamation and invitation cannot themselves provide the interior movement of grace. Only God can provide the grace that effectively moves a person to assent. On this point, Aquinas accepts the Gospel words at their face value: "Everything that the Father gives me will come to me, and anyone who comes to me I will never drive

---

62. Bede, *Homelia* 21 *in quadragesima* (Matth. ix, 9–13): "Ipse enim dominus qui eum foris uerbo uocauit intus inuisibili instinctu ut sequeretur edocuit infundens menti illius lumen gratiae spiritalis qua intellegeret quia is qui a temporalibus auocabat in terris incorruptibiles in caelis dare thesauros ualeret." *Corpus Christianorum Series Latina* vol. 122 (Turnhout: Brepols, 1955), p. 150, 71–75.

away" (John 6:37). And in his gloss on this verse from the Gospel of John, Aquinas writes:

> It might perhaps be objected that it does not follow necessarily that anyone will use God's gift, for many receive the gift of God who do not use it. How can he say, then, 'All that the Father gives to me shall come to me?' To reply: this giving means not only the *habitus*, faith and the like, but also an inner instinct [*instinctus*] to believe. Whatever works toward salvation is entirely of God's giving.[63]

Because faith inaugurates the theological life by establishing a personal relationship between God and the creature, only God can account for such an effect. Likewise, the free response of the justified person can arise only from God's moving the person to make that response within the context of the full Christian life. Again we are reminded of Thérèse of Lisieux's signature expression, "Tout est grâce!"—Everything is grace!

According to the plan of divine providence, a series of diverse agents can work together to bring a person to the assent of faith. The theological tradition, as in Bede's commentary on Matthew's conversion, recognizes these agents as efficient causes and further distinguishes them as either principal or instrumental causes.[64] In other words, God uses various intermediaries in bringing faith into the world. Of course, the one mediator who makes the entire process possible and upon whom all other instruments depend is the incarnate Word, our Lord and Savior Jesus Christ. The Second Vatican Council recognizes that the Incarnation governs the series of other mediators through whom God communicates faith to the world:

> He sent his Son, the eternal Word who enlightens all humankind, to live among them and to tell them about the inner life of God (see John 1:1–18). Thus it is

---

63. *In Johannem* chap. 6, lect. 4.

64. The general principle of efficient causality states that all contingent beings require an efficient cause for their existence, their continuance in existence, and any real, as distinguished from purely rational, changes that occur in them; this cause, moreover, remains really distinct from the contingent being that is its effect, for otherwise the world would be afloat in contingency. Furthermore, in order to complete the investigation in the line of efficient causality, the theologian must look at both the principal cause and the instrumental causes at work in producing any effect, such as causing a person to come to belief. Since formal causality specifies the kind of act that the believer exercises, the line of enquiry into efficient causality differs entirely from asking about the formal cause of faith.

that Jesus Christ, the Word made flesh, sent as a human being among humans, "speaks the words of God" (John 3:34) and accomplishes the work of salvation which the Father gave him to do (see John 5:36; 17:4).[65]

For the historical proposal of what is to be believed, the principal agents of the divine action in the world denote the subjects of revelation, namely, the prophets, who "prepared the way for the Gospel," and the apostles, who "handed on by their own preaching and examples and by their dispositions whatever they had received from Christ."[66]

The preaching Church continues her apostolic mission through her official preachers, namely the bishops, whom the apostles left behind as their successors, "handing on their own teaching function to them."[67] While the sole efficient cause of belief remains God himself, God provides, through the life and preaching of the Church, a whole series of dispositive efficient causes that render the person more suited to hearing the revealed message of salvation. To speak of persons as dispositive causes may appear to slight the particular human qualities that distinguish one person from another, but the opposite is actually true, for the notion of causality in this context simply means that God instrumentally uses everything that is human in order to achieve a result that surpasses the abilities that any single person possesses. The personalities of the saints are causes of grace, which is why we read their lives. All believers belong to the one causal order of divine instruction that leads to faith; as instruments of God, they share in the power of God himself.

In the case of the adult who has had no previous encounter with the preaching of the Gospel, we can envision, for purposes of analytical clarity, a sequence of events as descriptive of the movement from unbelief to fully formed faith. These acts may occur simultaneously in time, so that any priority suggested in listing them sequentially reflects an ontological pattern—the natural priority that a cause enjoys over its effect in any series of causing.

Both the prominent and the less-celebrated conversion stories illustrate that God provides a variety of preparations for justification, which in diverse ways dispose an individual to listen seriously to an announce-

---

65. The Dogmatic Constitution on Divine Revelation, *Dei verbum*, chap. 1, no. 4.

66. See *Dei verbum*, chap. 1, no. 3 & chap. 2, no. 7.

67. *Dei verbum*, chap. 2, no. 8, refers to Irenaeus of Lyons, *Adversus Haereses*, Bk. 3, chap. 3, no. 1.

ment of the Good News. One of the most common dispositions arises from a personal recognition of the disorder of sin. Openness to God's forgiveness can emerge with the recognition that one's own sinfulness entails an element of self-destructiveness that affects one's life, either as an individual or as a member of society. Theologians call this the experience of attrition. Consider the hypocrite—the man who habitually misrepresents himself and his true status in life to those whom he encounters in the course of his normal routine. Such habitual dissimulation effectively impedes this man from developing authentic interpersonal relations. But there comes a time when the subdolous man realizes to what extent this practice spells unhappiness for himself and for those who would seek to establish the bonds of true friendship with him. To the extent that this realization unfolds, the dissimulating man should come to recognize his need for forgiveness and to experience the ordinary human need for honest interpersonal relationships. The only alternative to receiving such a grace and instruction is to remain isolated from himself and others, absorbed in self-pity and suffused with unhappiness. But with a true experience of attrition, such a person is readied for the call of faith.

Take another example. A disposition for Christian belief can develop as well from positive experiences, for example, through learning, and especially through the pursuit of philosophical studies. Again, consider the woman who as a result of higher studies in philosophy or even other disciplines, such as history or medieval studies, comes to recognize intellectually the limits inherent in all rational endeavors. The twentieth-century Carmelite Blessed Edith Stein provides a good example. Even though she enjoyed the company of some of the leading intellectual figures of her age, she reached the conclusion that philosophical learning can provide only a limited fulfillment for the human person. In the designs of divine providence, reading the biography of the sixteenth-century Carmelite reformer St. Teresa of Jesus inspired the highly intellectual Edith Stein to forgo her secular pursuits and, in personal imitation of the saint, to seek a life of contemplative dedication where she would ponder the mysteries of the faith. The name she received upon entering the convent, Sr. Teresa Benedicta of the Cross, augured the sufferings that she would undergo in the course of remaining faithful to her vocation during an extraordinarily complex period of twentieth-century European history. Edith Stein died in a concentration camp during the Second World War.

The actual preaching of the Gospel inaugurates the process of justification. The spiritual biography of St. Augustine supplies the classic example of God using the most ordinary of circumstances to draw a person toward conversion. At a certain point in his life, Augustine began to experience attrition, which he describes with great sensitivity: "But when deep reflection had dredged out of the secret recesses of my soul all my misery and heaped it up in full view of my heart, there arose a mighty storm, bringing with it a mighty downpour of tears."[68] Augustine then goes on to recount that shortly thereafter he heard "a voice like that of a boy or a girl . . . chanting and repeating over and over, 'Take up and read. Take up and read.'" With that, Augustine picked up the Letter to the Romans and opened to the text, "Put on the Lord Jesus Christ, and make no provisions for the flesh, to gratify its desires" (Rom. 13:14).[69] From this moment, Augustine grew steadily in his resolve to seek the sacrament of baptism. His new life in the Church, which brought him into the liturgical assemblies, would provoke a different sort of emotion, as he himself again testifies:

How greatly did I weep during hymns and canticles, keenly affected by the voices of your sweet-singing Church! Those voices flowed into my ears, and your truth was distilled into my heart, and from that truth holy emotions overflowed, and tears ran down, and amid those tears all was well with me.[70]

The personal testimony of Augustine offers a paradigm for all Christian conversion stories. We could outline the principal moments of conversion as follows.

The initial moment in the process of coming to faith involves hearing the Word of God. St. Paul specifies this starting point when he declares in the Letter to the Romans: "So faith comes from what is heard, and what is heard comes by the preaching of Christ" (Rom. 10:17). Basing himself upon the scriptural revelation, the preacher who acts in virtue of the Church's mandate to carry on the work of Christ exteriorly pre-

68. *Confessions*, Bk. 8, chap. 12 (28), trans. John K. Ryan (New York: Image Books, 1960).
69. *Confessions*, Bk. 8, chap. 12 (29).
70. *Confessions*, Bk. 9, chap. 6 (14).

sents God's offer of salvation. Theologians refer to this as the *auditus exterior*, the outward hearing with the ears, or the *testimonium exterius*, the outward witness. St. Paul implies the distinction between the outward preaching and hearing of the Gospel and the interior grace that produces the inner obedience of faith, noting that some hear the preached word but do not believe: "They have not all obeyed the Gospel; for Isaiah says, 'Lord, who has believed what he has heard from us?'" (Rom. 10:16).

The preacher makes an offer. Then, according to the natural structure and process of human cognition, this offer is apprehended by the intellect and presented to the will, though merely under the common aspect of the good. In other words, the hearer recognizes in the Church's preaching something desirable, but from a natural point of view. This could mean the consolation involved in the forgiveness of sins, the sense of security that comes with the promise of a permanent rule of justice and peace, or the human affection aroused by the announcement that God exercises a paternal regard over his children. In promises such as these, the dissimulator recognizes a way out of his personal predicament and the chance to develop honest communication. Or, the woman philosopher discovers a way to surpass the limitations of human thought and the fallibility present in all human judgments. Because the Gospel reflects the ultimate intelligibility that divine Truth possesses, the one who hears the Gospel preached can perceive in every article of faith something of a promised human good, though the actual reality of the supernatural mystery entirely surpasses this created good.

Then follows the will's act of choosing the good of God's promises. This act of choice exemplifies what theologians refer to technically as an *operans operatum*, that is, an action that is free but remains instrumentally subordinated to a divine operative grace.[71] After its act of choice has been elicited (according to the intellect's natural perception of goodness), the principal agency of divine grace moves the will to

---

71. While this actual grace does not suppose the presence of habitual grace, it still represents a true gift from God. The divine movement is not intrinsically differentiated into operative and cooperative grace, for the very grace that is operative when it is met in pure passivity and in the complete absence of supernatural resources in the will becomes cooperative when it is met, subsequent to justification, by the supernatural resources of habitual grace and charity.

embrace the mysteries as such. In this moment, the will commands the intellect to assent judgmentally to the truth of God's promises (precisely as they are revealed by God to be true). The mind no longer distills from the preaching of the Gospel a natural perception of goodness, but embraces the full substance of supernatural truth. When this happens, the infusion of divine charity transforms the *pius credulitatis affectus*, the religious affect of credence, with the result that the believer no longer simply appreciates the promised good under the general aspect of some good thing but now fully embraces in love the revealed mystery about God and the things that pertain to God.[72] On the other hand, if the person at this point holds back from making a complete self-commitment to the message of salvation, he or she then abides in a state of unformed faith that has no power to save. St. Augustine recounts that his mother, St. Monica, purposefully delayed her son's baptism, though Augustine already knew the truths of the Christian religion. As he testifies, "Thus I already believed as did my mother and the whole household, except my father alone."[73] This happened because Monica feared that given his age and temperament the young Augustine was not yet ready to commit himself fully to God in love. Without commenting on the legitimacy of delaying baptism or the theology of sacramental efficacy that such a decision entails, we can note in Augustine's testimony an example of the distinction between unformed faith without charity (such as he possessed in his youth) and the faith formed by love that characterizes his later life. Augustine's personal journey to formed faith in fact produces one of the most celebrated laments in the history of Christian literature: "Too late have I loved you, O Beauty so ancient and so new, too late have I loved you!"[74]

In the ordinary working of divine providence, the initial affect of credence leads straightaway to formed faith. The pattern of priority, then, is one of logic, not time. At this moment, the intellect assents to what exceeds its natural capacities, and it does so not according to its own natural criteria of evidence but rather under the weight of the will's

---

72. The *habitus* of grace is considered operative up to the act of justification itself, but cooperative in as much as in synergy with an actual *gratia cooperans* and with infused charity it forms the principle of meritorious works.

73. *Confessions* Bk. 1, chap. 11 (18).

74. See *Confessions* Bk. 10, chap. 27 (38).

command. This assent to the truthfulness of God revealing, faith's formal object, takes place mediately through the statements of the Church's preaching of scriptural revelation. For a variety of pastoral reasons, the Church from time to time organizes the articles of faith into creeds or other formularies of faith.[75] The propositions or truth-bearing statements of faith seize the attention and motivate the assent of the intellect only as subsidiary material objects, that is, as a kind of "locale" in which First Truth is speaking. As is the case with all judg-mental acts, the intellect in "speaking" the "truth-word" of judgment surpasses the conceptual elements of the propositions or statements and dynamically signifies the being *(esse)* of the supernatural realities them-selves. Again it is St. Augustine who emphasizes this point, when he says, "the name of that reality is God."[76] Then there occurs the infusion of habitual grace in the essence of the soul and the infusion of the supernatural *habitus* of faith in the intellect and of hope and charity in the will.[77] With this grace, the person starts to enjoy a creature's share in the reality of the divine life, or the believer begins to live the theo-logical life.

In the sixteenth century, the Council of Trent summarized its teach-ing on the *habitus* of formed faith when it described the Christian life as the fruit of God's gratuity and at the same time the work of human freedom:

Thus, to those who work well right to the end and keep their trust in God, eternal life should be held out, both as a grace promised in his mercy through Jesus Christ to the children of God, and as a reward to be faithfully bestowed, on the promise of God himself, for their good works and merits. This, then, is that crown of righteousness which the Apostle says is laid up for him after his fight and his race, and will be awarded by the righteous judge not only to him but to all who love his appearing.[78]

75. For a brief account of this development, see *Catechism of the Catholic Church*, nos. 192–97.

76. St. Augustine, *Tractates on the First Letter of John* 4 (PL 35, 2008–2009; FOTC 92, 180).

77. This way of explaining justification takes account of Aquinas's distinction between the substance of the soul and its powers or capacities. The being of the human soul is not identical with its acting, or with its proximate capacities for acting; its substance is simple, whereas its capacities and activities are various in kind.

78. The Council of Trent, Session 6 (13 January 1547), "Decree on Justification,"

Virtue is a human quality; even the theological virtues still function within the limits established by the natural structures of human knowing and willing. They have God as their proper object and they account for a person's properly supernatural activities, but they respect the native structure of human intelligence and love. Moreover, the *habitus* of theological faith develops a disproportion between what even our elevated capacities can perform and the abundance of divine life that God is able to bestow on his sons and daughters. Even though the life of formed faith enables the believer to lay hold of the mysteries of the Godhead and of Christ, the Christian living a life of formed faith still requires additional assistance to be sustained amidst the hardships and difficulties he or she must face in the world. God unfailingly provides this assistance in the form of the Gifts of the Holy Spirit.

---

chap. 16, "On the fruit of justification, namely merit from good works, and on the nature of that merit."

₿ Chapter 5

The Impartings of the Holy Spirit

The graciousness of God toward his children, so St. Paul reminds us, surpasses all our imagining: "But, as it is written, 'What no eye has seen, nor ear heard, nor the human heart conceived, what God has prepared for those who love him'—these things God has revealed to us through the Spirit; for the Spirit searches everything, even the depths of God" (1 Cor. 2:9–10). Not only does God infuse virtues into the believer, he also imparts to them the gifts of the Holy Spirit. These graces render the Christian living by faith fully alert and readily docile to God. While authors throughout the patristic and medieval eras arranged the source materials for a theology of the gifts in various and often imaginative ways, a single objective guided their efforts: to account for the complete subordination of the Church to the Holy Spirit.[1] The Catholic tradition maintains the conviction that the visible mission of the Son and the invisible mission of the Holy Spirit always work together. So the Irish theologian Colman O'Neill states that "the gift of the Spirit to the community is inextricably linked with the personal mis-

---

1. For a general history of the theology of the gifts, see G. Bardy, F. Vandenbroucke, A. Bayez, M. Labourdette, C. Bernard, "Dons du Saint-Esprit" in *Dictionnaire de Spiritualité* 3, cols. 1641–1957. For the development of the doctrine in the patristic tradition, consult Albert Mitterer, "Die sieben Gaben des Hl. Geistes nach der Väterlehre," *Zeitschrift für katholische Theologie* 49 (1925), pp. 529–66 and Ambroise Gardeil, "Dons du Saint-Esprit II. Partie documentaire et historique," in *Dictionnaire de théologie catholique* IV, cols. 1748–1781. Although published in 1911, the latter work still remains a principal source for the period up to Aquinas.

sion of the divine Word and its sacramental continuation in the Eucharist."[2]

The Church teaches that the gifts of the Holy Spirit—wisdom, understanding, counsel, fortitude, knowledge, piety, and fear of the Lord—provide special assistance for developing and maintaining the theological life. Just as the human soul of Christ received the consolation of the Holy Spirit, so those who believe in Christ share in the gifts of his messianic anointing. The gifts are said to complete and perfect the virtues of those who receive them, making the Christian believer docile in readily obeying divine inspirations.[3] Christ's promise to send the third divine Person of the blessed Trinity as Comforter and Advocate, which comes at the center of his final discourse to the disciples (see John 16:12–15), grounds the theology of the gifts. The Christian knows that the Holy Spirit will continue to act within the Church, providing an assurance of its salvation: "And by this we know that Christ abides in us, by the Spirit that he has given us" (1 John 3:24). The gifts of the Holy Spirit—by initiating and expanding a unique kind of docility within the souls of believers—make it possible for the members of Christ's Body to act in a divine way.

Since the gifts belong in their fullness to the Son of David, Christ himself remains the principal model for this docility. Among those who have pursued inquiry into the gifts, Aquinas and his commentators merit special attention.[4] Aquinas revisited the biblical glosses and patristic

---

2. Colman E. O'Neill, O.P., *Sacramental Realism. A General Theory of the Sacraments* (Wilmington, DE: Michael Glazier, Inc., 1983), p. 195.

3. See *Catechism of the Catholic Church*, nos. 1830 and 1831.

4. Aquinas's views concerning the nature and function of these gifts continued to evolve as he composed the *Summa theologiae*. The final redaction of his gift-theology is found in the *secunda pars*. The only text in the *tertia pars* that says anything significant about the gifts is IIIa q. 7, a. 5 where Aquinas inquires concerning the grace of Christ. For more information, see Edward D. O'Connor, C.S.C., *The Gifts of the Spirit*, vol. 24 of the Blackfriars translation of the *Summa theologiae* (London/New York, Eyre & Spottiswoode/McGraw-Hill Book Company, 1974), especially appendix 4, pp. 110–30. The Thomist commentatorial tradition on the gifts includes the Italian Thomas de Vio Cajetan (1469–1534), *In primam secundae* q. 68, Leonine edition of Aquinas's *Opera omnia*, vol. VI (Rome, 1891), the Spanish theologians Francisco de Vitoria (c. 1485–1546), *In secundam secundae* q. 8, ed. Asociación "Francisco de Vitoria" (Salamanca, 1932–52), Bartolomeo Medina (1527–1580), *In primam secundae* q. 68, ed. Haeredum Mathiae Gastii (Salamanca, 1584), and Domingo Bañez (1528–1604), *In secundum secundae*, q. 8, ed. Bernardum Iuntam, (Venice, 1586). For a detailed study of the commentatorial tradition, see J. A. Aldama, "La

texts that treat of the gifts, especially in his commentary on the text of Isaiah: "And the Spirit of the Lord shall rest upon him, the spirit of wisdom and understanding, the spirit of counsel and might, the spirit of knowledge and the fear of the Lord. And his delight shall be in the fear of the Lord" (Isa. 11:2–3).[5] At times in the history of theology, the gifts have been presented as spiritual endowments reserved for those very advanced in the spiritual life.[6] Aquinas set an important example when he associated the gifts with everyday Christian life and taught that they form part of the life of every believer. His perspective controls the present discussion.

The tradition of the *Spiritus septiformis*, the sevenfold Spirit, dates from the Latin Church of the fourth century. From that time, theological reflection moved toward a fixed correspondence between the seven gifts and the seven main virtues of the theological life, the four cardinal moral and the three theological virtues.[7] The preferred paradigm, which already appears fully in the writings of St. Augustine, sets the gifts of the Holy Spirit alongside the infused virtues, the beatitudes, and the fruits of the Holy Spirit. It is worthwhile to remark that the vision of the moral life as shaped by gifts, fruits, and beatitudes differs sharply from narrow modern conceptions of moral theology, in which being ethical consists in making the right decision on the basis of formal principles or, what is worse, abiding by conventional moral values. When they insist that the Christian life requires the fruitful exercise of the seven gifts of the Holy Spirit, pastors and teachers of the faith emphasize that one cannot live the theological life, with its important moral requirements, outside of the full context of Trinitarian, Christological, and sacramental theology.

---

distinctión entre las virtudes y los dones des Espíritu Santo en los siglos XVI e XVII," *Gregorianum* 16 (1935), pp. 562–576. More recent commentators include R. Garrigou-Lagrange, *Perfection chrétienne et contemplation* (Paris, 1923), M.M. Philipon, *Le dons du Saint-Esprit* (Paris, 1954), and most recently, Benedict Ashley, O.P., *Thomas Aquinas-The Gifts of the Spirit* (Hyde Park, NY: New City Press, 1995).

5. The traditional list of seven gifts results from the fact that in verse 3 the Septuagint version used the Greek term for "piety" instead of repeating "fear of the Lord."

6. See Pinckaers, *Sources*, pp. 254–65; the author traces the omission of the treatise on the gifts to the sixteenth century and the beginnings of casuistry.

7. In 385, Pope Siricius, for instance, speaks of "the invocation of the sevenfold Spirit with imposition of hands by the bishop." See his *Letter to Himerius* (*DS* 183).

Some early medieval theologians, influenced by mystical numerology, held to the number seven with a certain methodological rigidity, and so sought a strict one-to-one correspondence between the seven virtues and the seven gifts. Thus, faith, hope, charity, prudence, justice, fortitude, and temperance were matched according to one scheme with wisdom, understanding, counsel, fortitude, knowledge, piety, and fear of the Lord. In his definitive conception, however, Aquinas chooses to associate the two gifts of understanding *(intellectus)* and knowledge *(scientia)* with the single theological virtue of faith. This creative theological decision does more than introduce a modest adjustment into a conventional theological schema. For by identifying the gift of knowledge with the virtue of faith, Aquinas qualifies the then-accepted Augustinian view that knowledge aids only the practical decisions of the moral life. The sharp distinction between dogmatic and moral theology is foreign to Aquinas, and so the gifts of both understanding and knowledge are put at the service of the act of belief, which covers dogma and morals. For Aquinas, the gift of knowledge renders us docile with respect to all the truths of faith, not just to those that guide the moral life.

The gifts associated with theological faith facilitate the believer's personal engagement with First Truth-Speaking. Aquinas teaches that judgment completes knowledge.[8] Both gifts, understanding and knowledge, aid the virtue of faith in bringing to completion its judgment about the Word of God revealing, which constitutes the act of belief. In order to appreciate the way in which the gifts accomplish this objective, we need to consider some general features of the gifts.

The Theology of the Gifts

The existence of the gifts of the Holy Spirit in the faithful who are conformed to Christ is not a solemnly declared dogma, but theological usage does enjoy ample support from both liturgical sources and the ordinary teaching authority of the Church.[9] The New Testament itself urges us to ponder the "impartings of the Holy Spirit" (Heb. 2:4). As

8. See *Summa theologiae* IIa-IIae q. 173, a. 2: "judicium est completivum cognitionis."
9. See the *Catechism of the Catholic Church*, nos. 1830–1831.

I have said, in taking leave of his disciples, Jesus told them, "It is good for you that I go away; for if I do not go away, the Paraclete will not come to you; but if I go, I will send him to you" (John 16:7). Theological reflection concerning the number, status, and purpose of the gifts of the Holy Spirit articulates the precise nature of this promised divine aid. The gifts shape the psychological powers of the believer so that he or she can respond positively to the movements of the Holy Spirit. Because no believer can advance without the aid of the Holy Spirit, the gifts remain an indispensable complement to the moral and theological virtues, even when these virtues enable the believer to act properly in the commonplace experiences of the Christian life.

Because they depend upon a separate kind of divine initiative, the gifts of the Holy Spirit differ intrinsically from the virtues. But it took time for the Church to learn how to explain the difference. The thirteenth-century Parisian master Philip the Chancellor was the first to introduce a clear-cut distinction between the virtues and the gifts; others subsequently came up with a variety of arguments to justify it.[10] The distinction between the virtues and the gifts reflects the different modes of activity they produce. In the practice of the behavioral virtues, the synergy of intellect and will works through infused prudence, so that grace moves the human powers according to their own dynamics. The gifts, on the other hand, prompt actions that more directly reflect God's plan, more of a "not I, but the grace of God that is with me" (1 Cor. 15:10). Explaining the psychology of the gifts, Aquinas takes his cue from a word of the Scriptures: The Latin Vulgate text employs the word "*spiritus*" for the spiritual endowments that Isaiah uses to describe the Davidic Messiah.[11] For Aquinas, this usage suggests an inherent

10. See Philip the Chancellor, *Summa de bono*, edited by Nicolai Wicki, *Corpus Philosophorum Medii Aevii. Opera Philosophica Mediae Aetatis Selecta*, vol. 2 (Berne: Editiones A. Francke, 1985), Pars Posterior, *De bono gratie in homine* II, D, "De septem donis Spiritus Sancti," Q. I "Utrum dona sint virtutes" [1106–1113]. For commentary, see O. Lottin, *Psychologie et morale aux XIIe et XIIIe siècles*, vol. 3 (Louvain: Duculot, 1929, 1930), p. 363. In his *In III Sententias*, ed. Borgnet (Paris, 1894), d. 34, A, a. 1 [614–20]: "An dona sunt virtutes?," Albert the Great catalogues the subsequent theologians' efforts to explain the distinction.

11. Aquinas presents some basic elements of his teaching on the gifts in question 68 of the *prima secundae*. Although the eight articles of this question assume a conception of

connection between spirit and movement. The gifts are designed to move the Christian in a godly direction. The Church describes the gifts as permanent dispositions in the believer to receive special divine inspirations or promptings that enable a person to surpass the basically human mode established by virtue.[12]

The infused virtues direct the Christian life according to a human mode, whereas the gifts direct the Christian life according to a divine mode. John of St. Thomas, whose commentary on the gifts inspires much of what is still said about them, states that this new mode of gift-activity produces some startling outcomes.[13] For example, he argues that once a virtuous act comes under the influence of the gifts, the action acquires an entirely new moral character or species. In simpler terms, this means that a virtuous action prompted by a gift of the Holy Spirit results in an entirely new sort of action. The grounds for this strong claim lie in the special regulatory principle that the gifts embody, the interior prompting that these graces bring. In order to illustrate how the same action can be performed in different ways, John of St. Thomas appeals to the simple image of a boat moved both by the rowing of oarsmen and by the force of the wind:

This interior illumination, this experiential taste of divine things and of other mysteries of the faith, excites our affections so that they tend to the object of

---

the gifts that Aquinas will later modify, a brief resumé of certain pertinent points nonetheless provides important basic information. In the plan of the *Summa theologiae*, the questions in Ia-IIae qq 68–70 treat the gifts of the Holy Spirit, the beatitudes, and the fruits of the Holy Spirit respectively.

12. See the *Catechism of the Catholic Church*, no. 1830.

13. The Portuguese-born Dominican John Poinsot (1589–1644) was a professor of theology at Alcalá de Henares, who began his teaching career at about the same time (c. 1614) that El Greco died. He thus epitomizes Spanish scholasticism at the end of the *siglo de oro*. Jacques Maritain considered him "one of the greatest metaphysicians in modern Western philosophy." The Iberian scholastic belongs to the school of late medieval and renaissance commentators on Aquinas. Though a near contemporary of Descartes, Poinsot's starting points are much different than the intuitions that inaugurate "la pensée moderne." Because he lived at a time when the Church (partly because of the insistence of the Protestant Reform) was required to look more directly at the personal element in religion, John of St. Thomas (as he has been more commonly known) can illumine aspects of the life of faith that earlier periods in theology failed to bring into such sharp focus. He analyzes Aquinas's distinction between the gifts of understanding and knowledge, showing different ways that these gifts aid theological faith. For a full presentation of the achievement of John Poinsot, see John Deely, *New Beginnings. Early Modern Philosophy and Postmodern Thought* (Toronto: University of Toronto Press, 1994).

virtue by a higher mode than these very same ordinary virtues do themselves. This happens to the extent that our affections obey a rule and measure dependent upon higher realities, namely, that interior prompting of the Holy Spirit—according to the rule of faith—and his illumination. As a result, the gifts effect a different kind of moral action, that is, they establish a distinctive moral specification; indeed, we are led to a divine and supernatural end by a mode that differs from the rule formed by our own efforts and labors (even in the case of infused virtue), that is, one formed and founded upon the rule of the Holy Spirit. In a similar way, the work of oarsmen moves a ship differently than the wind does, even if it moves through the waves toward the same port.[14]

The example is reminiscent of Luis de Molina (1535–1600) and his celebrated but misleading metaphor for the concurrence of divine and human causality in a work of grace. But in this text, John of St. Thomas engages an entirely different theological issue. He uses the example of two categorical causes, namely, oarsmen and wind, to explain two *modes* of a single divine activity in the person: a human mode, wherein the infused and theological virtues remain under the direction of our own ingenuity and resources, and a suprahuman mode, wherein the same virtues come under the influence of the gifts. For the graced person, then, two paths of virtuous activity lie open. Along the first path, the

14. See Joannes a Sancto Thoma, "De donis Spiritus Sancti," in *Cursus theologicus. In Summam Theologicam D. Thomae.* I-II, Disputatio XVIII in the Vivès edition, vol. 6 (Paris, 1885): "Ex ista autem interiori illustratione, et experimentali gustu divinorum, et aliorum mysteriorum fidei, inflammatur affectus ad hoc ut altiori modo tendat ad objecta virtutum, quam per ipsasmet ordinarias virtutes, quatenus sequitur regulationem, et mensurationem altiorem, scilicet ipsum instinctum interiorem Spiritus sancti juxta regulas fidei, et illustrationum ejus. Et sic diversam moralitatem ponit, et diversam specificationem, diverso quippe modo ducimur ad finem divinum, et supernaturalem ex regulatione formata nostro studio, et labore, etiam si virtus infusa sit, vel formata, et fundata in regulatione, et mensuratione Spiritus sancti, sicut diverso modo ducitur navis labore remigantium, vel a vento implente vela, licet ad eumdem terminum per undas tendat" (Disp. XVIII, a. 2, n. 29). Subsequent citations include the Disputatio (= Disp.); article (= a.); number (= n.), with the page number from this edition appended in brackets. An English translation was published under the title *The Gifts of the Holy Ghost* (New York: Sheed & Ward, 1951). Written in 1644, this commentary remains the acknowledged classic treatment in the Thomistic school; for example, the seventeenth-century Discalced Carmelite theologians at Salamanca—usually known as the "Salmanticenses"—wrote: "De hac materia tam docte, tam profunde et luculenter agit, ut palmam aliis, immo et sibi ipsi alia scribenti, praeripere videatur" (*Cursus theologicus, De spe,* Disp. 4, dub. 4, n. 43). For recent studies on the commentary, see Pinharanda Gomes, *Joao de Santo Tomás na filosofia do Século XVII* (Lisbon: Instituto de Cultura e Língua Poetuguesa, 1985), chap. 9, "Os Dons," and Javier Sese, "Juan de S.T. y su tratado de los dones del Espiritu Santo," *Angelicum* 66 (1989), pp. 161–84.

believer disposes of the gifts of God according to the resources of human ingenuity—*humano modo*, as the scholastics said—whereas along the other path, the believer deploys the gifts of God (in effect, the infused virtues) as God himself directs—*divino modo*. The second path is that of the gifts of the Holy Spirit, along which the Christian is moved by what John of St. Thomas calls an "interior prompting of the Holy Spirit and his illumination."

Common experience, moreover, supports this distinction: the evident contrasts in fervor among the members of the Church make clear that each justified believer remains free to govern even the spiritual resources of the life of faith. Human reason ordinarily remains the directive rule or measure for the infused moral and theological virtues, and much of the Christian life is constituted by divine grace acting within the ordinary movements of human reason, "consecrating" reason's perception and judgment by the truth of faith and the practical capacity of infused prudence. If we wish, however, to appreciate the need for the gifts of the Spirit, we need only recall that no adequate proportion exists between human nature and the goal of beatific fellowship with God. Therefore, the Holy Spirit, like a prompter on a theatrical set, inspires us to virtuous actions that surpass the bounds of human imagination. Cardinal Cajetan cites a text from 1 John as scriptural warrant for making a distinction between human and divine guidance even within the Christian life: "But the anointing which you received from him abides in you, and you have no need that any one should teach you; as his anointing teaches you about everything" (1 John 2:27).[15] Since participation in the divine life implies something that infinitely surpasses human reason, it is generally argued that the believer requires these special gifts so that a virtuous Christian life may achieve its full flourishing.[16] As everyday experience makes plain, Christians do engage in the pursuit of the created goods that remain proportionate to them, and they do this more easily than they aspire to the divine Good. Nevertheless, the good God alone leads to and finally constitutes their

15. Cajetan proposes this text in his commentary *In primam secundae* q. 68, a. 1.

16. For a brief essay that underscores the importance of the Holy Spirit in the Christian life, see Luc Somme, "La rôle du Saint-Esprit dans la vie chrétienne, selon saint Thomas d'Aquin," *Sedes Sapientiae* 26 (1988), pp. 11–29.

beatitude. On account of the utter disproportion between human capacities and the divine Good, Aquinas concludes that "the moving of reason is not sufficient to direct us to our ultimate and supernatural end without the prompting and moving of the Holy Spirit from above."[17] In short, even the life of faith and grace does not in itself ensure that Christian believers will use these divine gifts in a godly way.

The Holy Spirit—the Advocate and Comforter—pushes the believer beyond the restrictions of human inclination and judgment in matters that pertain to eternal life. This "leading" equals a kind of pedagogy in divine things. Aquinas helpfully compares the action of the Holy Spirit to that of a teacher who gradually leads an apprentice to a sure grasp of a particular discipline by providing moments of insight that elucidate both its methods and content. He writes, "But he who knows all things and has power over all things makes us safe by his movement from all foolishness, ignorance, dullness, harshness, and the like."[18] Aquinas undoubtedly has in mind the text from Acts that speaks about Christ first sending the Holy Spirit at Pentecost: "This Jesus God raised up, and of that all of us are witnesses. Being therefore exalted at the right hand of God, and having received from the Father the promise of the Holy Spirit, he has poured out this that you both see and hear" (Acts 2:32–33). The gifts continue the graces of Pentecost for the benefit of today's believer.

The biblical term *spiritus* of course suggests something transient, even charismatic. But since the theological life is sustained by the gifts of the Holy Spirit, they must form a permanent feature of the believer's moral character. The Christain should remain continually and actively receptive to the divine promptings that are indispensable for Christian perfection. Catholic teaching then asserts that the gifts themselves form distinctive *habitus*. According to Aquinas, the Gospel of John supports this claim when it recounts that Jesus reassures his disciples with the promise that the Counselor "dwells with you, and abides with you" (John 14:17). To illustrate this fusion between the spontaneity of an inspiration and the permanence of a settled disposition, John of St.

17. *Summa theologiae* Ia-IIae q. 68, a. 2.
18. See *Summa theologiae* Ia-IIae q. 68, a. 2, ad 3.

Thomas points out that the scriptural witnesses speak about the Spirit as "resting" on Christ.[19] As a permanent guest in the Christian soul, the Holy Spirit makes the faithful docile in readily obeying divine inspirations.

Since they are formed *habitus* in the believer, the gifts shape the moral character of the Christian in determined ways. As we noted earlier, the *habitus* of the virtues conform the different capacities of the person to their proper object, so that the person chooses what is good in a "natural" way—promptly, joyfully, and easily. The virtue of temperance, for example, so moderates the concupiscible powers of the soul that the truly temperate person performs actions according to the measure of right reason, but without the strain, interior struggle, and the determined effort that accompanies the exertion of those who do not possess the virtuous *habitus*. The gifts of the Holy Spirit, however, perfect the person in a more profound way, rendering the *sequela Christi*—the following of Christ—"connatural" to the believer. The gifts establish the psychological grounds for the Christian's concrete conformity to Christ, so that the believer need not struggle in order to heed the promptings of the Holy Spirit. At the same time, as the great variety that exists among the saints unmistakably indicates, the gifts do this without introducing a colorless uniformity into Christian living.

Like any philosophical concept, the notion of *habitus* takes on a certain analogical elasticity when used for theological purposes. An infused *habitus*, as we have seen, supplies certain personal dispositions in the believer which render the creative living of a Christian life prompt, joyful, and easy.[20] Even though the description of the gifts would seem to exclude the possibility that a Christian might reject a divine prompting, a *habitus* does not destroy human freedom. For the full deployment of divine grace never reduces human freedom; rather, as the case of Christ himself makes clear, the one who acts fully under the movement of grace achieves the highest exercise of freedom. "The Crucified Christ reveals the authentic meaning of freedom," writes Pope John Paul II, "he lives it fully in the total gift of himself and calls his disciples to share

19. See for example, Disp. XVIII, a. 2, n. 8.
20. For a neglected but still useful study on the notion of *habitus* in the Christian life, see Placide de Roton, O.S.B., *Les habitus. Leur caractère spirituel* (Paris: Labergerie, 1934), pp. 149–63.

in his freedom."[21] The gifts infallibly produce in the believer a sort of ordered spiritual liberty that characterizes New Testament existence.[22] St. John of the Cross seeks to capture the paradoxical status of the gift-*habitus* when he writes: "From the time I sought nothing because of what I myself wanted," he wrote, "everything was given to me by God, even though I did not ask for it."[23]

The gifts work only through love. "The gifts of the Holy Spirit," Aquinas writes, "are connected with one another in charity, in such wise that one who has charity has all the gifts of the Holy Spirit, while none of the gifts can be had without charity."[24] This means that the gifts of the Holy Spirit work only in a Christian whose faith is alive. How else can we explain the bold claim made about us in the Preface for the Christmas Mass at Midnight: "In the wonder of the Incarnation your eternal Word has brought to the eyes of faith a new and radiant vision of your glory. In him we see our God made visible and so are caught up in the love of the God we cannot see."[25] The gifts of knowledge and understanding help us realize this Christmas promise.

The Gifts Associated with Theological Faith

Understanding and knowledge are associated with theological faith, for these two gifts assist the Christian in faith's proper acts of belief and confession. As distinct *habitus* in the psychology of the Christian

21. Encyclical letter, *Veritatis splendor*, no. 85.

22. In more technical terms, as we have seen in chapter 4, the gifts are instances of a *gratia operans*, i.e., graces in which the divine initiative accounts for the direction of the human will. In the case of a *gratia operans*, the action of the will does not proceed because of a prior discursive process of the mind as regulated by the virtue of prudence. A movement of divine grace supplies for this ordinary working of our self-determination. Still, the will must consent to its own act. Hence, once the divine initiative is freely, though passively, received, the individual becomes the active cause of his or her own subsequent activity. The divine causality prolonging itself into this action forms a *gratia cooperans*.

23. For example, see his teaching in *Subida al Monte Carmelo*, Bk. 3, chap. 20.

24. *Summa theologiae* Ia-IIae q. 68, a. 5. The tradition correctly emphasizes that the gifts of the Holy Spirit work their effect on the moral life through the theological virtues, so that everything the Christian believes and hopes for plays an active role in the faithful exercise of Christian virtue.

25. *Missale Romanus*, editio typica altera (Vatican, 1975), Preface for Christmas I: "Quia per incarnati Verbi mysterium nova mentis nostrae oculis lux tuae claritatis infulsit: ut, dum visibiliter Deum cognoscimus, per hunc in invisibilium amorem rapiamur."

believer, the gifts associated with the virtue of faith operate in a mode that surpasses the ordinary process of human knowing. Aquinas argues that the fragility of the human mind justifies such interventions.[26] While the union between God and the believer effected by grace begins with a cognitive experience, loving affectivity plays a significant role in the knowledge of faith. According to the expression favored by John of St. Thomas, the believer performs out of a connaturalizing affectivity.[27] The gifts, then, are meant to develop an "experiential," "supra-rational," or "affective" way of laying hold of divine truth in the believer. They establish new habits of the heart, with the result that the person shaped by the gifts of the Holy Spirit experiences a transformation that steadies him or her in the pursuit of the theological life. But the journey always begins with believing the Word of God, who is First Truth-Speaking.

John of St. Thomas devotes more space to discussing the gifts of the Holy Spirit that advance our knowledge of divine things than he does to the gifts that succor the virtues of the affective capacities.[28] His longer treatment of the intellectual gifts undoubtedly reflects the preference that Aquinas himself shows to the work of intelligence in appropriating the saving doctrine and, especially, in advancing its development through the science of theology.[29] But as a genuine power of the human person, the human mind is not a separated intellect: the gifts of God's grace belong to the whole person. Therefore, the intellectual gifts of understanding and knowledge do not invite any rationalist interpretations of Christian doctrine, such as that generated by the spirit of seventeenth-century Cartesianism. On the contrary, the ancient Christian tradition unquestionably asserts that human cognition, when it comes face to face with divine truths, experiences its limits more than

26. See *Summa theologiae* Ia-IIae q. 68, a. 2.

27. See for example, Disp. XVIII, a. 3, n. 41.

28. John of St. Thomas treats the gifts of piety, fortitude, and fear of the Lord in a single article (a. 6) of his treatise on the gifts of the Holy Spirit. For further information on the gift of piety, see Horst Seidl, "Osservazioni al trattato di Giovanni di S. Tommaso sul dono della pietà," *Angelicum* 66 (1989), pp. 151–60.

29. For an original essay about the cognitive and the affective dimensions of Christian belief, see Richard Schaeffler, "Spiritus sapientiae et intellectus—spiritus scientiae et pietatis—Religionsphilosophische Überlegungen Verhaltnis von Weisheit, Wissenschaft und Frömmigkeit und ihrer Zuordnung zum Geiste" in *Weisheit Gottes—Weisheit der Welt. Festschrift für Kardinal Ratzinger zum 60. Gerburtstag* (St. Ottilien: EOS Verlag, n.d.) vol. I, pp. 15–35.

its prowess. The Christian needs not only to be taught the truth but to be confirmed in the truth. For this reason, the Church takes special comfort in the prayer that Jesus addresses to his heavenly Father shortly before his death: "Sanctify them in truth" (John 17:17).

Because the gifts of understanding and knowledge derive their energy from the virtue of charity, they are able to overcome the limitations that human reason imposes on our contemplation of the mysteries of salvation. According to the teaching of the New Testament, faith gives way to something greater, namely a vision "face to face," but theological charity perdures even in the life to come, for "love never ends" (1 Cor. 13:8–13). In other terms, charity already abides in the Church here below as the same reality that flourishes in the company of the saints above. This fact of the theological life explains why the tradition associates the highest intellectual gift of the Holy Spirit, namely wisdom, with the theological virtue that most perfectly embodies the divine reality: charity. "Since it develops out of connaturality for and union with divine things," explains John of St. Thomas, "the gift of wisdom does not supply a comprehensive knowledge concerning the highest causes; the gift rather deepens our grasp of these causes by way of a quasi-affective, mystical knowledge."[30]

Because the gifts depend on charity, both understanding and knowledge surpass the restrictions that our unaided intellectual capacities levy on the virtues of the mind. They accomplish this goal, however, without doing violence to the innate structure of cognition as intentional and without prejudicing the basic structure of the article as propositional. The articles of faith, in their propositional form, remain at every moment instruments of the new dispensation of God's truth.

The Gift of Understanding

The gift of understanding, explains Aquinas, "names a certain excellence of apprehension penetrating to inner reality."[31] As its etymo-

---

30. See Disp. XVIII, a. 4, n. 8 [636].

31. *Summa theologiae* IIa-IIae q. 8, a. 1, ad 3. In question 8, Aquinas's treatment takes into account four distinct elements: First, the nature of the gift of understanding (aa. 1–3); second, the subject in which the gift resides (aa. 4, 5); third, the relationship of understanding to the other gifts (a. 6); and lastly, the beatitude and fruit of the Holy Spirit that the medieval tradition associates with this gift (aa. 7, 8). The treatises on the gifts in the

logical components "*intus*" and "*legere*" suggest, the Latin term for understanding—"*intellectus*"—denotes a sort of intuitive reading between the lines. In the Aristotelian account of human knowledge, the intellectual *habitus* called understanding triggers the intellect to scrutinize the indemonstrable first principles from which the speculative intellect develops the process of thought. Even though these principles enter into every intelligent act that a person performs, they elude demonstrative argument. It is precisely as indemonstrable, however, that these first principles of the speculative intellect are compared with the articles of faith. Hence, Aquinas posits the analogy between natural understanding and the gift of *intellectus*. Just as natural understanding enables the human mind to grasp the first principles of speculative and practical reasoning, so the gift of understanding aids theological faith to penetrate what is contained in the articles of faith, whose substance no one can demonstrate.

Penetration does not mean comprehension. Rather, the gift of understanding aids our capacity to withstand the inevidence of theological faith. Even if the believer can neither immediately see nor demonstratively know the object of faith, he or she can still benefit from "the light [which] shines in the darkness" (John 1:5). Since the articles of faith serve as principles for the development of knowledge of faith, the gift of understanding enables the infused *habitus* of faith to fathom the truths expressed in these propositions as formulated. Understanding penetrates the underlayers of experience. For instance, faith assents to the factual truth that, in the blessed Eucharist, Christ is really, truly, and substantially present under the appearances of bread and wine. But the loving penetration of understanding achieves at least an oblique glimpse of why this real presence perdures, and of how the sacrament of the altar radiates Christ's personal and abiding love for the Church.

The act of belief, even when aided by the gift of understanding, still abides in faith's characteristic darkness. For the Spirit-inspired penetration of the articles of faith does not result in a discernment that destroys the mystery of faith. Since the virtue of faith is constituted precisely by its lack of evidence, the believer must still gaze on the Eu-

---

Summa theologiae offer a good example of Aquinas's organizational method and of his *via doctrinae*.

charist with the eyes of faith. To put it differently, the gift of understanding does not have a special object apart from theological faith. On the contrary, because the gift allows the believer to perceive more clearly the distance between the hidden reality and the truth-bearing statement that manifests it, the gift actually heightens the suspense of faith's inevidence. The gift accomplishes this goal, even as it bolsters the believer to adhere with greater precision and clarity to the truth that is believed.[32] Understanding helps the Christian grasp the true dimensions of the mysteries, so that the "substance of things hoped for" emerges from the shadows of mere appearances.

Only charity, of course, can account for the quasi-instinctive discernment that the gift of understanding brings to the act of believing.[33] "Just as by the gift of charity the Holy Spirit orders the human will that it be directly moved to some supernatural good, so also by the gift of understanding he illumines the human mind that it apprehend a certain supernatural truth, to which the right will must tend."[34] This happens because affective knowledge, according to its own proper dynamics, tends to detach itself from the human mode of conceptual knowledge. Love moves out to embrace the thing loved as it exists in the extramental world.

Understanding involves more than concepts. John of St. Thomas explains that the gift does not achieve its goal immediately as a result of simple apprehension. Rather, as a gift that aids the judgment of faith, the penetration of understanding itself involves a judgment. In order to distinguish the gift of understanding from the judgment of discursive reasoning (that the other intellectual gifts make), the same author calls

32. To arrive at knowledge by a means other than that of seizing a representation of the thing known accounts for the "quasi-experiential" character of such a knowledge. The mystics speak about a "ray of darkness" that strengthens the intellect in conformity to Truth.

33. The gift of understanding belongs to everyone who participates in divine charity. The function of a gift always remains "to aid" the act of its respective virtue. Thus, the act of "assent" that constitutes divine faith is complete in itself. According to the teaching of the Church, it can exist even in one who does not actually love God-thus, a "dead" faith, as it is called. The gift of understanding, however, supposes this assent. Charity moves the believer to an "understanding" of divine things, which results in concretely appreciating as a personal truth that which faith proposes for assent. See *Summa theologiae* IIa-IIae q. 8, a. 4.

34. *Summa theologiae* IIa-IIae q. 8, a. 4.

the judgment of understanding a simple or discriminative judgment. He describes this special kind of judgment as "a certain sympathy with spiritual things [that] arouses understanding to discern spiritual realities from corporeal ones."[35] For this reason, the saints who manifest special clarity in their understanding of the economy of salvation, of God's personal involvement in human history, are held up as examples of those who model the gift of understanding. Think of St. Francis of Assisi and his intuitive grasp that all creation reflects the glory of the Lord.

While we often look to the saints for concrete examples of the gifts, this sharpened and superior penetration of the terms that express the mystery opens up a special world of religious experience to each of the faithful. Consider the pronouncement that the Mother of God was preserved from every stain of sin from the first moment of her conception. Each element of this definition of faith invites a religious pondering and reflection. The gift of understanding shapes the human mind so that the believer enters into the meaning that "immaculate," "conception," and "mother" represent in the spiritual order. And understanding aids us likewise with all the other articles of faith, opening up a profoundly personal grasp of revealed truth while at the same time guaranteeing a unity of faith and practice within the one Body of Christ. Through the gift of understanding, the members of the Church again experience a Tabor vision of the Truth, even if, like the original disciples, we can only stammer, "Lord, it is good for us to be here" (Matt. 17:4).

The Aristotelian texts that clarify the two ways in which one can learn about virtue help to explain how a discriminative judgment develops out of a sympathy for spiritual things. The Aristotelian distinction between continence and true virtue points up a mode of judging that can help us to see how understanding works within the life of faith. On the one

---

35. Disp. XVIII, a. 3, n. 19 [609]. It is distinctive of Thomist epistemology to hold that the appetite cannot acquire knowledge. Even divine charity cannot know something except in a metaphorical way. So, in order to explain how the gift of understanding grows as a result of the union of the believer with God, who is the Highest Good, one must have recourse to *knowledge by conformity*. Formed faith observes the measure of faith as a knowing; it represents a human mode of knowing because the mind still must appropriate the articles of faith. Faith illumined by the gifts corresponds to a suprahuman mode of knowing. Love penetrates the representation of faith's Object. Nonetheless, the gift does not replace or subordinate the theological virtue. As a distinct gift of grace, understanding remains a cognitive attainment of First Truth, but as a Truth actually loved.

hand, a man can always acquire a moral virtue by studying its elements and principles, as when someone studies the various techniques for maintaining a healthy diet. If all he does, however, is grudgingly abide by the rules, then his dieting illustrates continence, an exercise of will only. On the other hand, a woman can also learn about temperance in food through close association with a person of moderate eating habits, and by observing closely how such a man or woman actually eats, thereby acquire the virtue of abstinence. For the truly temperate person knows the right amount of food to consume simply as a result of having made the right judgments concerning nourishment over a long period of time. Only such a person possesses the virtuous *habitus.* In this second example, the woman learns about temperance by experiencing the truth about temperate activity as it is lived out by the virtuous person. If this kind of knowing is possible in ordinary human experience, argues John of St. Thomas, "why cannot a person know and judge of divine truths from having experienced and loved them?"[36] As a gift that helps human intelligence, the discovery that the gift of understanding gives to the believer does not change the truth but transfigures it.

Experience is central to the theology of the gifts. John of St. Thomas asserts that "the gift of understanding sharpens and perfects the mind, not through study and metaphysical inquiry, but by mystical connaturality and union with divine truths."[37] In the case of the gift, divine love itself begets the desire for a right appreciation or estimate or understanding of the loved reality. John portrays this dynamic as follows:

Knowledge and judgment of spiritual and supernatural truths happens both through study and speculative inquiry ... and through connaturality, love, and experience. In his *On the Divine Names,* chap. 3, Dionysius wrote concerning Hierotheus that "he had not only attained to divine things, but had suffered them as well." Anyone suffers divine things when he is stirred to love and is moved by the Holy Spirit above the level measured by human rules.[38]

The saints even speak about the *"pondus amoris"*—the weight of love—which draws the believer toward God.

The gift of understanding grasps the Christian mysteries, especially those that disclose the actual happenings in the economy of salvation.

36. Disp. XVIII, a. 3, n. 48 [620].
37. Disp. XVIII, a. 1, n. 46 [619].
38. Disp. XVIII, a. 3, n. 45 [619].

Those believers who see into the events of Christ's life—the Annunciation, the Nativity, the Passion, the Resurrection, and the other mysteries—especially demonstrate the gift of understanding. Why? Because these persons love to meditate on the Scriptures and—in the apt phrase of St. Augustine—to "ponder with assent" the incarnate truths of salvation.[39]

It is important to mention the affinity between the gifts of the Holy Spirit and the universal call to holiness. For in the Christian life, personal holiness disposes one for a true and comprehensive vision of divine truth. The gift of understanding also penetrates moral truth in its relation to the final end of beatific vision.[40] Because the gifts bring a more profound experience of divine things, understanding aids the knowledge that moves the believer toward a right ordering of his or her loves, and so fosters the development of the theological life.[41] Only the Christian life communicates the Truth that gives ultimate meaning to the human vocation—the beatific vision.[42] For this reason, the Church insists that all the mysteries of the economy of salvation, such as those expressed in the articles of the Creed, pertain equally to her moral teaching. Every truth of faith points the believer toward the fruitful living out of the virtues and commandments.

The Gift of Knowledge

The gift of knowledge aids the operation of theological faith through a different sort of graced activity.[43] Just as science suggests a developed body of knowledge, so knowledge (scientia) adds the note of reflection and analysis to the intuition that comes from understanding. The certitude of all knowledge results from a judgment, but a person achieves

39. See his On the Predestination of the Saints, c. 2; Aquinas interprets this definition in Summa theologiae IIa-IIae q. 2, a. 1. For an application of this truth, see my Perpetual Angelus. As the Saints Pray the Rosary (New York: Alba House, 1995).

40. For example, see Summa theologiae IIa-IIae q. 8, a. 5: "Only the one who makes no mistake about the final end of human life possesses a correct appreciation of it, and firmly cleaves to this end as the greatest good."

41. Disp. XVIII, a. 3, n. 46 [619].

42. John of St. Thomas even considers that the gift of understanding segues into the light of glory (lumen gloriae). See Disp. XVIII, a. 3, n. 66 [627].

43. Aquinas treats the gift of knowledge in the four articles of Summa theologiae IIa-IIae q. 9 as follows: the nature and object of the gift (aa. 1,2); its speculative character (a. 3); and the associated beatitude (a. 4).

scientific knowing through making discursive judgments about reality on the basis of studied reflection. Often we think of the scientist as someone who studies reports and records that in turn generate theories or opinions. But if we consider the Aristotelian notion of science, then we are led to affirm the possibility of achieving sure knowledge of reality through causal principles. For the Christian believer, God's truthfulness guarantees this surety. The gift of knowledge is said to "resolve" the truths of faith, because it gathers together the apparently disparate truths acquired by faith and renders a settled vision about God's action in the world. It is a kind of infused science that judges the source of things in the divine plan.

Since both gifts that aid the virtue of faith involve judgments, we need to distinguish between the judgment of understanding and the judgment of knowledge. John of St. Thomas describes the proper activity of the gift of knowledge as resolutive or analytical judgment making: Knowledge "grounds a movement of the Holy Spirit which moves the mind not by a direct light, as if one were to shine a light into a dark room, but through an internal experience—an affective connaturality with the truth—by which it can supernaturally seize the realities about which it judges."[44] It is important to remember that connaturality lies at the heart of both understanding and knowledge. The gift of knowledge, however, enables the one who is united with God in love to scrutinize the causal explanations that underlie all of revealed truth as it is set forth by the Church.[45] Unlike the other intellectual gift of the Holy Spirit that is wisdom, the gift of knowledge principally concerns ascending relationships, those that start with effects and mount to their causes, and only obliquely with the descending relationships that link sovereign causes with their effects. In other words, the theological tradition reserves the highest explication of divine truth to the gift of wisdom, whereas the gift of knowledge looks toward God through the created effects of his divine agency in the world.[46] This means that the

44. Disp. XVIII, a. 4, n. 56 [653].
45. Disp. XVIII, a. 4, n. 1 [634].
46. John of St. Thomas briefly recapitulates this distinction in Disp. XVIII, a. 4, n. 50 [650]. He immediately remarks, however, that one must interpret this Augustinian distinction between divine and human things as referring to two formally distinct ways of thinking about reality.

gifts of knowledge and wisdom together strengthen the believer to interpret the world as God knows it to be. Hans Urs von Balthasar calls this the Christological form of knowledge.

Like all of the gifts, knowledge is linked with Christ's instrumentality in the Church. The gift of knowledge helps the believer escape the vicious circle of subjectivity that mistakes abstract concepts for the living truth about God. Through the judgment of knowledge, the mind is preserved from being confined to the closed world of its own creations and is led back to the open world of things as they actually exist in Christ. All authentic instruction given in the Church favors our developing this state of receptivity to divine truth. The gift of knowledge is "scientific," yet it scrutinizes the composition of a given article, as well as its possible relationship to other doctrines of faith in a mode different from that of discursive theology. As a "science of the saints," knowledge leads us to appreciate aspects of a divine mystery that argumentation in itself cannot disclose. The gift of knowledge, in its highest achievement, strengthens the believer's hold on the composition of the articles of faith.

To return to the example of the Immaculate Conception, the gift of knowledge facilitates our judging the implications of this doctrine for other mysteries of the faith. These implications can include both those that are articulated in propositions and those that are not. For example, one can consider Mary's unique privilege as a starting point for additional inquiries about her capacity to commit sin, about what she knew concerning Christ's person and his mission, about how the example of her virtues succors Christian living, and about still other developments of this faith proposition. Knowledge also illumines the relationship of this article of faith to other Marian doctrines, such as the Assumption or Mary's maternal mediation for the Church, as well as to all the other articles of faith. The one who lovingly contemplates the Immaculate Conception does not confront simply a "dogma" about the Mother of God, but the whole drama of salvation as the blessed Virgin personally embodies it.

The patristic tradition coupled the beatitude "Blessed are those who mourn" with the gift of knowledge. John of St. Thomas explains this connection in light of the judgment that knowledge enables the believer to make concerning the relative place that created goods hold in the theological life:

To have a perfect union with God and experience his immense goodness requires stripping oneself of creaturely things and possessing a *knowledge* of their poverty, humiliation, and bitterness; such considerations, furthermore, lead us to cling more closely to God, whom we come to know better as we distance ourselves from creatures.[47]

Knowledge, he continues, helps the believer to make accurate and precise judgments about created goods in the context of a Christian value system.[48] And since knowledge provides a correct estimate about created realities in themselves, it also allows the believer to recognize the privative results of misusing created goods. Thus Aquinas explains that "those only have the gift of knowledge who by the infusion of grace have certain judgment about things to be believed and things to be done, which judgment deviates in nothing from the rightness of justice."[49]

This does not mean, however, that the gift of knowledge leads to a dour moralism. On the contrary, the gifts bring "sweet refreshment from above." Nonetheless, because knowledge critically regards the entire body of revealed truth—and perhaps the Immaculate Conception serves as a good example in this context—this gift moves the believer to make the right judgment about human failures and their providential purpose in the Christian life. For in the truth of the Immaculate Conception, the believer discovers that this personal prerogative for the Mother of God represents a grace that abides at the heart of the Church and that lies open to each of Christ's members. The Church invokes Mary as the refuge of sinners because she personally embodies the integrity of life and purity of spirit that supplies an inexhaustible source of mercy and renewal for those who sin. We hail Mary as the Cause of our Joy because God unequivocally displays in her—one of our nature and race—the truth about the actual destiny of the world, namely, that Christ's salvation definitively triumphs over sin and death. The gift of knowledge aids the believer to put the Christian mysteries at the center of his or her life.

Only those who live fully the theological life can make this sort of judgment about the course of human events in the world. Why? We discover the answer in what the Holy Spirit teaches the Church about

---

47. Disp. XVIII, a 4, n. 57 [653].
48. Disp. XVIII, a. 4, n. 57 [653].
49. *Summa theologiae* IIa-IIae q. 9, a. 3 ad 3.

the truth of God's yearning: "Love, then, consists in this: not that we have loved God but that God has loved us and has sent his Son as an offering for our sins" (1 John 4:10). The Christian believer aided by the gifts of the Holy Spirit both knows and understands that God loves us, not because we are good but because he is. Life in the Spirit bears special fruit in the believer. These are the perfections that the Holy Spirit forms in us and that adumbrate eternal glory: charity, joy, peace, patience, kindness, goodness, generosity, gentleness, faithfulness, modesty, self-control, chastity.[50] In faith aided by the gifts of the Holy Spirit, the Christian already possesses God's mercy, his life, and his love. In his *Book on the Holy Spirit*, St. Basil writes: "As we contemplate the blessings of faith even now, like a reflection in a mirror, it is as though we already possessed the good things our faith tells us that we shall one day enjoy."[51] In the fruits and gifts of the Holy Spirit, we recognize a certain culmination of the theological life. And Blessed Elizabeth of the Trinity reminds us that the theological life leads to glory: "A praise of glory is a soul that gazes on God in faith and simplicity; it is a reflector of all that He is."

50. The tradition of the Church lists these as the twelve *fruits* of the Holy Spirit (see *Catechism of the Catholic Church*, no. 1832). In *Summa theologiae* Ia-IIae q. 70, a. 2, Aquinas says that a fruit of the Holy Spirit denotes an action that is ultimate and delightful, and that is descriptive of the life of eternal glory.

51. See *On the Holy Spirit*, chap. 15, 35–36; translation based on the French in *Sources chrétiennes* 17 bis, pp. 364–70. David Anderson, *St. Basil the Great on the Holy Spirit* (New York: St. Vladimir's Seminary Press, 1980) renders the text: "Even while we wait for the full enjoyment of the good things in store for us, by the Holy Spirit we are able to rejoice through faith in the promise of the graces to come."

Bibliography

Adams, Robert M. *The Virtue of Faith and Other Essays in Philosophical Theology.*
  New York: Oxford University Press, 1987.
Adels, Jill Haak. *The Wisdom of the Saints: An Anthology.* New York: Oxford
  University Press, 1987.
Albert the Great, Saint. *Commentary on the Third Book of the Sentences [In III
  Sententias].* Edited by Borgnet. Paris, 1894.
Aldama, J. A. "La distinctión entre las virtudes y los dones des Espíritu Santo
  en los siglos XVI e XVII." *Gregorianum* 16 (1935): 562–76.
Alfaro, Juan. "Fides in terminologia biblica." *Gregorianum* 42 (1961): 463–505.
Ambrose of Milan, Saint. *On Abraham.*
———. *Explanatio symboli.*
———. *On the Holy Spirit.*
Anscombe, G.E.M. *Ethics, Religion and Politics.* Vol. 3. Collected Philosophical
  Papers. Minneapolis, MN: University of Minnesota Press, 1981.
Aquinas, Thomas, Saint. *Collationes super Credo in Deum [In Symbolum Aposto-
  lorum expositio].*
———. *Compendium theologiae ad fratrem Reginaldum socium suum.*
———. *Expositio in librum Boethii De hebdomadibus.*
———. *Expositio et lectura super Epistolas Pauli Apostoli: In Romanos.*
———. *Expositio et lectura super Epistolas Pauli Apostoli: In Titum.*
———. *Expositio super Dionysium De divinis nominibus.*
———. *Expositio super librum Boethii De trinitate.*
———. *Expositio et lectura super Epistolas Pauli Apostoli: In Ephesios.*
———. *Lectura super Johannem. Reportatio.*
———. *Quaestiones disputatae De veritate.*
———. *Scriptum super libros Sententiarum.*
———. *Sententia super De anima.*
———. *Summa contra gentiles.*
———. *Summa theologiae.*

Aristotle. *Categories (Categoriae)*.
————. *Eudemian Ethics*.
————. *Metaphysics (Metaphysica)*.
————. *Nicomachean Ethics (Ethica Nicomachea)*.
————. *On Interpretation (De Interpretatione)*.
————. *On the Soul (De Anima)*.
————. *Prior Analytics (Analytica Prior)*.
Ashley, Benedict. *Thomas Aquinas: The Gifts of the Spirit*. Hyde Park, NY: New City Press, 1995.
————. "What Is the End of the Human Person? The Vision of God and Integral Human Fulfilment." In *Moral Truth and Moral Tradition. Essays in Honour of Peter Geach and Elizabeth Anscombe*. Edited by Luke Gormally. Dublin: Four Courts Press, 1994.
Augustine, Saint. *Confessions*.
————. *Contra Julianum haeresis Pelagianae defensorem*.
————. *De civitate Dei*.
————. *De doctrina christiana*.
————. *De gratia et libero arbitrio*.
————. *De praedestinatione sanctorum*.
————. *De sermone Domini in monte*.
————. *De spiritu et littera*.
————. *De Trinitate*.
————. *Enarrationes in Psalmos*.
————. *Epistolae*.
————. *In Epistolas Joannis ad Parthos*.
————. *In Genesim ad litteram*.
————. *In Joannis Evangelium*.
————. *Sermones ad populos*.
Balthasar, Hans Urs von. "Theology and Holiness." In *Explorations in Theology* I: *The Word Made Flesh*. San Francisco: Ignatius Press, 1989.
Bañez, Domingo. *In secundum secundae*. Edited by Bernardum Iuntam. Venice, 1586.
Bardy, G., et al. "Dons du Saint-Esprit." In *Dictionnaire de Spiritualité*. Vol 3. Paris: 19xx.
Basil the Great, Saint. *Letters*.
————. *On the Holy Spirit*.
Bede the Venerable, Saint. *Homelia 21 in qvadragesima* (Matth. ix, 9–13). In *Corpus Christianorum Series Latina* 122. Turnholt: Typographi Brepols, 1955.
Bedouelle, Guy, Romanus Cessario, and Kevin White, eds. *Capreolus (1380–1444) en son temps*. Mémoire dominicaine 1. Paris: Editions du Cerf, 1997.
Bellemare, R. "Credere: Note sur la définition thomiste." *Revue de l'Université d'Ottawa* 30 (1960): 37*–47*.
Benedict XII, Pope. *Benedictus Deus* (29 January 1336).
Boisselot, Pierre. "La lumière de la foi." *La vie spirituelle* 41 (1934).
Bonaventure, Saint. *Prologus* in *Opera omnia*.
Bourke, Vernon. "Habitus as a Perfectant of Potency in the Philosophy of St. Thomas Aquinas." Ph.D. diss., University of Toronto, 1938.
————. "The Role of Habitus in the Thomistic Metaphysics of Potency and

Act." In *Essays in Thomism*. Edited by R. E. Brennan, O.P. New York, 1942.

Boyer, Charles. "L'Image de Trinité. Synthèse de la Pensée Augustinienne." *Gregorianum* 5 (1946): 173–99; 333–52.

Bullinger, Heinrich. Introduction to *Summa of the Christian Religion*. N.p., 1556.

Cajetan, Thomas de Vio. *In primam secundae*. In Thomas Aquinas *Opera omnia*. Vol. 6. Rome: Leonine Edition, 1891.

Calvin, John. *Commentary on Romans*.

Catechism of the Catholic Church.

Cessario, Romanus. "Incarnate Wisdom and the Immediacy of Christ's Salvific Knowledge." In *Problemi teologici alla luce dell'Aquinate. Atti del IX Congresso Tomistico Internazionale. Studi Tomistici* Vol. 44. Vatican City: Libreria Editrice Vaticana, 1991: 334–40.

———. "Is Aquinas's *Summa* only about Grace?" In *Ordo Sapientiae et Amoris. Image et Message de Saint Thomas d'Aquin à travers les récentes études historiques, herméneutiques et doctrinales*, pages 197–209. Edited by Carlos-Josaphat Pinto de Oliveira, O.P. Fribourg: Editions Universitaires, 1993.

———. *The Moral Virtues and Theological Ethics*. Notre Dame/London: University of Notre Dame Press, 1991.

———. *Perpetual Angelus. As the Saints Pray the Rosary*. New York: Alba House, 1995.

Chenu, M.-D. "Psychologie de la foi dans la théologie du 13ème siècle." In *Etudes d'histoire littéraire et doctrinale du 13ème siècle*. Paris: J. Vrin, 1932.

Congregation for the Doctrine of the Faith. *Instruction on the Ecclesial Vocation of the Theologian* (1990).

Cottier, Georges. "Les motifs de crédibilité de la Révélation selon saint Thomas." *Nova et Vetera* (1990): 161–79.

Crosson, Frederick, and Bruce Marshall. "Postliberal Thomism Again." *The Thomist* 56 (1992): 481–524.

Cyril of Alexandria, Saint. *Commentary on the Gospel of John*.

Cyril of Jerusalem, Saint. *Catechetical Instructions*.

de Roton, Placide. *Les habitus. Leur caractère spirituel*. Paris: Labergerie, 1934.

Decrees of the Ecumenical Councils, Vol. 2: Trent to Vatican II. Edited by Norman P. Tanner, S.J. Washington, DC: Georgetown University Press, 1990: *Ad gentes; Dei Filius; Dei Verbum; Gaudium et Spes; Gravissimum educationis; Lumen gentium; Pastor aeternus; Presbyterorum ordinis; Unitatis redintegratio*.

Deely, John. *New Beginnings. Early Modern Philosophy and Postmodern Thought*. Toronto: University of Toronto Press, 1994.

Diderot. *Supplément au voyage de Bougainville*. In *Oeuvres philosophiques*. Paris: Garnier, 1964.

DiNoia, J. A. *The Diversity of Religions: A Christian Perspective*. Washington, DC: The Catholic University of America Press, 1992.

———. "Implicit Faith, General Revelation and the State of Non-Christians." *The Thomist* 47 (1983): 209–41.

Dionysius the Areopagite. *The Divine Names and The Mystical Theology*. Translated by C. E. Rolt. London: SPCK, 1979.

Dodd, C. H., et al. *Man in God's Design*. Newcastle upon Tyne: Studiorum Novi Testamenti Societas, 1953.

Dulles, Avery. *The Assurance of Things Hoped For: A Theology of Christian Faith.*
  New York: Oxford University Press, 1994.
––––––. *The Craft of Theology: From Symbol to System.* New York: Crossroad,
  1992.
––––––. *A History of Apologetics.* Washington, DC: Corpus Instrumentorum,
  1971.
Duns Scotus, John. *Quaestiones in librum III Sententiarum.* Paris: Vivès edition,
  n.d.
Dupré, Louis. "The Glory of the Lord. Hans Urs von Balthasar's Theological
  Aesthetic." In *Hans Urs von Balthasar. His Life and Work.* Edited by David L.
  Schindler. San Francisco: Ignatius Press, 1991.
––––––. "L'acte de foi chez Kierkegaard." *Revue Philosophique de Louvain* 54
  (1958): 418–55.
Duroux, Benoit. *La psychologie de la Foi chez S. Thomas d'Aquin.* Tournai: Des-
  cleé, 1963.
Elizabeth of the Trinity. "Heaven in Faith." In *I Have Found God.* Edited by
  Conrad De Meester, translated by Aletheia Kane. Vol. 1. Washington, DC:
  ICS Publications, 1984.
Erasmus of Rotterdam. *Erasmus' Annotations on the New Testament. Galatians to
  the Apocalypse.* Edited by Anne Reeve. Studies in the History of Christian
  Thought, vol. 52. Leiden: E. J. Brill, 1993.
Ernst, Cornelius. *The Gospel of Grace.* Vol. 30 of *Summa Theologiae.* New York:
  McGraw-Hill, 1972.
Eudes, John, Saint. Quoted in Jill Haak Adels, *The Wisdom of the Saints: An
  Anthology.* New York: Oxford University Press, 1987.
Farrell, Walter, and Dominic Hughes. *Swift Victory.* New York: Sheed and Ward,
  1955.
Gardeil, Ambroise. "Dons du Saint-Esprit II. Partie documentaire et histo-
  rique." In *Dictionnaire de théologie catholique.* Vol. 4.
Garrigou-Lagrange, Reginald. *De virtutibus theologicis.* Turin: Casa Editrice
  Marietti, 1949.
––––––. *Perfection chrétienne et contemplation.* Paris, 1923.
––––––. *The Theological Virtues.* Vol. 1. *On Faith.* St. Louis: B. Herder, 1965.
Gauthier, R.-A. "La date du Commentaire de saint Thomas sur l'Ethique à
  Nicomaque." *Recherches de Théologie ancienne et médiévale* 18 (1951).
Geach, P. T. *The Virtues.* Cambridge: Cambridge University Press, 1977.
Gilby, Thomas. *Consequences of Faith.* Vol. 32 of *Summa Theologiae.* New York:
  McGraw-Hill, 1975.
Gleason, Philip. *Keeping the Faith: American Catholicism Past and Present.* Notre
  Dame, IN: University of Notre Dame Press, 1987.
Gomes, Pinharanda. "Os Dons." Chapter 9 in *Joao de Santo Tomás na filosofia
  do Século XVII.* Lisbon: Instituto de Cultura e Língua Poetuguesa, 1985.
Gregory Nazianzen, Saint. *Orations.*
Gregory of Nyssa, Saint. *Vie de Moise.* Edited by Jean Daniélou, S.J. Paris:
  Sources chrétienne, 1942–43.
––––––. *On Christian Perfection.*
Guzie, Tad W. "The Act of Faith according to St. Thomas: A Study in Theo-
  logical Methodology." *The Thomist* 29 (1965): 239–80.

Hamlyn, D. W. "Behavior." *Philosophy* 28 (1953): 132–45

Hilary of Poitiers, Saint. *De Trinitate.*

Hill, William J. *Knowing the Unknown God.* New York: Philosophical Library, 1971.

———. *Proper Relations to the Indwelling Divine Persons.* Washington, DC: The Thomist Press, n.d.

———. *The Three-Personed God. The Trinity as a Mystery of Salvation.* Washington, DC: The Catholic University of America Press, 1982.

Irenaeus of Lyons, Saint. *Adversus Haeresis.*

Jerome, Saint. *In Psalmos XXXXI, Ad Neophytos,* In *S. Hieronymi Presbyteri Opera.* Pars II, Opera Homiletica. Turnholt: Brepols, 1958.

John Damascene, Saint. *De fide orthodoxa.*

John of the Cross, Saint. *Collected Works.*

John Paul II, Pope. *Fidei depositum.*

———. *Redemptor hominis.*

———. *Veritatis splendor.*

John of St. Thomas (John Poinsot). "De donis Spiritus Sancti." Disputatio XVIII in Vol. VI of *Cursus theologicus. In Summam Theologicam D. Thomae. I-II.* Paris: Vivès, 1885. English translation, *The Gifts of the Holy Ghost.* New York: Sheed & Ward, 1951.

Jordan, Mark D. *On Faith. Summa theologiae, Part 2-2, Questions 1–16 of St. Thomas Aquinas.* Notre Dame, IN: University of Notre Dame Press, 1990.

Kenny, Anthony. *What Is Faith?* Oxford: Oxford University Press, 1992.

Klubertanz, George. *Habits and Virtues.* New York: Appleton-Century-Croft, 1965.

Leo the Great, Saint. *Sermons.*

Leo XIII. *Aeterni Patris.*

Lindbeck, George A. *The Nature of Doctrine: Religion and Theology in a Postliberal Age.* Philadelphia: Westminster Press, 1984.

Lonergan, Bernard J. F. *Grace and Freedom: Operative Grace in the Thought of St. Thomas Aquinas.* New York: Herder and Herder, 1971.

———. *Verbum. Word and Idea in Aquinas.* Notre Dame, IN: University of Notre Dame Press, 1970.

Lottin, Odon. *Psychologie et morale aux XIIe et XIIIe siècles.* Vol. 3. Louvain: Duculot, 1929, 1930.

Luther, Martin. *Commentary on Galatians.*

Marmion, Dom. *Christ the Ideal of the Monk.* St. Louis: Herder, 1926.

Marshall, Bruce, and Frederick Crosson. "Postliberal Thomism Again." *The Thomist* 56 (1992): 481–524.

Maximus the Confessor. "The Chapters on Charity" in *Centuria* 1.

McDermott, John M. Introduction to *The Eyes of Faith* by Pierre Rousselot, S.J. Translated by Joseph Donceel, S.J., and Avery Dulles, S.J. New York: Fordham University Press, 1990.

McDermott, Timothy. *Summa Theologiae. A Concise Translation.* Westminster, MD: Christian Classics, 1989.

McIntyre, John P. Review of *Liber canonum diuersorum sanctorum patrum siue Collectio in CLXXXIII titulos digesta.* Edited by Joseph Motta. *Monumenta Iuris Canonici*; Series B: *Corpus Collectionum 7. Christianesimo nella Storia* 12 (1991): 420–22.

McKinnon, Alastair. "Søren Kierkegaard." Vol. 1 of *Nineteenth Century Religious Thought in the West*. Edited by Ninian Smart et alia. Cambridge: Cambridge University Press, 1985.

McNicholl, Ambrose. "On Judging." *The Thomist* 38 (1974): 768–825.

——. "On Judging Existence." *The Thomist* 43 (1979): 507–80.

Medina, Bartolomeo. *In primam secundae*. Edited by Haeredum Mathiae Gastii. Salamanca, 1584.

Melanchthon, Philipp. *Apology of the Augsburg Confession*, 1531.

Missale Romanus. Editio typica altera. Vatican, 1975.

Mitterer, Albert. "Die sieben Gaben des Hl. Geistes nach der Väterlehre." *Zeitschrift für katholische Theologie* 49 (1925): 529–66.

Molina, Luis de. *Concordia*.

More, Thomas. *Utopia*. Froben edition produced at Basle in 1518, reproduced by André Prévost.

Nichols, Aidan. "Walter Kasper and His Theological Program." *New Blackfriars* 67 (1986): 16.

Nicolas, Jean-Hervé. *Les profondeurs de la grâce*. Paris: Beauchesne, 1969.

O'Brien, T. C. *Faith*. Vol. 31 of *Summa Theologiae*. New York: McGraw-Hill, 1974.

——. "Premotion, Physical." In Vol. 7 of *The New Catholic Encyclopedia*: 740a–742b.

O'Connor, Edward. *The Gifts of the Spirit*. Vol. 24 of *Summa Theologiae*. London/New York: McGraw-Hill, 1974.

O'Neill, Colman. *Meeting Christ in the Sacraments*. Revised edition by Romanus Cessario. New York: Alba House, 1991.

——. *The One Mediator*. Vol. 50 of *Summa Theologiae*. New York: McGraw-Hill Book Company, 1965.

——. "The Rule Theory of Doctrine and Propositional Truth." *The Thomist* 49 (1985): 417–42.

——. *Sacramental Realism: A General Theory of the Sacraments*. Wilmington, DE: Michael Glazier, 1983.

Owens, Joseph. *Cognition: An Epistemological Inquiry*. Houston: Center for Thomistic Studies, 1992.

Parente, Pietro. "De munere rationis naturalis in actu fidei eliciendo." *Doctor Communis* 3 (1950): 10–21.

Philip the Chancellor. *Summa de bono*. Edited by Nicolai Wicki. *Corpus Philosophorum Medii Aevii. Opera Philosophica Mediae Aetatis Selecta*. Vol. 2. Berne: Editiones A. Francke, 1985.

Philipon, M. M. *Le dons du Saint-Esprit*. Paris, 1954.

Pinckaers, Servais. "Le désir naturel de voir Dieu." *Nova et Vetera* 51 (1976): 255–73.

——. *Sources of Christian Ethics*. Translated from the French by Sr. Mary Thomas Noble. Washington, DC: The Catholic University of America Press, 1995.

Pius IX, Pope. *Ineffabilis Deus*.

Pius XII, Pope. *Humani generis*.

——. *Divino afflante spiritu*.

Ramirez, Santiago. *De hominis beatitudine*. Vol. 3. Madrid, 1947.

Riga, Peter. "The Act of Faith in Augustine and Aquinas." *The Thomist* 35 (1971): 143–74.

Rousselot, Pierre. *The Eyes of Faith.* Translated by Joseph Donceel, S.J., and Avery Dulles, S.J. New York: Fordham University Press, 1990.

Schaeffler, Richard. Vol. 1 of *Weisheit Gottes—Weisheit der Welt. Festschrift für Kardinal Ratzinger zum 60. Gerburtstag.* St. Ottilien: EOS Verlag, n.d.

Schillebeeckx, Edward. "What Is Theology?" In Vol. 1 of *Revelation and Theology.* Translated by N. D. Smith. New York: Sheed and Ward, 1967–68.

Schmitz, Kenneth L. "St. Thomas and the Appeal to Experience." *Catholic Theological Society of America Proceedings* 47 (1992): 1–20:

Seidl, Horst. "Osservazioni al trattato di Giovanni di S. Tommaso sul dono della pietà." *Angelicum* 66 (1989): 151–60.

Sese, Javier. "Juan de S.T. y su tratado de los dones del Espiritu Santo." *Angelicum* 66 (1989): 161–84.

Simon, Yves. *The Material Logic of John of St. Thomas.* Translated by Yves R. Simon, John J. Granville, and G. Donald Hollenhorst. Chicago: University of Chicago Press, 1955.

Siricius, Pope. *Letter to Himerius.*

Somme, Luc. "La rôle du Saint-Esprit dans la vie chrétienne, selon saint Thomas d'Aquin." *Sedes Sapientiae* 26 (1988): 11–29.

Spicq, Ceslaus. *Connaissance et morale dans la Bible.* Paris: Editions du Cerf, 1985.

Sullivan, Edward. *The Image of God. The Doctrine of St. Augustine and Its Influence.* Dubuque, Iowa: Priory Press, 1963.

Tauler, John. *Institutiones.*

Taylor, Charles. *Sources of the Self. The Making of the Modern Identity.* Cambridge: Harvard University Press, 1989.

Therese of Lisieux. *Story of a Soul. The Autobiography of St. Therese of Lisieux.* A New Translation from the Original Manuscript by John Clarke, O.C.D. Washington, DC: ICS Publications, 1975.

Tindal, Matthew. *Christianity as Old as the Creation.*

Toland John. *Christianity Not Mysterious.*

Tyrrell, George. *Letters from a Modernist. The Letters of George Tyrrell to Wilfrid Ward, 1893–1908.* Edited by Mary Jo Weaver. London: Sheed and Ward, 1981.

———. *Religious Immanence.*

Vitoria, Francisco de. *In secundam secundae.* Edited by Asociación "Francisco de Vitoria." Salamanca, 1932–52.

Wallace, William A. *From a Realist Point of View. Essays on the Philosophy of Science.* Lanham, MD: University Press of America, 1979.

White, Victor. "Holy Teaching, The Idea of Theology according to St Thomas Aquinas." *Aquinas Papers* 33. London: Blackfriars Publications, 1958.

Index

Christian Faith and the Theological Life was composed in Ehrhardt by Brevis Press, Bethany, Connecticut; printed on 60-pound Natural Smooth and bound by Braun-Brumfield, Inc., Ann Arbor, Michigan; and designed and produced by Kachergis Book Design, Pittsboro, North Carolina.